EDUCATION IN A COMPETITIVE AND GLOBALIZING WORLD

# THE EDUCATIONAL SUPERINTENDENT

# BETWEEN TRUST AND REGULATION

## AN INTERNATIONAL PERSPECTIVE

# EDUCATION IN A COMPETITIVE AND GLOBALIZING WORLD

Additional books in this series can be found on Nova's website under the Series tab.

Additional e-books in this series can be found on Nova's website under the e-book tab.

# THE EDUCATIONAL SUPERINTENDENT BETWEEN TRUST AND REGULATION

## *AN INTERNATIONAL PERSPECTIVE*

**ADAM E. NIR**

**EDITOR**

**nova**
publishers
*New York*

For permission to use material from this book please contact us:
Telephone 631-231-7269; Fax 631-231-8175
Web Site: http://www.novapublishers.com

**NOTICE TO THE READER**

The Publisher has taken reasonable care in the preparation of this book, but makes no expressed or implied warranty of any kind and assumes no responsibility for any errors or omissions. No liability is assumed for incidental or consequential damages in connection with or arising out of information contained in this book. The Publisher shall not be liable for any special, consequential, or exemplary damages resulting, in whole or in part, from the readers' use of, or reliance upon, this material. Any parts of this book based on government reports are so indicated and copyright is claimed for those parts to the extent applicable to compilations of such works.

Independent verification should be sought for any data, advice or recommendations contained in this book. In addition, no responsibility is assumed by the publisher for any injury and/or damage to persons or property arising from any methods, products, instructions, ideas or otherwise contained in this publication.

This publication is designed to provide accurate and authoritative information with regard to the subject matter covered herein. It is sold with the clear understanding that the Publisher is not engaged in rendering legal or any other professional services. If legal or any other expert assistance is required, the services of a competent person should be sought. FROM A DECLARATION OF PARTICIPANTS JOINTLY ADOPTED BY A COMMITTEE OF THE AMERICAN BAR ASSOCIATION AND A COMMITTEE OF PUBLISHERS.

Additional color graphics may be available in the e-book version of this book.

**Library of Congress Cataloging-in-Publication Data**

ISBN: 978-1-62948-972-8

*Published by Nova Science Publishers, Inc. † New York*

# CONTENTS

# PREFACE

This book is the result of a joint effort conducted by a group of researchers coming from thirteen countries. Several meetings that took place during the University Council of Educational Leadership (UCEA) conference, the American Educational Research Association (AERA) conference and the European Conference for Educational Research (ECER) yielded a research initiative which was broadly defined "In search of the educational superintendent." The loose definition followed our understanding that the term "superintendent," which is frequently used in different educational and national settings, refers to different role expectations, duties and responsibilities, serving different purposes and ends.

This led to development of a survey instrument that was later on modified to meet the unique features of each educational system and distributed among superintendents. This process produced information which enabled researchers to establish a comparative perspective testifying to the control and trust mechanisms characterizing different educational systems using the role of the superintendent as a lens.

To enrich the description, additional researchers who were not part of the initial research team were asked to provide a description of the superintendency system in their country. This was done based on the set of guidelines used to create a common denominator with the other country descriptions.

Hence, the book brings a comprehensive description of the national and educational context and the superintendency system in each of the thirteen countries described, offering a rich and unique platform that may be used by readers to better understand the features and dynamics of various educational systems around the globe, and may also serve as a point of departure for those interested to further study trust and control mechanisms employed in public education.

This book could not have been completed without the joint effort conducted by many. I take this opportunity to express my gratitude to this wonderful group of researchers who have been instrumental in the successful completion of this project. Skill, commitment and enthusiasm were the driving forces which made this project possible. I would like to express my deepest appreciation to you all.

I would also like to acknowledge the Research Grant provided by the School of Education at the Hebrew University of Jerusalem which enabled me to bring this project to fruition.

*Adam E. Nir*

In: The Educational Superintendent
Editor: Adam E. Nir

ISBN: 978-1-62948-972-8
© 2014 Nova Science Publishers, Inc.

*Chapter 1*

# BLENDING TRUST AND CONTROL: A CHALLENGE FOR SCHOOL SUPERINTENDENTS

### *Adam E. Nir*

The Hebrew University of Jerusalem, Israel

Public education is one of the main forces that make a healthy and democratic society. In addition to educating and providing the younger generation with knowledge and skills that enable children to become contributing citizens to their society, public education is considered highly significant in consolidating the society and establishing its cultural and economic strength. For those reasons, governments invest a significant portion of the state's national resources in public schooling.

Taking into account the costs and political significance of public education, it is not surprising that governments tend to establish some formal mechanism responsible for the monitoring of schools, to ensure that public funds are spent efficiently and effectively and that schools operate professionally and in accordance with national goals and policies.

However, when considering the voices arguing that schools' autonomy should be broadened to better meet local needs and, at the same time, policy makers' inclination to ensure that schools follow national policies, a dilemma arises: how can educational systems pursue these two contradicting demands simultaneously? This dilemma is obviously applicable to all public education systems. Therefore, it is not surprising that they all have a formal monitoring mechanism with individuals holding a position often called "superintendent" in spite of the inherent differences among them. Nevertheless, substantial dissimilarities may be found in the role expectations and degrees of regulation that superintendents are expected to enforce when supervising schools in different national contexts. In this sense, the role definition and expectations attributed to the superintendency are in fact a reflection and a vivid expression of the way trust and control are conceived and translated in a given educational system. Inevitably, this also has practical implications for superintendents and for school level educators: when schools operate in a highly regulated institutional environment and superintendents are expected to closely monitor school processes and outcomes, local educators are more likely to experience mistrust resulting from their limited degrees of freedom. This in turn may increase their frustration following their constrained ability to initiate and produce educational processes according to their professional judgment.

The superintendents' role definition in public educational systems may therefore reflect a unique and fragile equilibrium that each particular system generates between the inclination to enforce national policies on schools as a means for ensuring their implementation and the tendency to enable school level educators to act in accordance with local needs, initiatives and considerations.

Hence, to better understand the challenge facing superintendents and explain the differences in superintendents' role expectations and professional conduct in different educational settings, more needs to be said about trust, control and the relation between these two qualities which has continuously been a puzzling issue (Jagd, 2010).

## WHAT IS TRUST?

Despite the growing interest in trust, there does not appear to be a solid consensus regarding the role of trust in organization theory (Douglas Creed & Miles, 1996). Accordingly, there is a lack of shared definition of the notion of trust. Castaldo (2007) found in the literature dozens of different definitions for this concept. In essence, however, trust involves positive expectations regarding the actions of others and the willingness to be vulnerable to these actions (Jagd, 2010).

It is a belief or cognitive stance that may be quantified by a subjective probability (Braynov & Sandholm, 2002). The difficulty to clearly pinpoint the meaning of trust in organizational and institutional contexts may be further explained in considering that trust is not a static phenomenon: it may increase or decrease, depending on the ongoing interactions with others and on the context within which these interactions occur (Bijlsma-Frankema & Costa, 2005). In this respect, it is also important to acknowledge that the construction and destruction of trust are not equivalent processes: while the development of trust is a slow and incremental process (Möllering, 2006), mistrust may follow a single negative incident (Bijlsma-Frankema & Costa, 2005).

## HOW IS TRUST CREATED?

Trust involves a conscious decision to rely on another party's behavior and judgment. Undoubtedly, this is not an easy thing to do as this act involves risk and uncertainty, especially if the trustee errs or betrays the trust. Therefore, it seems that some facilitating conditions must exist if trust is likely to develop. Among these conditions are: the ability to suspend disbelief and mistrust (Bachmann, 2001; Möllering, 2005a) and promote positive expectations, the willingness to become vulnerable (Bijlsma-Frankema & Costa, 2005), the willingness to cope with risk (Bachmann, 2001), and some personal acquaintance with the trustee (Bachmann, 2001; Lewicki & Bunker, 1995) with particular emphasis on the trustee's integrity and assumed ability (Schoorman, Mayer & Davis, 2007). Nevertheless, as argued by Luhmann (1979) and Gambetta (1988), in many cases trust begins where rational prediction ends.

# FORMS OF TRUST

Trust is about the willingness of one party to rely on the actions of another party (the trustee) and abandon control over the trustee's actions to a certain degree, based on the assumption that the trustee will act in accordance with one's expectations. Nevertheless, the literature suggests that trust is not uniform but, rather, a quality which may take various forms. Shapiro, Sheppard and Cheraskin (1992) distinguish between three forms of trust in organizational settings: *deterrence-based* trust follows an assumption that people will do what they say they are going to do. This form of trust is sustained by the threat of punishment which will follow inconsistent behavior. *Knowledge-based* trust relies on the information we have about others and the extent to which it enables us to assume we understand them and are able to predict their behavior. And finally, *identification-based* trust which evolves from empathy with the other party's values desires and intentions. In considering that trust is an ever evolving phenomenon, these forms of trust may change over time from one form to the other (Lewicki & Bunker, 1995).

# TRUST IN HIERARCHICAL STRUCTURES

As research on trust gradually becomes vast, there is a growing recognition of its importance in social, economic, political legal and organizational relations. The growing interest in trust in organizational settings evolves from the notion that trust is associated with organizational effectiveness (Barnes, 1981). As Fukuyama (1995) argues, the ability to form trusting relationships with diverse strangers is organizational social capital. Specifically, it is argued that organizations characterized by high levels of trust will have more adaptive organizational structures (Rousseau, Sitkin, Burt & Camerer, 1998), strategic alliances (Das & Teng, 1998; Jones & Bowie, 1998), will be more effective in crisis management (Webb, 1996) and will be characterized by reduced internal conflict and administrative expenditures (Shockley-Zalabak & Ellis, 2000).

In hierarchical settings characterized by a long and diversified chain of command, trust even plays a more significant role since control is more complicated and individuals have greater opportunities for consideration and judgment.

Trust is important for individuals located in both higher and lower levels of the hierarchy. Individuals in lower status positions typically experience fear that those above will exploit and treat them unfairly. High ranking individuals typically suspect that their subordinates will become engaged in acts that are not in line with the organizational policy and mission (Kramer, 1996). Therefore, in considering the reciprocal vulnerabilities and uncertainties that are inherent to hierarchical relationships (Kramer, 1996), trust becomes a crucial element (Kanter, 1977; Sitkin & Roth, 1993).

Building trust in large-scale hierarchies is not a simple task since trust typically follows face to face encounters through which individuals gain knowledge about each other's personal capabilities, values and preferences (Bachmann, 2001). This last argument may be better explained in considering that in large-scale hierarchies, individuals occupying positions in different echelons hardly know each other. Therefore, trust between individuals located at different hierarchical levels cannot be based on personal acquaintance. Moreover, trust which is grounded on personal acquaintance may not be sufficient to produce the qualities and quantities of trust needed in highly diversified systems (Zucker, 1986). Hence, trust in diversified hierarchical structures must also rely on institutional arrangements (Bachmann, 2001) which include standards of expertise, regulations and procedures, creating the foundation for a "system trust" (Giddens, 1990).

# TRUST VS. CONTROL: A ZERO-SUM GAME?

Trust is viewed as highly significant for coordinating relations in organizational systems and decreasing uncertainty and risk. The problem with trust is that even after it has been established successfully, it always remains a fragile mechanism.

It is important to acknowledge, however, that trust is not the only means organizations employ in order to reduce uncertainty and promote adequate performance. The use of power as a means for control is another mechanism typically employed to reduce uncertainty and ensure that individuals act in accordance with organizational guidelines and regulations. While these two mechanisms are rather distinct, they seem to operate on the basis of a similar principal (Bachmann, 2001) as they both create an influence which regulates individual behaviors and establishes the quality of interactions among organizational members. The main difference between these two concepts may be evident in the degrees of freedom individuals have: when trust is involved, compliance is based on individual ethics and integrity, leaving much space for personal judgment. As far as control is concerned, those in high level positions leave limited degrees of freedom for their subordinates. Instead, they construct an undesirable scenario regarding the subordinate's future behavior and connect it with threats and sanctions (Bachmann, 2001). Hence, as Bachmann (2001) argues, "…trust works on the basis of positive assumptions about *alter ego's* willingness and ability to cooperate, while power is constitutively based on the selection of a *negative* hypothetical possibility regarding *alterego's* (re-)actions…" (p. 350). In practice, systems characterized by a low level of institutional trust are more likely to choose power as a means for controlling relationships (Bachmann, 2001). This is also the case of modern complex organizational systems which may not be controlled merely on the basis of trust and individual goodwill.

Although trust and control are two concepts that focus much attention when individual and organizational behavior is considered, the exclusive meaning of each of them is not entirely clear (Costa & Bijlsma-Frankema, 2007) in spite of the large number of empirical endeavors which attempted to differentiate between them (de Man & Roijakkers, 2009; Ferrin, Bligh & Kohles, 2007; Khodyakov 2007; Long & Sitkin, 2006; Möllering, 2005b). Nevertheless, the literature advocates two main perspectives to describe the relationship between the two concepts: the substituting or the complementing (Jagd, 2010).

The substituting perspective argues that the two concepts are inversely related so that the presence of trust reduces the need for control and vice versa (Dekker, 2004; Jagd, 2010). According to this perspective, organizations wishing to regulate individual behaviors must choose between these two mechanisms (Costa & Bijlsma-Frankema, 2007).

The complementing perspective argues that trust and control allow organizations to achieve improved performance that either mechanism may provide on its own (Poppo & Zenger, 2002). According to this perspective, these two mechanisms do not exclude each other and, therefore, may be employed simultaneously (Bachmann, 2001). Moreover, the simultaneous reliance on trust and control is assumed to contribute to the effectiveness of both governance strategies (Das & Teng, 2001; Jagd, 2010). Möllering (2005a) argues that one main reason for the confusion between control and trust and for the tendency to see them as two contradictory notions rests in their different focus: while trust is defined mainly in terms of the expectations one party has regarding the other, control is defined in terms of the level of constraints imposed on the other. Such definitions foster the notion of dualism arguing that control and trust cannot coexist. However, Möllering (2005a) suggests that duality rather than dualism reflects the actual relationship between the two concepts. This means that trust and control assume each other's existence in the sense that you cannot have one without the other (Sydow & Windeler, 2003). Control and trust exist in a reflexive relationship where trust may produce control. This last statement may be better explained in considering that the generalization of trust in the sense it is no longer tied to particular individuals but rather to the entire system turns trust into a control-like quality as it becomes a social reality characterizing the system as a whole (Zucker, 1986). And finally, trust and control are irreducible to each other in the sense that trust cannot be understood as a subcategory of control and control cannot be understood as a form of trust. Möllering concludes that the duality perspective for trust and control enables obtaining richer amounts of positive expectations where other approaches remain simplistic, linear and deterministic (Möllering, 2005a).

The duality perspective which assumes that trust and control are complementary and therefore may coexist implies that supervision processes conducted in organizational systems may take a dynamic form. Specifically, every system may adopt a different blend of trust and control and may change this blend according to the circumstances, policies and the level of commitment and involvement of subordinates. The qualities of this blend may be evident in the degrees of freedom and empowerment that role holders located at the lower levels of the hierarchy have and in the type of mechanism that each system adopts for the purpose of regulation. Hence, the duality perspective for trust and control may explain the differences likely to be found in the function and scope of supervision between hierarchies and organizational systems.

## THE CHALLENGE OF TRUST BUILDING IN PUBLIC EDUCATIONAL SYSTEMS

Trust building is an incremental process requiring several facilitating conditions in order to evolve. While trust depends on the way individuals are perceived by others and on the willingness of one party to rely on the actions and judgment of others, one cannot ignore the circumstances or the type and quality of the issues involved. Specifically, when individuals operate in an institutional environment characterized by high ambiguity and complexity, establishing trust as a main mechanism for behavior regulation is likely to be more difficult since such circumstances lack clear standards for action success or failure.

Such is the case of schools operating in public educational systems. Schools strive to achieve goals which are systematically ambiguous (Wildavsky, 1979). The relation between ends and means tends to be vague (Rose, 1984) and the measures for goal achievement are inherently unreliable (Hogwood & Peters, 1985; March & Olsen, 1976; Pressman & Wildavsky, 1984). The complexity of the educational system is aggravated by the inherent essence and nature of its issues and problems (Elboim-Dror, 1970). Using Rittel and Webber's classification, educational issues are mostly "wicked" rather than "tame": they are ill-defined; there is no ultimate test for their solutions; they are unique; they are symptoms of other issues and educators are held liable for any consequences obtained by their actions, since social tolerance for undesired outcomes and mistakes is low when wicked issues are involved (1973). It is difficult, therefore, to articulate holistic solutions for educational problems since it is difficult to differentiate between problems and their symptoms (Kaufman, 1972). Moreover, educational problems have typically multiple correct solutions and there may be multiple methods of obtaining each (Wagner, 1994). Hence, when facing ill-defined problems, educators must first spend considerable effort identifying the problem and the values at stake in the solution. When they have achieved such clarification, they may still be uncertain about the goals to be accomplished, the adequate solution process and constraints or obstacles to solutions that they are likely to encounter. For this reason, least structured problems are difficult to solve and are considered frightening and stressful (Leithwood & Stager, 1989). Complexity also characterizes social and political interests that educational systems are expected to satisfy. Schools are exposed to a variety of contradictory interests and to complex interwoven problems which characterize the turbulent environment in which they operate (Drucker, 1980; Schon, 1983). A significant number of school problems are unpredictable and unclear (Leithwood, 1994) and must be solved in contexts that are highly variable (Leithwood & Steinbach, 1994). Consequently, schools need to be flexible so as to enable their adaptation when conditions or circumstances change (Lane, 1995). As a result, public schools experience deep tension between the need for stability and the need for flexibility, since in their stability society finds its order, and yet that order depends upon their capacity to change (Stewart & Ranson, 1994). Consequently, such characteristics may undermine the construction of trust and, at the same time, make trust a critical factor in considering the complexity and ambiguity of educational issues, the structural fragmentation of the system and, therefore, the critical role that individual judgment plays.

## THE EDUCATIONAL SUPERINTENDENT

Public education is one of the main and most influential institutions that western democracies sponsor and maintain. Therefore, the role of the state in controlling public schools and the conflict between governmental versus local control has always been at the center of the debate in modern states (Nir, 2009). In this sense, creating a balance and reconciling between these two clashing objectives has long ago been detected as a major challenge for policymakers (Weiler, 1990).

Superintendents play a major role in this respect. Holding one of the most influential leadership positions in public education, they strive to combine the loosely coupled fragments typically characterizing educational systems (Weick, 1976), to ensure that educational processes conducted at the school level are professionally adequate, effective and in line with state goals.

Nevertheless, while research on educational leadership at the school level is abundant, studies on the educational superintendent are relatively sparse. Studies that focused on the educational superintendent suggest that this role is certainly not a walk in the park. Rather, evidence suggests that the role of the superintendent has evolved into one of the "most complex positions seen today" (Short & Scribner, 2002, p. 1). Kowalski (2006) found that most superintendents consider their position demanding and complex following their need to cope with a variety of challenges and multiple expectations which occasionally create a hostile environment. Unsurprisingly, the superintendent's role is considered a high-conflict managerial position (Blumberg, 1985; Boyd, 1982; Jackson, 1995; Kowalski, 1995; Leithwood, 1995; Nir & Eyal, 2003; Thody, 1997), since superintendents serve as mediators between conflicting demands and expectations coming from various stakeholders. Thus, superintendents are "immersed in a vague and uneasy harmony of opposing forces" (Carter & Cunningham, 1997, p. 33) and are "awash in contradictions and anomalies" (Crowson, 1987). These unique role circumstances portray the notion that conflict is "a built-in element of the superintendent job" (Crowson, 1987) and a component of "the DNA of the superintendency" (Cuban, 1985). Hence, over the years, the superintendent role has transformed from "community leader to school manager to education manager to scapegoat" (Houston, 2007, p. 30).

A review of the literature reveals that school superintendents typically face many fronts: They serve as educational and instructional leaders, as political leaders, as managerial leaders and as communicators (Cuban, 1985; Johnson, 1996; Kowalski, 2005). Their role duties include a wide variety of tasks: involvement in the daily affairs of school classrooms and interaction with teachers and principals; strategic planning; budget preparation, vision setting and human resource management (Johnson, 1996; Peterson & Barnett, 2006, p. 124). Edwards (2007) lists six role commonalities which seem to characterize American superintendents: 1. serving as chief executive officer of the school board; 2. providing leadership planning and evaluating instructional programs; 3. selecting and hiring personnel; 4. preparing the budget for submission to the board and monitoring its use after approval; 5. administering building and facilities operation and maintenance; 6. serving as leader in improving the education system (pp. 10-11).

The need to cope with a large variety of tasks while experiencing conflicting demands exposes school superintendents to high pressure and risk. In considering the complicated and unstable role circumstances they face, it is not surprising that job security is called into question. And, indeed, research conducted in the American educational context suggests that the superintendency is characterized by rapid turnover (Chapman, 1997, p. 3): the average period of service for superintendents within their respective districts is six years (Glass, Bjork & Brunner, 2000) and 64% of school districts had three or more superintendents during a single decade (Glass & Bjork, 2003). Similar findings have been obtained in a longitudinal study that tracked superintendents' tenure since the 1970s (Kowalski, 2006, p. 316). Moreover, specific conditions such as high poverty districts or low financial support may even have a stronger negative impact on superintendents' tenure (Byrd, Drews & Johnson, 2006; Natkin, Cooper, Alborano, Padilla & Ghosh, 2002).

It appears, as a result, that the superintendent's role is complicated, difficult and often characterized by an ambiguous professional horizon. Nevertheless, differences are likely to be found among national educational systems in the patterns of control and supervision applied to schools and, therefore, also in superintendents' role expectations. Conceptually, such differences may evolve from two basic orientations that construct the infrastructure for supervision: *control* and *trust*. Control aims at establishing regulation based on a set of guidlines or standards in pursuit of some desired objectives (Das & Teng, 2001). Formal control will attempt to enforce compliance and will therefore strive to limit the degrees of freedom granted to school level educators. Such orientation will encourage superintendents to closely monitor schools' conduct to ensure they operate in accordance with policy plans and regulations. Superintendents will be expected to use their formal authority so that potential deviations will be decreased and to exercise their power through the use of sanctions when such deviations occur.

Trust is the second orientation for supervision. It is assumed to help subordinate the professional behavior of individuals (Bachmann, 2001) and is likely to take place in educational systems that attempt to promote school educators' autonomy and degrees of freedom to allow local considerations and values to influence and shape school level processes. Such an orientation will encourage superintendents to serve as facilitators and to use their proficiency and expertise to assist schools to meet national as well as local goals most effectively.

Bearing in mind that public educational systems are loosely coupled (Weick, 1976), a trust oriented supervision seems more adequate since power and coercionare are less capable of producing goodwill (Bachmann, 2001) which is essential for highly fragmented organizational systems. In this sense, establishing supervision on the basis of strong control and coercion might be counterproductive since power does not enjoy high reputation in day to day praxis (Bachmann, 2001). Therefore, initiating strong control may be interpreted by school level educators as mistrust which is known to reduce efficiency, creativity, self-directedness and interest in work tasks (Tyler & Kramer, 1996).

However, in line with the duality perspective which argues that trust and control are complementary and therefore may coexist, supervision processes conducted in educational systems are likely to be dynamic and may reflect a blend of these two orientations. Specifically, such blends may analytically produce four different cultures of supervision in educational systems, as the following conceptual model illustrates:

# Cultures of supervision

**Control**

|             | low           | high       |
|-------------|---------------|------------|
| **low**     | Idiosyncratic | Regulation |
| **high**    | Autonomy      | Conflict   |

**Trust**

*Autonomy* – This culture of superintendency is characterized by a tendency to express high trust in schools evident in the limited efforts to control and closely monitor schools' conduct. This pattern grants school level educators considerable degrees of freedom, allowing them to act in accordance with their professional judgment within a predetermined framework set by state policies and regulations.

*Conflict* – This culture reflects a blend of high trust and high control, testifying to the inclination to ensure that policy plans are carried out as planned while allowing for local considerations to shape school level processes. This pattern of superintendency will result in conflict for superintendents who will be expected to grant teachers and school leaders a high degree of professional freedom, and yet ensure that school level activities and processes are in line with state policy plans, regulations and ideologies.

*Idiosyncratic*– This culture of superintendency reflects a blend of low trust and low control that superintendents are expected to exert while interacting with school level educators. This pattern may follow the high fragmentation characterizing the structure of schools and the educational system and, as a result, the difficulty it creates for control and external monitoring activities. Such circumstances may produce a culture of supervision that mainly treats exceptions such as extreme and unanticipated events which cannot be ignored. Under the idiosyncratic culture of supervision, school level educators will experience high degrees of freedom which may lead them to assume that superintendents have high trust in them, although in practice this culture of supervision will typically reflect the limitations that structural fragmentation produces for external control.

*Regulation*– This culture of supervision will follow low trust in school level educators and, therefore, a tendency to exert high control whenever possible in spite of the structural fragmentation characterizing schools and the educational system as a whole. This pattern will be characterized by a vast number of strict regulations followed by external measurements which will strive to restrict teachers' and principals' degrees of freedom as a means for ensuring that schools' performance meets state policies.

As previously noted, supervision processes may take a dynamic form. In practice, the blend of trust and control may change, leading to a transformation of the culture of supervision characterizing a given educational system. Such transformations are likely to follow innovative policy plans which foster structural changes and therefore also modifications in the structure of control. School empowerment initiatives and school-based management policy plans may serve as good examples for these types of change, especially when introduced in centralized educational systems (Nir, 2003). Such initiatives may lead to modifications in the culture of supervision mainly, from regulation which typically characterizes centralized structures, to conflict (Nir & Eyal, 2003), or even to a supervision culture of autonomy if these policy plans are implemented rigorously.

# TRUST AND SUPERINTENDENCY IN CONTEXT

While each of the described superintendency cultures reflects a unique duality between trust and control, it is important to note that in reality patterns of supervision in different educational systems will always be influenced by social cultural and circumstantial occurrences. Therefore, each educational system is likely to be characterized by a superintendency system portraying an exclusive blend of this duality.

Moreover, this duality is likely to also be shaped by the way trust is perceived and articulated in different social realms and cultural settings since trust is context dependent and its qualities are often formed by norms, values and qualities of the cultural setting (Bachmann, 2001). National cultures influence the maintenance and development of trusting relations (Harris & Moran, 1996) through their values that impact individual perception, reasoning and trust. For example, different societies have different assumptions regarding the nature of individuals: some societies see people as a mixture of good and evil. Others see individuals as basically good or as basically evil, and trust is associated with these world views (Adler, 1997). As a consequence, countries may be classified according to the level of trust that typically characterizes their cultures (Parkhe, 1998).

In search of mechanisms that explain how trust differs across cultures (Den Hartog, 2004) and how cultures foster or prevent the development of trust relations, it is further argued that different societies are characterized by different orientations likely to impact individual predisposition to trust. Specifically, task-oriented cultures seem to have a higher initial trust of strangers while relationship-oriented cultures need time to develop a relationship prior to working on the task (Schoorman, Mayer & Davis, 2007). Other studies suggest that the cultural variable of uncertainty avoidance is another well-established predictor often mentioned in relation to trust: it predicts the predisposition to take risks which is highly significant in determining the level of trust (Sully de Luque & Javidan, 2004).

Bearing in mind the contextual influences shaping trust, this book attempts to provide international audiences of policymakers, planners, district as well as school-level educators and obviously researchers substantial multicultural evidence regarding mechanisms and processes of control characterizing different educational systems, using the superintendent's role as a lens. Each chapter focuses on a single state so that readers may obtain an insider's perspective of the superintendency system in light of the structural, institutional and cultural characteristics of each educational system.

All chapters are written by leading scholars representing thirteen countries and educational systems, which differ from each other in almost every possible respect: size, quality of achievements, structure and patterns of authority (centralized/decentralized), financial investment, social fragmentation and many other features.

As expected, the chapters show that control is employed in all countries and educational systems. Yet, the superintendency system and superintendents' influence and expected contribution to schools and the educational system significantly differ in light of the unique characteristics of each cultural setting.

In realizing the differences in the way trust and control are conceived in various cultural and social settings, it is possible to conclude that national contexts have a critical influence on the way trust is conceptualized and articulated, on the duality and particular blend created between trust and control and, therefore, on the role expectations that superintendents are supposed to meet.

And so, the Russian proverb "*trust, but verify*" (*Doveryai, no proveryai*), which tackles the duality between trust and control, seems to be relevant to all public educational systems. However, its significance and practical implications are likely to take various shapes and forms, producing unique implications for school superintendents operating in different systems and educational settings.

# REFERENCES

Adler, N. J. (1997). *International dimensions of organizational behaviour*. Cincinnati: South Western College Pub.

Bachmann, R. (2001). Trust power and control in trans-organizational relations. *Organization Studies*, 22 (2), 337-365.

Barnes, L. B. (1981). Managing the paradox of organizational trust. *Harvard Business Review*, 59 (March-April), 107-116.

Bijlsma-Frankema, K., & Costa, A. C. (2005). Understanding the trust-control nexus. *International Sociology*, 20 (3), 259-282.

Blumberg, A. (1985). *The school superintendent: Living with conflict.*New York: Teachers College Press.

Boyd, W. L. (1982). The politics of declining enrollments and school closings. In: N. H. Cambron-McCabe & A. Odden (Eds.), *The changing politics of school Finance* (pp. 231-267). Cambridge, Mass.: Ballinger.

Braynov, S., & Sandholm, T. (2002). Contracting with uncertain level of trust. *Computational Intelligence*, 18 (4), 501-514.

Byrd, J., Drews, C., & Johnson, J. (2006, October). *Factors impacting superintendent turnover: Lessons from the field.* Paper presented at the annual meeting of the University Council of Educational Administration, Texas.

Carter, G. R., & Cunningham, W. G. (1997). *The American school superintendent: Leading in an age of pressure.* San Francisco: Jossey-Bass Publishers.

Castaldo, S. (2007). *Trust in market relationships*. Cheltenham: Edward Elgar.

Chapman, C. H. (Ed.). (1997). *Becoming a superintendent: Challenges of school district leadership.*Upper Saddle River, N.J.: Merrill.

Costa, A. C., & Bijlsma-Frankema, K. (2007). Trust and control interrelations: New perspectives on the trust-control nexus. *Group & Organization Management*, 32 (4), 392-406.

Crowson, R. L. (1987). The local school district superintendency: A puzzling administrative role. *Educational Administration Quarterly*, 23 (3), 49-69.

Cuban, L. (1985). Conflict and leadership in the superintendency. *Phi. Delta Kappan*, 67 (1), 28-30.

Das, T. K., & Teng, B. S. (2001). Trust control and risk in strategic alliances: An integrated framework. *Organization Studies*, 22 (2), 251-284.

Das, T. K., & Teng, B. S. (1998). Between trust and control: Developing confidence in partner cooperation in alliances. *Academy of Management Review*, 23 (3), 491-512.

de Man, A. P., & Roijakkers, N. (2009). Alliance governance: Balancing control and trust in dealing with risk. *Long Range Planning*, 42 (1), 75-95.

Dekker, H. C. (2004). Control of inter-organizational relationships: evidence of appropriation concerns and coordination requirements. *Accounting, Organization and Society*, 29 (1), 27-49.

Den Hartog, D. N. (2004). Assertiveness. In: R. J. House, P. J. Hanges, M. Javidan, P. Dorfman & V. Gupta (Eds.), *Culture, leadership and organizations: The GLOBE study of 62 societies* (pp. 395-431). Thousand Oaks, Cal.: Sage.

Douglas Creed, W. E., & Miles, R. E. (1996). Trust in organizations: A conceptual framework linking organizational forms, managerial philosophies and the opportunity costs and controls. In: R. M. Kramer, & T. R. Tyler (Eds.), *Trust in organizations* (pp. 16-38). Thousand Oaks, Cal.: Sage.

Drucker, P. F. (1980). *Managing in turbulent times*. New York: Harper and Row.

Edwards, M. (2007). *The modern school superintendent: An overview of the role and responsibilities in the 21st century*. Lincoln, Neb.: iUniverse, Inc.

Elboim-Dror, R. (1970). Some characteristics of the education policy formation system, *Policy Science*, 1 (1), 231-253.

Ferrin, D. L., Bligh, M. C., & Kohles, J. C. (2007). Can I trust you to trust me? A theory of trust, monitoring and cooperation in interpersonal and intergroup relationships. *Group Organization Management*, 32 (4), 465-499.

Fukuyama, F. (1995). *Trust: The social virtues and the creation of prosperity*. New York: Free Press.

Gambetta, D. (Ed.), (1988). *Trust: Making and breaking co-operative relations*. Oxford: Basil Blackwell.

Giddens, A. (1990). *The consequences of modernity*. Stanford: Stanford University Press.

Glass, T., & Bjork, L. (2003). The superintendent shortage: Findings from research on school board presidents. *Journal of School Leadership*, 13(3), 264-287.

Glass, T., Bjork, L., & Brunner, C. (2000). *The study of the American superintendency, 2000: A look at the superintendent in the new millennium*. Arlington, Va.: American Association of School Administrators.

Harris, P. R., & Moran, R. T. (1996). *Managing cultural differences*. Houston: Gulf Publishing.

Hogwood, B. W., & Peters, G. B. (1985). *The pathology of public policy*. Oxford: Oxford University Press.

Houston, P. (2007). From custodian to conductor.*School Administrator*, 64 (3), 28-33.

Jackson, B. L. (1995). Balancing act: *The political role of the urban school superintendent*. The Joint Center of Political and Economic Studies, Washington, DC.

Jagd, S. (2010). Balancing trust and control in organizations: Towards a process perspective. *Society and Business Review*, 5 (3), 259-269.

Johnson, S. M. (1996). *Leading to change: The challenge of the new superintendency*. San Francisco, Cal.: Jossey-Bass, Inc.

Jones, T. M., & Bowie, N. E. (1998). Moral hazards on the road to the virtual corporation.*Business Ethics Quarterly*, 8 (2), 272-292.

Kanter, R. (1977). *Men and women of the corporation*. New York: Basic Books.

Kaufman, R. A. (1972). *Educational system planning*. New Jersey: Prentice-Hall.

Khodyakov, D. (2007). The complexity of trust-control relationships in creative organizations: Insights from a qualitative analysis of a conductorless orchestra. *Social Forces*, 86 (1), 1-22.

Kowalski, T. J. (2006). *The school superintendent: Theory, practice, and cases* (2nd ed.). Upper Saddle River, N.J.: Merrill, Prentice Hall.

Kowalski, T. J. (2005). Evolution of the school superintendent as communicator. *Communication Education*, 54 (2), 17.

Kowalski, T. J. (1995). *Keepers of the flame: Contemporary urban superintendents*. Thousand Oaks, Cal.: Corwin Press.

Kramer, R. M. (1996). Divergent realities and convergent disappointments in the hierarchic relation. In: R. M. Kramer, & T. R. Tyler (Eds.), *Trust in organizations* (pp. 216-245). Thousand Oaks, Cal.: Sage.

Lane, J. E. (1995). *The public sector: concepts, models and approaches.* London: Sage.

Leithwood, K. (1995). *Effective school district leadership: Transforming politics into Education.*Albany, New York: State University of New York Press.

Leithwood, K. (1994). Leadership for school restructuring. *Educational Administration Quarterly*, 30, (4), 498-518.

Leithwood, K., & Stager, M. (1989). Expertise in principals' problem solving.*Educational Administration Quarterly*, 25, (2), 126-161.

Leithwood, K., & Steinbach, R. (1994). The relationship between variations in patterns of school leadership and group problem-solving processes. In: P. Hallinger, K. Leithwood & J. Murphy (Eds.), *Cognitive perspectives on educational leadership* (pp. 102-129). New York: Teachers College Press.

Lewicki, R. J., & Bunker, B. B. (1995). Developing and maintaining trust in work relationships. In: R. M. Kramer & T. R. Tyler (Eds.), *Trust in organizations* (pp. 114-139). Thousand Oaks, Cal.: Sage.

Long, C., & Sitkin, S. B. (2006). Trust in the balance: how managers integrate trust building and task control. In: R. Bachmann & A Zaheer (Eds.), *Handbook of trust research* (pp. 87-107). Cheltenham: Edward Elgar.

Luhmann, N. (1979). *Trust and power.* New York: John Wiley.

March, J. G., & Olsen, J. P. (Eds.) (1976). *Ambiguity and choice in organizations.* Bergen, Norway: Bergen Universitetsforlaget.

Möllering, G. (2005a). Rational, institutional and active trust: Just do it!? In: K. M. Bijlsma-Frankema & R. J. A. Klein Woolthuis (Eds.), *Trust under pressure: Empirical investigations of the functioning of trust and trust building in uncertain circumstances* (pp. 24-51). Cheltenham: Edward Elgar.

Möllering, G. (2005b). The trust/control duality: An integrative perspectives on positive expectations of others. *International Sociology*, 20 (3), 283-305.

Möllering, G. (2006). *Trust: reason, routine, reflexivity.* Elsevier: London.

Natkin, G., Cooper, B., Alborano, J., Padilla, A., & Ghosh, S. (2002, April). *Predicting and modeling superintendent turnover.* Paper presented at the Annual Meeting of the American Educational Research Association, New Orleans, La..

Nir, A. E. (Ed.) (2009). *Centralization and school empowerment: From rhetoric to practice.* New York: Nova Science Publishers.

Nir, A. E. (2003). The impact of school-based management on public schools in Israel. *Curriculum and Teaching,* 18 (1), 65-80.

Nir, A. E., & Eyal, O. (2003). School-based management and the role conflict of the school superintendent.*Journal of Educational Administration,* 41 (5), 547-564.

Parkhe, A. (1998). Understanding trust in international alliances. *Journal of World Business,* 33 (3), 2190-240.

Petersen, G., & Barnett, B. (2005). The superintendent as instructional leader. In: L. G. Bjork & T. J. Kowalski (Eds.), *The contemporary superintendent: Preparation, practice, and development* (pp. 107-136). Thousand Oaks, Cal.: Sage.

Poppo, L., & Zenger, T. (2002). Do formal contracts and relational governance function as substitutes or complements? *Strategic Management Journal*, 23 (8), 707-725.

Pressman, J., & Wildavsky, A. (1984). *Implementation.* Berkeley: University of California Press.

Rittel, H. W., & Webber, N. M. (1973). Dilemmas in general theory of planning. *Policy Science,* 4 (2), 155-169.

Rose, R. (1984). *Understanding big government: The program approach.* London: Sage.

Rousseau, D. M., Sitkin, S. B., Burt, R. S., & Camerer, C. (1998). Not so different after all: A cross discipline view of trust. *Academy of Management Review,* 23 (3), 393-404.

Schon, D. A. (1983). *The reflective practitioner.* New York: Basic Books.

Schoorman, F. D., Mayer, R. C., & Davis, J. H. (2007). An integrative model of organizational trust: Past, present and future. *Academy of Management Review,* 32 (2), 344-354.

Shapiro, D., Sheppard, B. H., & Cheraskin, L. (1992). Business on a handshake. *Negotiation Journal,* 8 (4), 365-377.

Shockley-Zalabak, P., & Ellis, K. (2000). *Measuring organizational trust: Cross cultural survey and index.* International Association of Business Communicators IABC, San Francisco.

Short, P. M., & Scribner, J. R. (Eds.) (2002). *Case studies of the superintendency.* Lanham, Md.: Scarecrow Press.

Sitkin, S. B., & Roth, N. L. (1993). Explaining the limited effectiveness of legalistic "remedies" for trust/distrust.*Organizational Science,* 4 (3), 367-392.

Stewart, J., & Ranson, S., (1994). Management in the public domain. In: D. McKevitt & A. Lawton (Eds.), *Public sector management* (pp. 54-84). London: Sage.

Sully de Luque, M., & Javidan, M., (2004). Uncertainty avoidance. In: R. J. House, P. J. Hanges, M. Javidan, P. Dorfman, & V. Gupta (Eds.), *Culture, leadership and organizations: The GLOBE study of 62 societies* (pp. 603-644). Thousand Oaks, Cal.: Sage.

Sydow, J., & Windeler, A. (2003). Knowledge trust and control: Managing tensions and contradictions in the regional network of service firms. *International Studies of Management and Organization,* 33 (2), 69-99.

Thody, A. (1997). Leadership of schools: Chief executives in education.Wiltshire, U.K.: Redwood Books.

Tyler, T. R., & Kramer, R. M. (1996). Whither trust? In: R. M. Kramer, & T. R. Tyler (Eds.), *Trust in organizations* (pp. 1-15). Thousand Oaks, Cal.: Sage.

Wagner, R. K. (1994). Practical problem-solving. In: P. Hallinger, K. Leithwood & J. Murphy (Eds.): *Cognitive perspectives on educational leadership* (pp. 88-102). New York: Teachers College Press.

Webb, E. J. (1996). Trust and crisis: Trust in organizations – frontiers of theory and research. In: R. M. Kramer, & T. R. Tyler (Eds.), *Trust in organizations* (pp. 288-301). Thousand Oaks, Cal.: Sage.

Weick, K. E. (1976). Educational organizations as loosely coupled systems, *Administrative Science Quarterly,* 21 (1), 1-19.

Weiler, H. N. (1990). Comparative perspectives on educational decentralization: An exercise in contradiction? *Educational Evaluation and Policy Analysis,* 12 (4), 433-448.

Wildavsky, A. (1979). *Speaking truth to power: The art and craft of policy analysis.* Boston: Little, Brown & Co.

Zucker, L. G. (1986). Production of trust: Institutional sources of economic structure. *Research in Organizational Behavior*, 8, 53-111.

In: The Educational Superintendent
Editor: Adam E. Nir

ISBN: 978-1-62948-972-8
© 2014 Nova Science Publishers, Inc.

*Chapter 2*

# THE SCHOOL DISTRICT SUPERINTENDENT IN THE UNITED STATES OF AMERICA

*Lars G. Björk[1], Theodore J. Kowalski[2]*
*and Tricia Browne-Ferrigno[1]*
[1]University of Kentucky, KY, US
[2]University of Dayton, OH, US

The role of school-district superintendents in the United States of America has evolved since the introduction of the position during the middle of the 19th century. Since that time, the pace of demographic and economic change has accelerated. These circumstances not only had a profound effect on the nature of schooling in the nation but also contributed to defining then redefining superintendents' work. As the nation shifted from an agricultural to an industrial economy people migrated in ever-increasing numbers from rural farming communities and small towns to urban centers. Cities increased in size and then grew exponentially following unprecedented waves of immigration. Over the next several decades, these demographic shifts increased the complexity of urban life and altered the way cities were organized, managed and governed—which had a profound impact on the nature of public education. Immigrants arrived with a diverse array of economic beliefs, political experiences and cultural traditions. These differences raised concern among some segments of society but inspired others to find ways to forge common ground and facilitate assimilation. In this crucible of change, the purpose of schooling was redefined, shifting from simply ensuring that students were literate and numerate to broadening access and nurturing understanding of the American society and established values and beliefs.

Economic, social, political and technological changes that ensued over successive eras continued to influence how superintendents' work was defined. Initially, they were regarded as teacher scholars who focused their efforts on academic quality. When the size and complexity of school districts exceeded the capacity of school board members to provide direct oversight of school district affairs, superintendents became managers. In the post-World War I era, when corporate management was in ascendency, school district superintendents assumed the mantle of the chief executive officer (CEO), and school boards mimicked those in the private sector in form and function. After the Great Depression of the

1930s, superintendents embraced the notion of parent involvement as they reclaimed their role in the education of children and youth. This changed orientation required considerable political acumen to negotiate new terrain.

During the post-World War II period, a broad array of influences enhanced the importance of public education including expansion of science and mathematics curricula and the pursuit of desegregation and equal rights in the 1950s-1970s. Beginning in the mid-1980s, a protracted era of educational reform and high stakes accountability—unparalleled in its intensity, duration and magnitude—was launched. Thus, throughout its recent history, the role of superintendent is inextricably intertwined with the changing nature and purpose of schooling. Scholars have observed several important dynamical relationships between context and superintendent roles. First, the nature of their work is intertwined with the economic, social and political shift occurring in the nation, states and local communities. Second, the prominence of roles is variable. Roles that were prominent in one era were eclipsed in another, but none of these roles has disappeared. Rather, they became less conspicuous as dictated by a shift in demands on the office or by the determination of the school boards and communities they serve.

The notion that superintendents' work may be characterized as consisting of five major roles is grounded in historical and empiricalevidence. These data indicate the complexity of superintendents' roles and provide a measure of insight into how superintendents may use their position to launch and sustain educational reform. Thus, examining the evolution of the role of superintendents in its historical context and testing the viability of assertions provides a template for understanding the nature of their work, characteristics and responsibilities. To accomplish this, we situate the superintendent in time and place in the American education system, examine educational reform initiatives that are changing the nature of their work, briefly describe the characteristics of those who serve as school district CEOs, and then discuss role characterizations as tested against historical discourse, professional standards and research findings.

## EDUCATIONAL REFORM REPORTS: IMPLICATIONS FOR SUPERINTENDENTS

During the past three decades, "widespread concern for the quality of public education launched what is arguably is the most intense, comprehensive and sustained effort improve education in America's history" (Björk, 2001a, p. 19). Since 1983, national commission and task force reports linked the quality of public schooling to the well-being of the country immersed in a highly competitive, global economy. These reports not only examined the condition of education but also heightened expectations for schooling, called for improving instruction, and contributed to fundamentally altering the manner in which schools are organized, administered and governed. These recommendations for improvement coupled with those emerging from state-level investigations stimulated a wide array of reform measures by federal and state legislatures, departments of education, school districts and schools. Taken as a whole, these recommendations and mandatesnot only challenged conventional assumptions about the nature of schooling but also increased awareness of the importance of school and district leadership. Since the early 1990s interest in large-scale, district-level systemic reform heightened interest in the role of superintendents in launching and sustaining educational change. The scope, intensity and complexity of calls for change not only challenged superintendents (Brunner, Grogan & Björk, 2002) but also heightened concerns about how their roles had changed and may change.

According to Firestone (1990), serious efforts to correct school deficiencies began in the late 1970s before release of *A Nation at Risk* (National Commission on Excellence in Education, 1983). Although the content and often strident claims made by the authors of *A Nation at Risk* were disputed, media coverage created a widespread public perception that schools had not only failed the nation's children but also triggered the nation's recent economic decline. Citizens, policymakers and parents called for an investigation of public education and demanded that schools be held accountable for student learning. Thus, *A Nation at Risk* is not only credited with launching an era of educational reform but also serving as a metaphor for its vulnerability. Analysts agree that educational reform reports were released in three successive waves, each having distinct yet related themes (Björk, 1996; Björk, Kowalski &Young, 2005; Firestone, Furhman & Kirst, 1990; Murphy, 1990). The first wave of educational reform reports (1983-1986) commenced with release of *A Nation at Risk* (National Commission on Excellence in Education, 1983) and followed in rapid succession by similar documents including *Making the Grade* (Twentieth Century Fund, 1983), *High School* (Boyer, 1983), *Action for Excellence* (Task Force on Education for Economic Growth, 1983), and *Educating Americans for the 21st Century* (National Science Board Commission, 1983). These first-wave reports called for increasing student academic performance, holding schools accountable for student test scores, increasing graduation requirements, lengthening the school day and year, and increasing the rigor of teacher licensure requirements. Most states incorporated many of these recommendations through education reform legislation and regulatory controls that often reached into the classroom. Policy analysts often refer to this time period as the introduction to an era of high stakes accountability. It is important to note that these legislative initiatives shifted responsibility for policymaking from local school district boards of education to state-levelgovernmental agencies, which limited opportunities for school-level policymaking, expanded the size and research of state and district bureaucracies, and increased the workload of superintendents, principals and teachers (Björk, 1996).

The second wave of education reform reports, released between 1985 and 1989, not only fueled the national debate on public education but also reinvigorated reformers. A sample of five prominent reports was selected from those released to illustrate an uncommon level of consistency in thinking about what needed to be done: *Investing in Our Children* (Committee for Economic Development, 1985), *A Nation Prepared* (Carnegie Forum on Education and the Economy, 1986), *Tomorrow's Teachers* (Holmes Group, 1986), *Time for Results* (National Governors Association, 1986), and *Children in Need* (Committee for Economic Development, 1987). An analysis of these reports revealed several recurring themes. First, they affirmed the need to institute standards-based assessments to hold individual schools accountable for improving student test scores, used as a proxy for evidence of student learning. Second, recommendations called for an emphasis on higher-order thinking skills, problem solving and computer competency, and cooperative learning. Third, these reportsrecognized that demographic trends in the nation's populationand the percentage of children living in poverty had important implications for learning and teaching. Fourth, the reports collectively made a compelling case for radically redesigning teaching and learning processes to ensure that all children progress academically—including those viewed as at risk for not achieving (Murphy, 1990). Fifth, these reports concluded that bureaucratic school structures and rigid state regulatory controls had a numbing effect on schools, discouraged creativity, and contributed to low academic achievement and high student failure rates. Consequently, they recommended decentralizing decisionmaking by instituting school-based management councils to increase teacher participation, ownership and professionalism (Björk, 1996).

The third wave of education reform reports, released between 1989 and 2003, was highly critical of previous prescriptive and solution driven recommendations (Clark & Astuto, 1994; Peterson & Finn, 1985) focused on organizational and professional issues rather than on the well-being of students and their learning. Prominent reports released during the third wave included *Beyond Rhetoric: A New American Agenda for Children and Families* (National Commission on Children, 1991), *Turning Points:Preparing American Youth for the 21ˢᵗ Century* (Carnegie Corporation of New York, 1989), *Visions of a Better Way: A Black Appraisal of Public Schooling* (Franklin, 1989), *Education That Works: An Action Plan for the Education of Minorities* (Quality Education for Minorities Project, 1990), *National Excellence: A Case for Developing America's Talent* (U.S. Department of Education, 1993) and *Great Transitions: Preparing Adolescents for a New Century* (Carnegie Corporation of New York, 1995). These reports offered two canons for genuine reform. First, improving education had to focus on children and learning rather than on organizational bureaucracies, administration or teacher professionalism. Second, providing support to parents was viewed as central to enhancing children's capacity to learn. In this regard, they advocated that schools be redesigned to serve as the hub of integrated service systems (Murphy, 1990). Many of these concepts were subsequently embodied in Professional Development Schools, Cities in Schools, Sizer's Coalition of Essential Schools, and Comer's School Development Programs (Fullan, 1983).

Following the third wave of education reform, a series of reportswas published, such as*America 2000: An Education Strategy* (Alexander, 1991), and federal legislation was passed, including *Goals 2000: Educate America Act* (1994), and *No Child Left Behind Act* (2002). Despite the considerable media fanfare when released, these offered many recommendations found in previous reform reports. In some instances, new legislation negated improvement efforts in progress, thus creating considerable confusion and frustration for educators and parents (Ravitch, 2010). Nonetheless, policymakers raised concerns anew and called for serious reform. This fourth wave of reform reiterated previous reports on the changing demographic characteristics of the nation's social fabric and confirmed significant implications for learning and teaching, particularly for children at risk. A unique aspect of this reform era, however, was the acknowledged importance of leadership and its centrality to the success of school change.

Although NCLB was heralded as groundbreaking educational reform legislation, analysts and practitioners however take exception to this view. While they concur that its focus on learning for all children is laudable, they decry policymakers' penchant for top-down, coercive mandates (Kowalski, McCord, Petersen, Young & Ellerson, 2010). Contrary to findings from social science research indicating that bottom-up collaboration is central to successful re-culturing and organizational restructuring, NCLB was both highly prescriptive in its requirements and narrow in how progress would be measured. For example, Kowalski and colleagues (2010) observe that superintendents are responsible for "determining the real needs of local schools and engaging a broad spectrum of stakeholders to determine how those needs would be met" (p.5). This and other NCLB requirements had profound implications for superintendents who were expected to play pivotal leadership roles in its implementation. Further, NCLB implementation coincided with districts experiencing dramatic demographic shifts; unprecedented levels of students living in poverty (Anyon, 2005); greater numbers of immigrant students (Fix & Passel, 2003); political divisiveness and factional opposition to NCLB (Kirst & Wirt, 2009); increasing local crime rates and need for social services resulting in increasing operational costs (Kowalski et al., 2010). The confluence of these circumstances exponentially increased the difficulty of launching and sustaining the NCLB agenda.

## DECENTRALIZED SYSTEM OF EDUCATION IN THE U.S.

A national, unitary system of education does not exist in the U.S. in the way that it does in most European countries where education is centralized and controlled through a ministry of education and operates under the auspices of provincial or municipal government structures. The U.S. Constitution makes no mention of education; however, under provisions of the Tenth Amendment, it reserves to states all powers not specifically delegated to the federal government or prohibited by the Constitution. This *reserve clause* is the basis for allocating responsibility for public education to individual states (Pulliam & Van Patten, 2006). Education statutes and regulations are enacted by state legislatures and administered by state-level boards of education and state departments of education. The notion of local control of education dates from the nation's colonial period and remains a powerful concept, particularly when applied to funding public schools and governance. Consequently, state departments of education defer responsibility for district-level governance and administration to local school boards and superintendents. In addition local taxes are levied by school districts, county or municipal government (primarily through real estate taxes) that provide approximately 60% of the district's annual budget. Thus, in the U.S. there are 50 different state education systems composed ofapproximately 15,000 local school districts. Although all school districts are required to adhere to federal and state laws and policies, many differences exist among each district within a state because they often promulgate their own philosophy and goals.

## ROLE OF THE FEDERAL GOVERNMENT IN EDUCATION

The notion of local control is rooted in the nation's colonial era traditions which explain why schools have always been a responsibility of towns and cities. However, the federal government has always had some say in public education. For example, the general welfare clause of the U.S. Constitution gives Congress the right to act to serve the common good and ensure the general welfare of the nation. The language is broad enough for the federal government to use public tax monies to support specific education programs that Congress agrees serves the broad interest of the nation. For example Congress passed the first Elementary and Secondary Education Act (ESEA) in 1963, and federal money was used to advance science and mathematics education during eras known as the Cold War and the Space Race. When Congress passed the Civil Rights Act in 1964, it allowed federal funds to be used in support of school desegregation during the Civil Rights Movement. In addition, Congress passed the Education of All Handicapped Children Act in 1997 (commonly known as PL 94-142), then extended its provisions through enactment of the 1990 Individuals with Disabilities Education Act (IDEA) to ensure that handicapped children are adequately served by schools. Although the federal government is prohibited from providing for the general support of education (i.e., reserve clause in the Tenth Amendment), the federal government provides approximately 7% of school budgets through state governments that transfer funds to local schools. The U.S. Department of Education, which is administered by a presidential-appointed secretary of education, provides oversight of federal education programs (i.e., distribution of tax funds), collects data on the condition of education in the nation, and supports long-term research on important issues facing schools.

## ROLE OF THE STATE GOVERNMENT IN EDUCATION

Each state in the nation's federal system has its own Constitution, laws and tax codes that provide for the support and maintenance of education within its respective borders. States give local boards of education responsibility for managing school districts, and the public schools within the districts are funded by state allocations that typically amount to approximately 33% of district budgets. Because state legislatures are responsible for schools, they promulgate education laws, determine how state taxes are allocated to schools, and establish the manner in which financial support is provided to local districts.

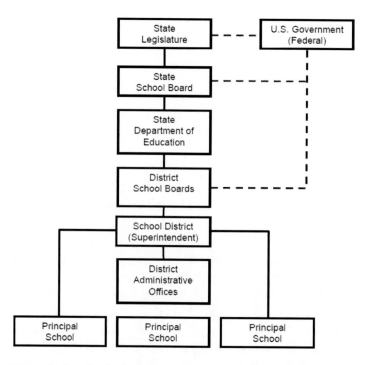

Figure 1. The structure of education in the U. S. A.

In addition, state legislatures set minimum standards for teacher and administrative licensure and personnel salaries, the elementary and secondary curriculum, and special services (e.g., buses, books, programs). Each state's school code is thus a compilation of laws that guide the operation of school districts and conduct of education in states.

State constitutions and laws provide for the establishment of a uniform system of schools and specify how they are governed. The typical state hierarchy includes a school board that may either be elected or appointed by the governor (see Figure 1). The state board of education hires a commissioner or secretary of education to oversee the state department of education. State departments of education are divided into categorical areas that are aligned with different responsibilities defined by state statute (e.g., elementary, middle and secondary schools; special education; student transportation; testing and accountability) and provide oversight of local school operations. The organizational structure of state departments of education will vary state by state.

*Local school districts:* The local school district is the basic administrative unit in state education systems (Björk, 2005). It exists at the pleasure of the state, which has complete control of its boundaries, jurisdiction, funding and defining powers of the board of education. Local school boards are elected, and members hold staggered terms to ensure continuity of decisions over time. A local school board typically has 5-9 citizens elected by local residents; however, cities may have school boards composed of 12-15 members. Historically, they have served as the primary point of access for citizens and parents to influence education policymaking. Although a local school board serves as a forum for mitigating differences, outcomes must comply with the Constitution of the United States of America, respective state constitutions, applicable court decisions as well as state rules, regulations and policies. The primary responsibility of each local school board is legislative—particularly, making policy and providing oversight of school district operations. Because citizens who are not experts in school affairs are elected members of boards of education, they must ensure that school district personnel carry out these responsibilities. Local school districts may provide education at several levels including pre-schools, elementary schools (grades 1-5), middle schools (grades 6-8), high schools and vocational schools (grades 9-12). The school board oversees school district operations through its hiring of the superintendent.

*District superintendent:* The superintendent serves as CEO of the district and manages its day-to-day affairs. They are typically hired on multiple-year contracts (usually three years in length) and serve in two to three districts over an average career spanning 16 years (Kowalski et al., 2010). They have a central office staff (middle management) that varies in size according to population of the community served. The variation in district size thus influences the degree to which the superintendent engages directly in activities within individual schools or oversees the work completed by central office staff (Björk, 2005; Browne-Ferrigno & Glass, 2005).

As the CEO of the school district, the superintendent is responsible for ensuring that legislated mandates, policies and regulations are implemented properly and for providing oversight and support to local schools. Their duties thus include:

- advising the board of education on education and policy matters;
- making recommendations to the board regarding personnel hiring;
- ensuring compliance with directives of state and federal authorities;

- preparing district budgets for board review and adoption;
- leading long-range planning activities;
- providing oversight of instructional programs and student performance;
- determining the internal organizational structure of the district; and
- making recommendations regarding school building maintenance and new construction needs (Kowalski, 2006).

In sum, superintendents must be cognizant of a wide array of economic, social and political changes unfolding in the nation as well as the state where they serve; be well-versed in national, state-level and local policy initiatives; and have the capacity to translate that knowledge into a systemic implementation plan that will withstand the rigors of continuous public inspection and criticism. Consequently, the nature of superintendents work is as complex as it is intense, requiring multiple and diverse roles (Björk, 2005).

## EVOLUTION OF THE AMERICAN SUPERINTENDENT: A DISCURSIVE ANALYSIS OF ROLES

The position of school district superintendent in the U.S. was created during the late 1830s. By 1850, 13 large city school systems already had employed an administrator in this capacity with the first district superintendents being appointed in Buffalo, New York and Louisville, Kentucky (Grieder, Pierce & Jordan, 1969). By the turn of the century (1900), most city school districts had appointed a district administrator. Scholars concur that this action was in response to numerous conditions including the consolidation of rural school districts into larger ones, an establishment of state-mandated minimum curricula, passage of compulsory attendance laws, demands for increased financial accountability, and the press for efficiency (Kowalski & Keedy, 2005).

Some discrepancies in historical accounts of the evolution of the office and role of superintendents are noted by Petersen and Barnett (2003, 2005) who attribute differences to three conditions: (a) use of different historical sources, (b) differing interpretations of historical accounts, and (c) variances in the analytical approaches used. For example, some scholars (e.g., Tyack & Hansot, 1982) relied on a developmental or linear approach that is grounded in the notion that superintendent's role matured over time. On the other hand, Callahan (1966) employed a discursive analysis that relied on rhetoric and writings to define role expectations. Brunner, Grogan & Björk (2002) acknowledged merits of both approaches, but they concluded that the discursive approach provided a more detailed account of superintendents' work and consequently resulted in a greater number of developmental stages. They also closely examined the debate over the earliest role conceptualization of the district superintendent and note that they as well as Carter and Cunningham (1997) identify it as being a school board's clerk. This role characterization is thought to have existed for several decades prior to 1850 and is predicated on the belief that big city school boards were reluctant to relinquish power. Consequently, they relegated their superintendents to performing modest clerical and administrative tasks. Historical evidence also suggests that this role was temporary, a condition that may explain why some historians (e.g., Callahan, 1966) did not view it as being relevant to contemporary practice.

# SUPERINTENDENTS' ROLE CHARACTERIZATIONS

Five role conceptualizations are addressed in this chapter to demonstrate how the position of district superintendent evolved and to show why none has become irrelevant to modern practice (Kowalski & Björk, 2005). The first four roles emerged from a review of the literature described by Callahan (1966): *teacher-scholar* (1850 to early 1900s), *organizational manager* (early 1900s to 1930), *democratic leader* (1930 to mid-1950s), and *applied social scientist* (mid-1950s to mid-1970s). The fifth role, *communicator* (mid-1970s to present), was recently added by Kowalski (2003, 2005, 2006). He argues persuasively that in practice, separating these five characterizations is impossible because practitioners often assume two or more of them at any given time. In other words, the five roles are woven into the fabric of superintendents' work. Taken together, these role conceptualizations provide an important framework for understanding the complexity of the position as well as define the knowledge and skills required for effective practice. An examination of findings from historical discourse on the superintendency (Brunner, Grogan & Björk, 2002) and data reported in the last two ten-year studies authorized by AASA (Glass, Björk & Brunner, 2000; Kowalski et al., 2010) were used to inform the discussion of the nature and validity of the five role conceptualizationsin the context of contemporary practice.

# SUPERINTENDENT AS TEACHER-SCHOLAR

Since the turn of the 20th century, the primary foci of district superintendents were (a) implementing a minimum, mandated state curriculum and (b) supervising teachers. Having district schools deliver a set of uniform subjects and courses enhanced efforts to assimilate children into the American culture; however, this goal of commonality required increasing levels of centralization and standardization to ensure compliance (Spring, 1994). In this context, the earliest superintendents were basically master teachers (Callahan, 1962). In addition, superintendents in larger school districts were often viewed as intellectual leaderswhoauthored professional journal articles about philosophy, history and pedagogy (Cuban, 1988). Some district supervisorseventually became state superintendents, professors and college presidents, which not only affirmed their role as teacher-scholars but also enhanced prestige of the profession (Petersen & Barnett, 2005).

The superintendentrole as teacher-scholar was summarized in an 1890 report on urban superintendents by Cuban (1976a):

> It must be made his recognized duty to train teachers and inspire them with high ideals; to revise the course of study when new light shows that improvement is possible; to see that pupils and teachers are supplied with needed appliances for the best possible work; to devise rational methods of promoting pupils. (p. 16)

Early superintendents were astute and used the aura of their professionalism to shield themselves from rough and tumble politics of the era and to deflect efforts by community power elites who wanted to usurp their authority. In other words, superintendents diligently avoided being cast as politicians or managers. Conceptualization of the district superintendent as teacher-scholar waned after 1910, but it never become totally irrelevant. Over the past century, expectations that superintendents should serve as instructional leaders fluctuated. However, since the early 1980s, school reform initiatives not only have heightened these expectations but also made it an enduring aspect of their work. Currently, superintendents are expected to provide visionary leadership and planning necessary to produce academic gains at the school district level. In many instances, districts and states have incorporated improving student academic test scores as part of superintendent evaluations and contract renewal criteria (Kowalski & Björk, 2005).

The AASA report by Glass, Björk & Brunner (2000) found that the teacher-scholar role is increasing in importance. For example, in 2000 over 40% of superintendents responding to the AASAsurvey indicated that the school board's primary expectation of them was to serve as an educational leader. Among the superintendents responding to the AASA survey administered ten years later (Kowalski et al., 2010), 60% reported that their school boards placed a substantial emphasis on the superintendent serving as an instructional leader. Additionally, the 2000 data indicate that this role expectation was more pronounced in larger districts, particularly those serving more than 3,000 students, and by gender. Among female superintendent respondents, 51.4% viewed being educational leader as their most important responsibility. Further, the responsibilities associated with the teacher-scholar role were prominent among challenges faced by superintendents in 2000 (Glass, Björk & Brunner, 2000).

## SUPERINTENDENT AS ORGANIZATIONAL MANAGER

During the latter part of the $19^{th}$ century (1890s), community elites who served as district school board members expressed reservations about the ability of superintendents to administer large city districts. These concerns focused primarily on a perceived lack of managerial knowledge and skills. Heated debates ensued and "the lines of argument crystallized over whether the functions of a big-city superintendent should be separated in to two distinct jobs, i.e., business manager and superintendent of instruction" (Cuban, 1976b, p. 17). Interestingly, this aspect of the debate resurfaced in 2010 when the Chicago Public Schools adopted a bipartite model.

During the late 1800s, an era characterized by an infusion of industrial concepts of scientific management and efficiency into public education, debates centered on whether or not schools operated efficiently, at least not in comparison to successful businesses (Kowalski, 1999). Over the next two decades, many leading education administration scholars, such as Ellwood Cubberly, George Strayer and Franklin Bobbitt, promoted the adoption of scientific management in public schools (Cronin, 1973). Efforts to reconfigure the role of superintendentsas district business managers were criticized by mayors, city council members and members of other political parties because they were apprehensive that it would increase the stature, influence and power of superintendents (Callahan, 1962). Conversely, some leading scholars opposed adoption of the managerial role because they believed that a shift towards adopting principles of industrial management would be accompanied by notions of board authority and executive control that were perceived as ill-suited to education organizations. Concern centered around the issue that corporate management models would erode the public's belief in ownership of schools and influence in how their children were educated (Björk & Gurley, 2005; Glass 2003).

Notwithstanding, business-dominated school boards assigned superintendents several management responsibilities (e.g., budget development and administration, standardization of operation, personnel management, facility management). Adoption of the business model for school administration was increasingly criticized after 1930 for three major reasons. First, the stock market crash and Depression of the 1930s tarnished the aura of the efficiency of captains of industry. Second, many parents objected to their perceived loss of involvement in the governance process (Kowalski, 2006). Third, earlier proponents of scientific management, including George Sylvester Counts, openly criticized the infusion of business values into school district administration, claiming it incongruous with the core values of democracy (Van Til, 1971). Several decades later, educators and policymakers compromised, noting that effective administrators had to be both managers and instructional leaders (Kowalski, 1999).

Superintendents' management role remains a core aspect of their work (Browne-Ferrigno & Glass, 2005; Kowalski & Glass, 2002). For example, more than a one-third (36.4%) of superintendents responding to an AASA survey indicated that their school board members expected them to be an effective manager (Glass et al., 2000). Nonetheless, superintendents also reported that management-related issues posed challenges, such as inadequate financial resources (96.7%), student-learning accountability (87.5%), and compliance with state and federal mandates (82.2%). These findings affirm that the superintendent's management role is an integral aspect of their work.


## SUPERINTENDENT AS DEMOCRATIC-POLITICAL LEADER

The role conceptualization of superintendent as democratic-political leader is grounded in the political reality of their work. Since 1923, inadequate financial support for public education has been perceived as being the most significant challenge facing superintendents. As the intensity of competition between public education and other public agencies for scarce resources increased, the nature of superintendents' political role became more evident. Although politics was regarded as an anathema during previous decades (Björk & Lindle, 2001; Kowalski, 1995), in the turbulent 1930s such convictions were displaced by the need for district superintendents to serve as lobbyists and political strategists to secure financial support and engage communities and parents bent on restoring democracy in the larger school districts that had adopted corporate models of management and governance (Melby, 1955). In essence, superintendents were urged to galvanize policymakers, employees and other taxpayers to support their districts' initiatives (Howlett, 1993) and mitigate interest group political pressure (Björk & Lindle, 2001; Kowalski, 1995). Through a national AASA survey study, Glass et al. (2000) found that 58% of superintendents acknowledged that interest groups tried to influence them and school board decisions, which tends to be more prevalent in large school districts than small districts. In addition, 83% of superintendents identified administrator-board relations (i.e., micro-politics) as one of the greatest challenges they face. Collectively, these outcomes demonstrate that working with the board and public remains a primary role expectation.Since the 1930s, it has been evident that the issue facing superintendents was not whether they should be politicians, but rather how they carry out that role and responsibilities (Björk & Gurley, 2005).

## SUPERINTENDENT AS APPLIED SOCIAL SCIENTIST

The view of superintendent as applied social scientist largely has been defined by both societal conditions and professional dispositions. Several societal forces were identified by Callahan (1966) such as (a) a growing dissatisfaction with democratic leadership after World War II that ignored realities of practice and (b) the emergence of findings from social science research applicable to organizations including public education. In the professional sphere, Callahan acknowledged the contributions of support during the 1950s from the Kellogg Foundation that enabled professors of school administration to conduct social science research and build a knowledge base for the profession, which is often referred to as the theory movement. In addition, he noted a resurgence of criticism of public schools during the early 1950sthat focused on persistently inadequate schooling for large segments of the nation's economic underclass and minority, which suggested that administrators failed to use social science data on the condition of schooling and learning. According to Argyris (personal communication, 1982), this linked to the emergence of the information society in which previously unavailable data on organizations shed new light on public and private entities. It not only shattered long-standing organizational myths but also and most notably contributed to a decline in public esteem for the profession.

Two additional elements influenced acceptance of the superintendents' role as applied social scientist. First, concurrent with the Kellogg Foundation supported research during the 1950s, superintendents and principals were portrayed as applied social scientists and leaders in the field. They pushed to make school administration an established academic discipline like business management and public administration (Culbertson, 1981). Consequently, courses shifted away from internal organizational operations (i.e., practical aspects of school administration) to those that reflected social science research and theory (Crowson & McPherson, 1987).

In this new preparation milieu, practitioners were expected to embrace notions of empiricism, predictability and scientific certainty in their research and practice (Cooper & Boyd, 1987). Second, interest in systems thinking and relationships among events in internal and external environments of organizations grounded efforts to link legal, political, social and economic dimensions to enhance administrator effectiveness (Getzels, 1977). The intent was to create a new normal for practice for superintendents; that is, they were expected to apply scientific inquiry to identify and solve problems of practice.

More recently, the notion of the superintendent as applied social scientist captured the interest of critical theorists. They conclude that the social sciences provide a foundation for understanding the relationship between society and schooling and eradicating social injustices in public institutions (Johnson & Fusarelli, 2003). Consequently, school superintendents are expected to be aware of contextual issues such as changing demographics, poverty, racism, drugs and violence (Fusarelli & Fusarelli, 2005; Kochan, Jackson & Duke, 1999) and ensure that schools are simultaneously socially just, democratic and productive (Goldring & Greenfield, 2002; Sergiovanni, 1992; Starratt, 1991).

## SUPERINTENDENT AS COMMUNICATOR

The nation's emergence as an information-based society in the mid-1950s (Kowalski, 2001) directly heightened expectations for superintendents to master the art of communication and support the use of technology in learning, teaching and administration. By the 1980s, the era of administrators working in isolation ended as educational reform and restructuring emphasized collaboration, organizational restructuring and distributing leadership. System-wide reform required broad-based stakeholder engagement and systemic thinking that is explicated by the social systems perspective (Chance & Björk, 2004; Murphy, 1991; Schein, 1996). As noted by Schlechty (1997), "systemic thinking requires us to accept that the way social systems are put together has independent effects on the way people behave, what they learn, and how they learn what they learn" (p. 134). Thus, highly effective superintendents reframed school-district change as holistic and developmental.

Scholars concur that communication and organizational culture are reciprocal relationships. According to Conrad (1994), "Cultures are communicative creations. They emerge and are sustained by the communicative acts of all employees, not just the conscious persuasive strategies of upper management. Cultures do not exist separately from people communicating with one another" (p. 27). Further, Axley (1996) asserts that "communication gives rise to culture, which gives rise to communication, which perpetuates culture" (p. 153). As such, culture influences communicative behavior, and communicative behavior is instrumental to building, maintaining and changing culture (Kowalski, 1998). In the case of local school districts, normative communicative behavior for superintendents is shaped largely by two realities: (a) the need for them to assume leadership in the process of school restructuring (Björk, 2001b; Murphy, 1994), and (b) the need for them to change school culture as part of the restructuring process (Heckman, 1993; Kowalski, 2000).

Superintendents' communicator role is shaped by two conditions—the need to restructure school cultures and the need to access and use information in a timely manner to identify and solve problems of practice. Among respondents to an AASA national survey (Glass et al., 2000), nearly all superintendents (95%) acknowledged that they were their board's primary source of information. Moreover, a majority of superintendents reported having engaged regularly in communication-intensive interactions with parents and other citizens, such as setting district objectives and priorities (69%), strategic planning (61%), fundraising (60%), and curricular and program decisions (60%). In this era of emerging technologies, superintendents are compelled to communicate more adroitly using social media (e.g., electronic mail, blogs), engage a broader range of stakeholder groups, and deliver performances of unprecedented quality (Kowalski & Keedy, 2005).

## SUPERINTENDENT CHARACTERIZATIONS AND PROFESSIONAL STANDARDS

These five role characterizationsdiscussed have been affirmed by Kowalski and Björk (2005) using historical data and findings from two national studies sponsored by the AASA (Glass et al., 2000; Kowalski et al. 2010). A summary of knowledge and skills associated with each of the superintendents'role conceptualizations is provided in Table 1.

**Table 1. Knowledge and Skills Associated with Superintendent
Role Conceptualizations**

| Role | Pertinent Knowledge and Skills |
|---|---|
| Teacher-scholar | Pedagogy; educational psychology; curriculum; instructional supervision; staff development; educational philosophy |
| Manager | Law; personnel administration; finance/budgeting; facility development/maintenance; collective bargaining/contract maintenance; public relations |
| Democratic leader | Community relations; collaborative decision making; politics |
| Applied social scientist | Quantitative and qualitative research; behavioral sciences |
| Communicator | Verbal communication; written communication; listening; public speaking; media relations |
| Multi-role * | Motivation; organizational theory; organizational change and development; leadership theory; ethical/moral administration; technology and its applications; diversity/multiculturalism; human relations |

* This category includes knowledge and skills pertinent to all or nearly all roles.
** From Kowalski & Björk (2005).

In addition, superintendent role conceptualizations were examined using the *Professional Standards for the Superintendency* (Hoyle, 1993) promulgated for superintendents by the AASA and later incorporated into the Interstate School Leadership Licensure Consortium (ISLLC) *Standards for School Leaders* (Council of Chief State School Officers [CCSSO], 1996). In 2005, Hoyle, Björk, Collier and Glass published a research-based textbook focused on the knowledge and skills aligned with the AASA standards required for superintendents to become high performing CEOs. Both sets of standards are widely regarded as being comprehensive and highly relevant for guiding preparation, state-level licensure and evaluating superintendents' performance. Thus, they provide a useful template for examining the interface between knowledge and skills associated with licensure and practice. It is evident that the role conceptualizations discussed in this chapter are closely aligned with AASA and ISLLC standards (see Table 2 and Appendix A). A consequence of testing the authenticity of these role conceptualizations against historical and empirical data as well as professional standards is gaining confidence that, taken together, they reflect the reality that superintendents' work and roles are highly complex.

# CHALLENGES FACED BY SUPERINTENDENTS IN THE U.S.A.

Examining the characteristics and challenges faced by American school district superintendents provides insight into who serves as school district CEOs. Findings from the most recent decennial study of the superintendency supported by AASA (Kowalski et al., 2010) affirm that superintendent career patterns remain similar over the past three decades and identify three main paths to the office. The majority (49%) of superintendents moved from being a classroom teacher to assistant principal or principal and then to a central office administrative position before assuming a position as a school district CEO.

**Table 2. Interface of Knowledge and Skills and the AASA and ISLLC Standards**

| Pertinent knowledge/skills | ISLLC | AASA |
|---|---|---|
| *Teacher-scholar* | | |
| Pedagogy | 6 | 2 |
| Educational psychology | 6 | 2 |
| Curriculum | 5 | 2 |
| Instructional supervision | 6 | 2,5 |
| Staff development | 6, 7 | 2 |
| Educational philosophy/history | 2 | 5 |
| *Manager* | | |
| School law | 2, 4, 7 | 3, 6 |
| Personnel administration | 7 | 3 |
| Finance/budgeting | 4 | 3 |
| Facility development/maintenance | 4 | 3 |
| Collective bargaining/contract maintenance | 4, 7 | 3, 5 |
| Public relations | 3, 4 | 3, 6 |
| *Democratic leader* | | |
| Community relations | 3 | 1, 4, 6 |
| Collaborative decision making | 1, 2 | 1, 4 |
| Politics | 1, 2, 8 | 1, 6 |
| Governance | 2 | 6 |
| *Applied social scientist* | | |
| Quantitative and qualitative research | 4, 5 | 1 |
| Behavioral sciences | 1, 8 | 4, 6 |
| Measurement and evaluation | 5, 6 | 2 |
| *Communicator* | | |
| Verbal communication | 3 | 1, 4, 6 |
| Written communication | 3 | 1, 4, 6 |
| Media relations | 3, 8 | 6 |
| Listening | 3 | 1, 6 |
| Public speaking | 3 | 1, 6 |
| *Multi-role* * | | |
| Motivation | 5, 6, 7 | 2 |
| Organizational theory | 1, 2, 7 | 1, 2, 5 |
| Organizational change and development | 1 | 1, 4, 6 |
| Leadership theory | 1 | 1, 2, 5 |
| Ethical/moral administration | 8 | 5 |
| Technology and its applications | 3, 4, 6 | 2, 3 |
| Diversity/multiculturalism | 1, 3, 8 | 1, 2, 4 |
| Conflict management | 1, 2 | 1, 4, 6 |

* This category includes knowledge and skills pertinent to all or nearly all roles.

Note: Numbers in the AASA and ISLLC columns refer to the standards number. See Appendix A for reference.

Originally published in Kowalski & Björk (2005).

The second pattern indicated that 31% of surveyed superintendents also moved from teacher to assistant principal or principal, but they were then appointed as a superintendent (i.e., became CEO without central office administrative experience). The third career path was reported by approximately 9% of superintendents; they acquired district responsibilities by moving from the classroom to the board office. The last two patterns are more common in small, rural school districts that have a limited number of central office (i.e., middle management) positions that enable prospective superintendents to gain relevant management experience.

According to survey data, the median age of superintendents is 55 years, and their careers typically encompass the last 18 years of their professional lives. They typically serve two or three districts for six years in each location (i.e., they complete two 3-year contracts). Most respondents (70%) hold at least a master's degree in educational administration (Glass & Franceschini, 2007), which is reasonable as most states require a graduate degree for administrator certification or licensure. During the past four decades, the percent of superintendents holding a doctorate—either a Doctor of Education (EdD) or Doctor of Philosophy (PhD)—has increased significantly moving from 29% in 1971 to 45% in 2010 (Kowalski et al., 2010). Perhaps the most startling aspects of demographic data on superintendency are that are 76% are male and 94% are Caucasian (Kowalski et al., 2010). These statistics are disturbing in a nation in which more than half of the population (50.9%) is female and over one-fourth identify themselves as members of racial groups other than Caucasian (e.g., African American, Asian, Native Hawaiian or other Pacific Islander) (U. S. Census Bureau, 2010).

Superintendents face a number of problems, many of which are persisting and intractable. Data from the 2010 decennial study commissioned by AASA (Kowalski et al., 2010) identify these issues. They are listed in rank order with those being most important at the top: (a) financing schools, (b) school board relations, (c) assessment of student learning outcomes, (d) planning and goal setting, (e) changing priorities in the curriculum, (f) management problems, and (g) accountability and credibility. Interestingly, inadequate financial support for schools has been listed as being the most serious issue facing superintendents since the 10-year studies were instituted in 1923. In addition, maintaining good working relationships with school district board members remains a concern for CEOs, especially as school district meetings often serve as public platforms upon which contested state and national issues are debated. The remaining issues taken together (i.e., student assessment, planning and goal setting, changing priorities in the curriculum, system accountability) directly reflect decades-long emphasis on launching and sustaining school reform. Addressing these multiple and diverse issues while simultaneously managing schools is often described as trying to build the plane while it is in flight.

The history of the superintendency suggests that the superintendent's roles and responsibilities are defined by emerging social, economic and political conditions, which in turn establish performance expectations for schools and studentsthat are aligned with perceived national needs and transformational efforts. In large measure, historical events have defined an American system of public education framed by federal, state and local community expectations. How those are structured, funded and governed and how the superintendent's roles are defined influences the trajectory of career patterns and issues faced. During the last two decades, the rise of a global economy heightened concern for the future well-being of the nation, fueled demands for improving education, and stimulated interest in the role of superintendents in large-scale, system-wide reform.This brief description of the school district superintendent in the United States may prove useful as a starting point in making cross-national comparisons; however, we caution that while superintendents may share some characteristics with regard to roles and work responsibilities, contexts matters significantly. Consequently, it is incumbent upon international scholars to ascertain where commonalities converge and where their work is unique in time and place. Working collaboratively offers a singular opportunity to advance our understanding on a global scale.

# APPENDIX A

## Superintendent Preparation and Licensing Standards

*American Association of School Administrators (Focused Specifically on Superintendents)*

- Standard 1: Leadership and district culture
- Standard 2: Policy and governance
- Standard 3: Communications and community relations
- Standard 4: Organizational management
- Standard 5: Curriculum planning and development
- Standard 6: Instructional management
- Standard 7: Human resources management
- Standard 8: Values and ethics of leadership

*Interstate School Leadership Licensure Consortium (Focused on All School Administrators)*

- Standard 1: A school administrator is an educational leader who promotes the success of all students by facilitating the development, articulation, implementation and stewardship of a vision of learning that is shared and supported by the school community.
- Standard 2: A school administrator is an educational leader who promotes the success of all students by advocating, nurturing and sustaining a school culture and instructional program conducive to student learning and staff professional growth.
- Standard 3: A school administrator is an educational leader who promotes the success of all students by ensuring management of the organization, operations and resources for a safe, efficient, and effective learning environment.
- Standard 4: A school administrator is an educational leader who promotes the success of all students by collaborating with families and community members, responding to diverse community interests and needs and mobilizing community resources.
- Standard 5: A school administrator is an educational leader who promotes the success of all students by acting with integrity, fairness and in an ethical manner.

- Standard 6: A school administrator is an educational leader who promotes the success of all students by understanding, responding to, and influencing the larger political, social, economic, legal and cultural context.

# REFERENCES

Alexander, L. (1991). *America 2000: An education strategy*. Washington, DC: U.S. Department of Education.

Anyon, J. (2005). What "counts" as educational policy? Notes toward a new paradigm. *Harvard Educational Review*, 75(1), 65-88.

Axley, S. R. (1996). *Communication at work: Management and the communication-intensive organization*. Westport, Conn.: Quorum Books.

Björk, L. G. (1996). The revisionists' critique of the education reform reports. *Journal of School Leadership, 6,* 290-315.

Björk, L. G. (2001a). Preparing the next generation of superintendents: Integrating formal and experiential knowledge. In C. C. Brunner & L. G. Björk (Eds.), *The new superintendency: Advances in research and theories of school management and educational* (pp. 19-54). Greenwich, Conn.: JAI Press.

Björk, L. G. (2001b). The role of the central office in decentralization. In T. J. Kowalski & G. Perreault (Eds.), *21st century challenges for schooladministrators* (pp. 286-309). Lanham, Md.: Scarecrow Press.

Björk, L. G. (2005).Superintendent-board relations: An historical overview of thedynamics of change and sources of conflict and collaboration. In G. J. Petersen & L. D. Fusarelli (Eds.), *The district superintendent and school board relations: Trends in policy development and implementation* (pp. 1-22). Charlotte, N.C.: Information Age Publishing.

Björk, L. G., & Gurley, D. K. (2005).Superintendent as educational statesman and political strategist. In L. G. Björk & T. Kowalski (Eds.), *The contemporary superintendent: Preparation, practice, and development* (pp.163-185). Thousand Oaks, Cal.: Corwin Press.

Björk, L. G., Kowalski, T. J., & Young, M. D. (2005). National reports and implications for professional preparation and development. In L. G. Björk & T. J. Kowalski (Eds.), *The contemporary superintendent: Preparation, practice and development* (pp. 45-70). Thousand Oaks, Cal.: Corwin Press.

Björk, L., & Lindle, J. C. (2001). Superintendents and interest groups. *Educational Policy,* 15(1), 76-91.

Boyer, E. L. (1983). *High school: A report on secondary education in America*. New York, N.Y.: Harper and Row.

Browne-Ferrigno, T., & Glass, T. E. (2005). Superintendent as organizational manager. In L. G. Björk & T. J. Kowalski (Eds.), *The contemporary superintendent: Preparation, practice and development* (pp.137-161). Thousand Oaks, Cal.: Corwin Press.

Brunner, C. C., Grogan, M., & Björk, L. G. (2002). Shifts in the discourse defining the superintendency: Historical and current foundations of the position. In J. Murphy (Ed.),

*The educational leadership challenge: Redefining leadership for the 21st century* (pp. 211-238). Chicago, Ill.: University of Chicago Press.

Callahan, R. E. (1962). *Education and the cult of efficiency: A study of the social forces that have shaped the administration of public schools.* Chicago, Ill.: University of Chicago Press.

Callahan, R. E. (1966). *The superintendent of schools: A historical analysis.* Unpublished manuscript, Graduate Institute of Education, Washington University, St. Louis, Mo. (ERIC Document Reproduction Service No.ED 0104 410).

Carnegie Corporation of New York (1989, June). *Turning points: Preparing American youth for the 21st century* [Report of the Task Force on Education of Adolescents]. Waldorf, Md.: Author.

Carnegie Corporation of New York (1995, October). *Great transitions: Preparing adolescents for a new century.* Waldorf, Md.: Author.

Carnegie Forum on Education and the Economy Task Force on Teaching as a Profession (1986). *A nation prepared: Teachers for the 21st century.* New York, N.Y.: Carnegie Forum on Education and the Economy.

Carter, G., & Cunningham, W. (1997). *The American school superintendent: Leading in the age of pressure.* San Francisco, Cal.: Jossey-Bass.

Chance, P. L., & Björk, L. G. (2004).The social dimensions of public relations. In T. J. Kowalski (Ed.), *Public relations in schools* (3rd ed., pp.125-148). Upper Saddle River, N.J.: Merrill, Prentice Hall.

Clark, D. L., & Astuto, T. A. (1994). Redirecting reform: Challenges to popular assumptions about teachers and students. *Phi Delta Kappan, 75*(7), 512-520.

Committee for Economic Development (1985). *Investing in our children.* New York, N.Y.: Author.

Committee for Economic Development (1987). *Children in need.* New York, N.Y.: Author.

Conrad, C. (1994). *Strategic organizational communication: Toward the twenty-first century* (3rded.). Fort Worth, Texas: Harcourt Brace College.

Cooper, B. S., & Boyd, W. L. (1987). The evolution of training for school administrators. In J. Murphy & P. Hallinger (Eds.), *Approaches to administrative training in education* (pp. 3-27). Albany: State University of New York Press.

Council of Chief State School Officers (1996). *Interstate School Leaders Licensure Consortium: Standards for school leaders.* Washington, DC: Author.

Cuban, L. (1976a). *Urban school chiefs under fire.* Chicago, Ill.: University ChicagoPress.

Cuban, L. (1976b). *The urban school superintendent: A century and a half of change.* Bloomington, Ind.: Phi Delta Kappa Educational Foundation.

Cuban, L. (1988). *The managerial imperative and the practice of leadership in schools.* Albany: State University of New York Press.

Culbertson, J. A. (1981). Antecedents of the theory movement.*Educational Administration Quarterly, 17*(1), 25-47.

Cronin, J. M. (1973). *The control of urban schools: Perspective on the power of educational reformers.* New York, N.Y.: Free Press.

Crowson, R. L., & McPherson, R. B. (1987). The legacy of the theory movement: Learning from the new tradition. In J. Murphy & P. Hallinger (Eds.), *Approaches to administrative training in education* (pp. 45-64). Albany: State University of New York Press.

Firestone, W. W. (1990). Continuity and incrementalism after all: State responses to the excellence movement. In J. Murphy (Ed.), *The educational reform movement of the 1980s: Perspectives and cases* (pp. 143-166). Berkeley, Cal.: McCutchan.

Firestone, W. A., Furhman, S., & Kirst, M. W. (1990). An overview of educational reform since 1983. In J. Murphy (Ed.), *The educational reform movement of the 1980s: Perspectives and cases* (pp. 349-364). Berkeley, Cal.: McCutchan.

Fix, M. & Passel, J. S. (2003). *U.S. immigration: Trends and implications for schools.*Presentation at the National Association for Bilingual Education NCLB Implementation Institute, New Orleans, La.

Franklin, J. H. (1989). *Visions of a better way: Black appraisal of public schooling.* Washington, DC: Joint Center for Political and Economic Studies.

Fullan, M. (1983). *Change forces: Probing the depths of educational reform.* London, England: Falmer Press.

Fusarelli, B. C., & Fusarelli, L. D. (2005). Reconceptualizing the superintendency: Superintendents as social scientists and social activists. In L. G. Björk & T. J. Kowalski (Eds.), *The contemporary superintendent: Preparation, practice, and development* (pp. 187-206). Thousand Oaks, Cal.: Corwin Press.

Getzels, J. W. (1977). Educational administration twenty years later, 1954-1974. In L. Cunningham, W. Hack & R. Nystrand (Eds.), *Educational administration: The developing decades* (pp. 3-24). Berkeley, Cal.: McCutchan.

Glass, T. E. (2003). *The superintendency: A managerial imperative?* Paper presented at the annual meeting of the American Educational Research Association, Chicago, Ill.

Glass, T. E., Björk, L. G., & Brunner, C. C. (2000). *The study of the American superintendency 2000: A look at the superintendent in the new millennium.* Arlington, Va.: American Association of School Administrators.

Glass, T. E., & Franceschini, L. A. (2007). *The state of the American school superintendency: A mid-decade study.* Arlington, Va.: American Association of School Administrators.

Goldring, E., & Greenfield, W. (2002). Understanding the evolving concept of leadership in education: Roles, expectations, and dilemmas. In J. Murphy (Ed.), *The educational leadership challenge: Redefining leadership for the 21st century* (pp. 1-19). Chicago, Ill.: University of Chicago Press.

Grieder, C., Pierce, T. M., & Jordan, K. F. (1969).*Public school administration* (3rd ed.). New York, N.Y.: Ronald Press.

Heckman, P. E. (1993). School restructuring in practice: Reckoning with the culture of school. *International Journal of Educational Reform, 2*(3), 263-272.

Holmes Group (1986). *Tomorrow's teachers.* East Lansing, Mich.: Author.

Howlett, P. (1993). The politics of school leaders, past and future. *Education Digest, 58*(9), 18-21.

Hoyle, J. (1993). *Professional standards for the superintendency.*Arlington, Va.: American Association of School Administrators.

Hoyle, J. R., Björk, L. G., Collier, V., & Glass, T. (2005). *The superintendent as CEO: Standards-based performance.* Thousand Oaks, Cal.: Corwin Press.

Johnson, B. C., & Fusarelli, L. D. (2003, April). *Superintendent as social scientist.* Paper presented at the annual meeting of the American Educational Research Association, Chicago, Ill.

Kirst, M. W., & Wirt, F. M. (2009). *The political dynamics of American education* (4[th]ed.). Berkeley, Cal.: McCutchan.

Kochan, F. K., Jackson, B. L., & Duke, D. L. (1999).*A thousand voices from the firing line: A study of educational leaders, their jobs, their preparation and the problems they face.* Columbia, Mo.: University Council for Educational Administration.

Kowalski, T. J. (1995). *Keepers of the flame: Contemporary urban superintendents.* Thousand Oaks, Cal.: Corwin Press.

Kowalski, T. J. (1998). The role of communication in providing leadership for school reform. *Mid-Western Educational Researcher, 11*(1), 32-40.

Kowalski, T. J. (1999). *The school superintendent: Theory, practice, and cases.* Upper Saddle River, N.J.: Merrill, Prentice Hall.

Kowalski, T. J. (2000). Cultural change paradigms and administrator communication. *Contemporary Education, 71*(2), 5-10.

Kowalski, T. J. (2001). The future of local school governance: Implications for board members and superintendents. In C. C. Brunner & L. G. Björk (Eds.), *The new superintendency* (pp. 183-201). Oxford, U.K.: JAI Press.

Kowalski, T. J. (2003). Superintendent shortage: The wrong problem and the wrong solutions. *Journal of School Leadership, 13*(3), 288-303

Kowalski, T. J. (2005). Evolution of the school district superintendent position.In L. G. Björk & T. Kowalski (Eds.), *The contemporary superintendent: Preparation, practice, and development* (pp. 1-18). Thousand Oaks, Cal.: Corwin Press.

Kowalski, T. J. (2006). *The school superintendent: Theory, practice and cases* (2[nd]ed.). Thousand Oaks, Cal.: Sage.

Kowalski, T. J., & Björk, L. G. (2005). Role expectations of district superintendents: Implications for deregulating preparation and licensing. *Journal of Thought, 40*(2), 73-96.

Kowalski, T. J., & Glass, T. E. (2002).Preparing superintendents in the 21st century. In B. S. Cooper & L. D. Fusarelli (Eds.), *The promises and perils facing today's school superintendent* (pp. 41-60). Lanham, Md.: Scarecrow Education.

Kowalski, T. J., & Keedy, J. L. (2005). Preparing Superintendents to be Effective Communicators. In L. G. Björk & T. J. Kowalski (Eds.), *School district superintendents: Role expectations, professional preparation, development and licensing* (pp. 207-226). Thousand Oaks, Cal.: Corwin Press.

Kowalski, T. J., McCord, R. S., Petersen, G. J., Young, I. P., & Ellerson, N. M. (2010). *The American school superintendent: 2010 decennial study.* Lanham, Md.: Rowma & Littlefield Education.

Melby, E. O. (1955). *Administering community education.* Englewood Cliffs, N.J.: Prentice Hall.

Murphy, J. (1990). *The reform of American pubic education in the 1980s: Perspectives and cases.* Berkeley, Cal.: McCutchan.

Murphy, J. (1991). *Restructuring schools: Capturing and assessing the phenomena.* New York, N.Y.: Teachers College Press.

Murphy, J. (1994). The changing role of the superintendency in restructuring districts in Kentucky.*School Effectiveness and School Improvement, 5*(4), 349-375.

National Commission on Children (1991). *Beyond rhetoric: A new American agenda for children and families.* Washington, DC: Author.

National Commission on Excellence in Education (1983). *A nation at risk: The imperative for educational reform.* Washington, DC: U.S. Government Printing Office.

National Governors Association (1986). *Time for results.* Washington, DC: Author.

National Science Board Commission on Precollege Education in Mathematics, Science and Technology (1983). *Educating Americans for the 21st century.* Washington, DC: National Science Foundation.

Petersen, G. J., & Barnett, B. (2003, April). *The superintendent as instructional leader: History, evolution, and future role.* Paper presented at the annual meeting of the American Educational Research Association, Chicago, Ill.

Petersen, G. J., & Barnett, B. G. (2005). Superintendent as instructional leader: Current practice, future conceptualizations, and implications for preparation. In L. G. Björk & T. G. Kowalski (Eds.), *The contemporary superintendent: Preparation, practice, and development* (pp. 107-136). Thousand Oaks, Cal.: Corwin Press.

Peterson, K. D., & Finn, D. E. (1985, Spring). Principal, superintendents and administrator's art. *The Public Interest,* 79, 42-62.

Pulliam, J. D., & Van Patten, J. D. (2006). *History of education in America* (9th ed.). Upper Saddle River, N.J.: Pearson Education.

Quality Education for Minorities Project (1990). *Education that works: An action plan for the education of minorities.* Cambridge: Massachusetts Institution of Technology.

Ravitch, D. (2010). *The death and life of the great American school system: How testing and choice are undermining education.* New York, N.Y.: Basic Books.

Schein, E. H. (1996). Culture: The missing concept in organization studies. *Administrative Science Quarterly,* 41(2), 229-240.

Schlechty, P. C. (1997). *Inventing better schools: An action plan for educational reform.* San Francisco, Cal.: Jossey-Bass.

Sergiovanni, T. J. (1992). *Moral leadership: Getting to the heart of school improvement.* San Francisco, Cal.: Jossey-Bass.

Spring, J. H. (1994). *The American school, 1642-1993* (3rd ed.). New York, N.Y.: McGraw-Hill.

Starratt, R. K. (1991). Building an ethical school: A theory for practice in educational leadership. *Educational Administration Quarterly,* 27(2), 185-202.

Task Force on Education for Economic Growth (1983). *Action for excellence: A comprehensive plan to improve our nation's schools.* Denver, Col.: Education Commission of the States.

Twentieth Century Fund Task Force on Federal Elementary and Secondary Education Policy (1983). *Making the grade.* New York, N.Y.: Twentieth Century Fund.

Tyack, D., & Hansot, E. (1982). *Managers of virtue: Public school leadership in America, 1820-1980.* New York, N.Y.: Basic Books.

U.S. Census Bureau (2010). *American FactFinder.* Washington, DC: U.S. Department of Commerce. Retrieved from http://factfinder2.census.gov/faces/tableservices/jsf/pages/productview.xhtml?pid=DEC_10_DP_DPDP1&prodType=table retrieved: 14 April, 2013.

U.S. Department of Education (1993, October). *National excellence: A case for developing America's talent.* Washington, DC: Author.

Van Til, W. (1971). Prologue: Is progressive education obsolete? In W. Van Til (Ed.), *Curriculum: Quest for Relevance* (pp. 9-17). Boston, Mass.: Houghton-Mifflin.

In: The Educational Superintendent
Editor: Adam E. Nir

ISBN: 978-1-62948-972-8
© 2014 Nova Science Publishers, Inc.

*Chapter 3*

# MEDIATING TENSIONS BETWEEN STATE CONTROL, LOCAL AUTONOMY AND PROFESSIONAL TRUST: NORWEGIAN SCHOOL DISTRICT LEADERSHIP IN PRACTICE

## *Jan Merok Paulsen[1] and Guri Skedsmo[2]*
[1]Hedmark University College, Norway
[2]University of Oslo, Norway

During the last decades several strategies have been used to renew the Norwegian educational system and improve its quality. Introducing Management by Objectives (MBO) and distributing tasks and responsibilities to local authorities and schools were important strategies during the 1990s. Parallel to this, state curriculum reforms have been launched, the latest reform, the Knowledge Promotion (K06) in 2006, shortly after a national system to measure and monitor educational quality was introduced in 2004. In spite of the emphasis on local autonomy and the responsibility of the municipalities as school owners in the policy discourse, several scholars have pointed to the fact that this national system and the latest reform have led to increased centralization within a decentralized educational system (Aasen et al., 2012) or that even centralization and decentralization have been used as twin reform strategies (Møller & Skedsmo, 2013). In this respect it can be argued that the national standardized tests introduced as part of the national quality assessment system in particular have contributed to this development. Student outcomes on these tests are perceived as the main indicator of educational quality, and local school administrations and schools experience increasing pressure to improve student outcomes (Skedsmo & Hopfenbeck, in progress).

In many ways, recent developments illustrate a rather complex relationship between national and local authorities characterized by mutual dependency and collaboration, as well as tensions. On the one hand, the municipalities are responsible for implementing state policy and providing public services for their citizens (Bukve, 1997; Engeland, 2000; Offerdal, 1992). On the other hand, they are the components of local government that can be considered as a meeting ground for different local interests which are formulated and prioritized by local politicians. In this chapter we address how key actors at the local level experience their role in school governing processes. In particular, we focus on the role of the superintendents and how they mediate tensions embedded in the professional, social and political context in which their management and leadership roles are situated.

The school superintendent, who holds a managerial position in the municipality, i.e.,in the school district's hierarchy, firstly, is responsible for primary and secondary education within the entire municipality and thereby for authority over school principals; secondly, the superintendent is subordinate to a municipal school committee or school board; thirdly he or she leads a central school office in the municipal hierarchy; and finally, the superintendent is part of the top level of the municipal hierarchy through membership in the senior leadership team (Johansson, Moos, Nihlfors, Paulsen & Risku, 2011). In line with this conceptualization, the superintendent is a holder of a middle-position that makes him or her uniquely positioned to mediate between conflicting views and interests (Floyd & Wooldridge, 1997) of administrative levels and different stakeholders. Although there is large variation in formal jobtitles and work descriptions, the empirical data from Norwegian municipalities (Johansson et al., 2011) cluster and cohere around a leadership and management role conceptually close to the school superintendent as portrayed in the literature (Johansson, 2010). We assume that by focusing on this position, its relation to the local political system and its function as the superior of the principals within the municipalities, it will be possible to capture, at least partially, important preconditions for local school development (Nihlfors, 2003; Nihlfors, Johansson, Moos, Paulsen & Risku, 2013). Moreover, the school superintendent is considered a key agent in school governing processes, quality assurance of schools, and change and quality development.

We first look at different expectations directed towards the role of superintendent and the areas of responsibility of local authorities as these are formulated in key policy documents. In addition, we report on empirical findings from a survey conducted among superintendents in 2009. Altogether 291 out of 429 municipalities responded to the survey, giving a response rate of 68%.[1] To add some illustrative points, a small selection of data from the school board survey undertaken in 2011 is shown. Finally, we discuss different tensions related to responding to diverse expectations but also tensions and even paradoxes embedded in the national educational policy.

## KEY CHARACTERISTICS OF SCHOOL GOVERNING IN NORWAY

The Norwegian educational system is predominantly public, which means that most schools and universities are run by public authorities. Education at all levels is free. There is no streaming according to abilities, gender or other factors, and more than 95% of Norwegian students are enrolled in regular classes. This is based on the ideology that all children, irrespective of physical or mental disabilities or learning difficulties, should be integrated as much as possible into the regular school system.

With respect to the structure of the Norwegian educational system, the National Assembly (*Stortinget*) determines the basic pattern of education by legislating the aims and

---

[1] The non-response rate is assumed to be influenced by demography in the Norwegian municipal sector, where 159 municipalities have fewer than 3,000 inhabitants and in many cases were found to have no central school office at all.

structure. The Ministry of Education and Research is in turn responsible for formulating the national educational policy. The main tasks of the National Directorate for Education and Training are to implement the national educational policy, to develop subject curricula, and to ensure quality. The overall responsibility for the supervision of schools is delegated to the Regional Educational Offices. There are 18 such offices altogether, one office located in each county (there are 19 counties in Norway, but only 18 Regional Educational Offices, since there is one common office for the counties of Oslo and Akershus).

The 428 municipalities in Norway are responsible for the 10 years of compulsory education at the primary and lower secondary school levels. The municipalities vary in size as well as in socio-economic level. About 40% of the national budget goes to the municipalities, which in turn provide public services comprising compulsory education, health care and social services. In educational policy documents published after 2004, the municipalities are defined as "school owners." Their main responsibilities within the area of education are as follows:

- adapt the national curriculum to local needs,
- run in-service training for teachers and school leaders, and
- ensure the quality of schooling.

The schools are considered self-governing units that report to the municipalities as well as to the state.

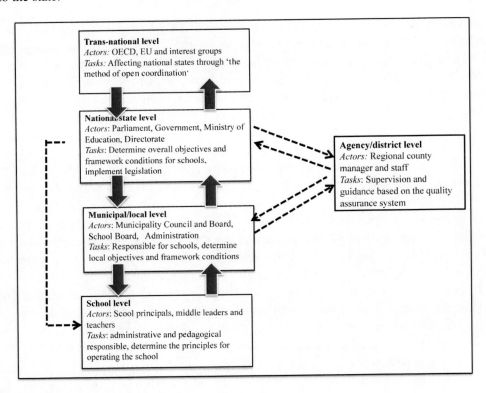

(Source: Nihlfors et al., 2013).

Figure 1. Key actors in the transnational educational system model.

The principals have the overall responsibility for the development of school practice, to follow up on state and local priorities, and to follow up on educational outcomes achieved. Moreover, important tasks of the principals are personnel management, administration and resource allocation. During the last decade we have seen a shift from traditional government structures towards a more complex and unclear governance model in the Nordic countries (Moos, 2006). The Norwegian educational system is increasingly influenced by transnational bodies such as the EU, OECD, etc. Schools are expected to implement national and transnational (e.g., European) citizenship education, using state resources, but also contributions from the local political level. Along with this development, the aim has shifted over time from contributing to developing a democratic society to strengthening the national economy in the global competition. An overview of the organizational structure of the Norwegian educational system is provided in Figure 1.

The transnational agencies operate on a *soft governance* model, inspiring national agencies from governments and downwards by comparisons, benchmarks and European programs. National parliaments legislate and governments carry out and implement the legislation when issuing regulations and setting the educational agenda. The transnational agencies have only existed for a few decades, with the overarching aim to further the creation of a European community and European citizens (Moos, 2009).

## New Modes of School Governing

Recent changes in the Norwegian educational policy may be evident in the introduction of the national evaluation system that includes evaluations and standardized achievement tests. These measures increase focus on educational outcomes in terms of students' performance on achievement tests indicating new modes of school governing (Helgøy & Homme, 2006). These new modes are often described as an orientation towards output based means of governing characterized by several features. Initially, these new modes of governing comprise new concepts of educational quality. The increased focus on educational outcomes in terms of students' performance on achievement tests include concepts of educational quality which seem to be defined by expectations for specific outcomes. It also indicates a belief that any discrepancy between the expected outcomes and the level of achievements can be identified (Skedsmo, 2009).

Secondly, as a consequence, information associated with educational outcomes, produced through evaluations and measurements, can be seen as the point of departure for school governing (Skedsmo, 2009). This information established expectations for improved educational outcomes which in most cases are also performance oriented.

To help schools and municipalities to improve, the national authorities initiate school development programs and educational programs focusing on the development and improvement of basic competencies. Thirdly, the new governing modes provide new input defined by the outcomes achieved (Afsar, Skedsmo & Sivesind, 2006; Karseth & Sivesind, 2009; Sivesind & Bachmann, 2008; Skedsmo, 2009).

Fourthly, an important aspect related to the increased focus on evaluation and measurement is the need to make key actors such as superintendents, principals and teachers accountable (Skedsmo, 2009). In this case, accountability often refers to when an actor, by virtue of contractual obligations, has the right to hold another actor responsible to a set of standards, to judge whether the standards have been met, and to intervene or impose sanctions if the standards are deemed unfulfilled (Johansson et al., 2013).

The municipalities are required to establish a system for quality assurance comprised of evaluating, documenting and following up the results of the schools. In key national policy documents published over the last decade, this is pointed out as the main area of responsibility (Skedsmo, 2009). Different types of data about the schools and the education sector are collected and integrated in a status report which in the final round is submitted to the County Governor, located in each of the regional counties. This report forms the basis for supervision practices, which ensures that the municipalities follow up on their responsibilities as *school owners* (Royal Ministry of Education and Research, 2007-2008).

Compared to inspection-driven systems found in many other Western democracies, this approach does not imply direct control of educational quality in terms of teaching and learning in schools. The state supervision follows a system revision approach and aims to expose cases where legal regulations are not followed (Sivesind, 2009). So far, state supervision has focused on areas such as the right to special education and adapted teaching, to secure a safe school environment and the extent to which the municipalities have established a system for quality assurance.

## THEORETICAL PERSPECTIVES

This chapter draws on different sets of theoretical perspectives. Our point of departure is that school governing processes are reflexive. The superintendents' perceptions represent, in many ways, the social effects of the meaning of the policy to which they are being called upon to respond (Ball, 1994, 2008). This means that policies will be implemented according to how they are perceived, interpreted and acted upon. Also, governing processes in the Norwegian school system reflect in certain ways loosely coupled system features (cf. Rowan, 2002), especially when analyzing policy implementation and change across various administrative levels (cf. March & Olsen, 1984). Weick (2001) conceptualizes loose coupling as a multi-level organizational system "when the components of a system affect each other (1) suddenly rather than continuously, (2) occasionally rather than constantly, (3) negligibly rather than significantly, (4) indirectly rather than directly, and (5) eventually rather than immediately" (Weick, 2001, p. 383).

The crucial point in Weick's (1976) theoretical proposition is that one can expect significant lack of correspondence between the formal system's architecture, in terms of plans, goals, implementation strategies and quality assurance systems developed by state agencies, and the negotiations, decisions, power distribution and operational activities carried out by the actors in the municipalities (March & Olsen, 1976; Weick, 1996). Despite the "messages" from the national school legislation about monitoring, auditing, quality assurance related to student learning and test data, it is not guaranteed that these demands will be imposed on principals and teachers by superintendents. On the contrary: superintendents and school boards in Norwegian municipalities may mediate some of these centrally imposed policy demands by employing buffering strategies (Thompson, 1967), through the re-translation of policy goals and symbolic implementation (Forsell, 2001). Loose coupling in the school governance system is, not surprisingly, observed by the numerous cases showing that reforms are seldom "transplanted" from one social context to another (Datnow, 2002). And, school superintendents are uniquely positioned to take an active part in mediating between system levels and schools, by performing gatekeeper roles (Tushman & Katz, 1980), bridging among various actors' interests and in some cases buffering and sheltering schoolteachers through lack of implementation (Meyer, 1992; Yan & Louis, 1999).

Weick (1976) has an important, although overlooked, point that loose coupling is a dialectical phenomenon; organizational systems are typically both loosely and tightly coupled. This mixed pattern is visible, for example, in the Norwegian quality assurance system. The couplings between the state level and the county level are fairly tight, whereas the couplings between the counties and the next layer, i.e., the municipalities, are looser. Moreover, the relation between the municipalities and the schools is further loosened because the system allows mediating practices, e.g., autonomous selection of items for the municipal quality report, which makes sense, given the diversity in size, demography and political orientation in the Norwegian landscape. For the purpose of maintaining the necessary insight, transparency and control of public institutions, a certain degree of tight coupling is needed. Examples may be evident in the national quality assessment system and, in particular, in the national standardized tests, the increased demand for reporting and accountability, and in the competency aims, all representing new ways of governing the outputs of national programs. Thus, school governance in practice can be conceived as a blend of tightening and loosening done simultaneously although in different areas.

## AN EMPIRICAL FOUNDATION

This analysis, building on different methodological approaches and outlining new modes of governing (that describe tensions between the national and local levels and the working context of superintendents), draws on literature review and analysis of key policy documents published over the last decade.[2] Findings from two surveys conducted in 2009 and 2011,[3] one among superintendents and one among representatives from municipal educational committees, are reported. The analysis of the data is mainly descriptive, where open-ended questions to both groups are analyzed and categorized, based on existing research literature within this field. Moreover, the paper is informed by data sets from the Norwegian Research Database on Municipality Organization (Blåka, Tjerbo & Zeiner, 2012; Hovik & Stigen, 2004, 2008).

## THE SUPERINTENDENT IN THE GOVERNANCE SYSTEM – AN EDUCATOR

In our superintendent study a strong professional core is reflected in superintendents' education and career path. They are primarily educators with a career path extending from

---

[2] Some of this work was conducted as part of GuriSkedsmo's PhD, which was published in 2009.
[3] These surveys were conducted by researchers at Hedmark University College, Norway.

teacher education, professional work as teachers, school leadership positions and, then, superintendency.

### Table 1. Background of Norwegian school superintendents

| Background item | Frequency | Percent |
|---|---|---|
| Recruited from primary education | 215 | 73.88 |
| Recruited from other parts of the education system | 23 | 7.90 |
| Teacher related professional education | 268 | 92.10 |

When it comes to career path, the superintendents in our sample are mostly recruited to their first school superintendent job from the educational sector, as Table 1 illustrates.

Thus, the Norwegian school superintendent is typically an educator (cf. Bjørk & Kowalski, 2005), with most of his or her training and career path embedded in the schooling system. Our data support the notion that school leadership at the municipal level is seen more as an enterprise of professional expertise, and that the managerial rhetoric of the New Public Management (cf. Christensen & Lægreid, 2002; Røvik, 1996) did not have a significant impact on the recruitment of school superintendents.

## MISMATCHING AGENDAS?

*Prioritized tasks and issues in the dialogue with school principals:* Superintendents were asked to rank three most important tasks on the job in their relationship with school principals. Their responses are categorized and presented in Appendix 1. These responses are grouped into seven main broad categories: Quality management, human resource management, administration and coordination, financial management, pedagogical leadership and school improvement, student learning and strategic leadership.

Superintendents' responses initially show that quality management plays a relatively minor role in superintendents' agendas with their school principals (11.91%). Also within this theme, we can see a tendency in the rhetoric to avoid the control aspect and greater tendency to use softer terms such as "quality development" and "quality system development." Administrative themes including human resource management (19.95%), financial management (16.33%), administration and coordination (9.77%) make up 46.05% of the responses, displaying a relatively strong administrative work profile among the superintendents in the sample. Third, pedagogical leadership and school development tasks account for 31.86% of the total tasks representing superintendents' interactions with school principals, indicating a strong orientation towards the professional domain. Fourth are tasks related to the "end product" of schooling, namely, student achievement, school climate, special needs and learning environment. These responses (7%) do not display a strong direct focus on student learning in daily task priorities characterizing the dialogue superintendents have with school principals. Although parental involvement is hardly mentioned, this is not surprising considering other published works on this theme (Bæck, 2010a; Paulsen, 2012).

The responses obtained support an image of an administrative and educational leadership profile of the Norwegian superintendent. The prioritized tasks and agendas accentuate state-initiated quality supervision of schools, school development, and accountability. At the same time, the local quality management focus seems to be rather weak, and so is the focus on student achievements. Bearing in mind that data are based on self-report statements about organizational behavior, these reports reveal a gap between policy makers' preferences and superintendents' task preferences when it comes to managerial accountability (e.g., inspection, quality assurance, followup of student achievement data) as well as the relationship to parents. Both domains are, however, relatively high on the national policy agenda.

## RANKED EXPECTATIONS IMPOSED BY THE SCHOOL BOARD

In the school board survey of 2011[4] we asked board members to rank, firstly, their most important tasks, and secondly, the three most important issues they would hold the superintendent accountable for. Three trends emerged. First, in addition to budgeting and financial management, which are standard demands, quality assurance issues were highly prioritized. These included *raising the quality of the teachers' work* and *improving national test achievements of the students in our municipality*. In a similar vein, *monitoring the schools' level of goal achievements* was a highly prioritized task as expressed by the school board members in the sample. Second, when school board members were asked about their expectations from the superintendents, quality assurance issues were again quite apparent, and board members tended to express high expectations in relation to superintendents' accountability for the quality of student learning. Hence, although quality assurance is hardly mentioned in superintendents' discourse with school principals, the two data sets support the notion that school superintendents are active mediators of local policy expectations.

## A LOOSELY AND TIGHTLY COUPLED GOVERNANCE CHAIN

The empirical evidence gathered in two national surveys of superintendents and school board members portray a governing system that is both loosely and tightly coupled in respect to different domains. They give rise to the assumption that there are some degrees of disconnection between central policies and local priorities. The prioritized tasks support the notion that certain issues are mediated and filtered out when central policies meet the local government level. This is evidently the case when it comes to parental involvement (Bæck, 2010b; Paulsen, 2012). More noteworthy, at the local level, we also see that the superintendents filter out and mediate priorities defined by the local politicians. Quality control and quality assurance issues make up a significant portion of the agenda as perceived in school board members' task preferences and in their expectations of their superintendents. However, these areas seem to have a low priority when superintendents are requested to

---

[4] The school board survey was undertaken in 2011, collecting responses from school board members from about a third of Norwegian municipalities.

conceptualize their work areas. There is some question whether quality control and quality assurance are mediated in terms of creating a greater focus on superintendents' need to support school development.

## MEDIATION AS AN IMPORTANT LEADERSHIP FUNCTION

The data show that school superintendents in Norway are typically educators with a task preference structure anchored in a professional educational discourse. Moreover, the data give support to the notion that mediation is a central leadership and management function as exerted by school superintendents. Supplemental data from the superintendent survey on professional network engagement underscore that the superintendents are active network players, and they are also members of the municipality's senior leadership team. They are, thus, uniquely positioned to buffer, translate priorities and change the structure of preferences according to what they view to be most important. Whereas the national agenda is relatively "infused" with strong quality rhetoric, this agenda is nearly absent when superintendents rank their tasks and issues they see as important in the daily leadership dialogues with their school principals.

## SUPERINTENDENTS IN THECROSSFIRE

Superintendents' position in the national quality assurance system contextualizes their leadership role in the *crossfire* between the state and local government priorities (Johansson et al., 2011). Further, superintendents are also placed at the interface between political and professional demands made of school principals and teachers (Lundgren, 1990). Thus, the superintendents' position is embedded in a context constituted by a blend of demands for professional trust on the side of teachers and school leaders, local autonomy expected by local politicians and legitimized state control through the quality assurance system. Implicitly, we assume that a main function for school superintendents is to filter and mediate between political and administrative managers, on one side, and educational practitioners, especially school leaders, on the other.

## THE BLUEPRINT ASSUMPTION: ABSENCE OF POLICY FORMATION IN NORWEGIAN MUNICIPALITIES

Inherent in the Norwegian school institution is the longstanding norm that the municipalities should counterbalance the state's power in practical school policy (Engeland, 2000). Several authors argue that in the present situation, across different national systems, the state has increasingly struck back and tightened its grip by indirect steering conceived as soft governance (Hudson, 2007; Moos, 2009). It is a growing trend in Norway, although less visible than in Sweden, that the state utilizes a sort of "licence to bypass" the municipalities by means of forwarding directives and initiatives directly to the schools and principals (Nihlfors et al., 2013). The evaluation of the implementation of K06 policy shows that the state administrative level increasingly regards the local level as a tool to implement national policies (Aasen et al., 2012).

Moreover, in a review of Norwegian school government 1970-2007, Engeland and Langfeldt (2009) conclude that independent school policy formation and policy initiatives are very seldom observable in Norwegian municipalities. Noteworthy, the time-span of their review encompasses the implementation phase of the systemic school reform labelled the Knowledge Promotion (K06), which paradoxically presumes a substantial local engagement in policy formation through delegation and decentralization. Specifically, the government presumed that the municipalities should "fill in the gaps" in vague and underspecified goal formulations in the curricula of the (K06) with their own local strategies, policy initiatives and prioritizations.

However, in reality, this was not the case. For example, municipal policy goals and local educational strategies, as observed in written documents, have tended to have a general and vague nature leaving the impression that they are "blueprints" of national policies (Engeland & Langfeldt, 2009). Specifically this has been the case when it comes to the content of the curriculum, i.e., the ideological steering of schools: locally developed evaluation criteria (towards school principals and teachers) as well as local curriculum development have seldom been found. Further, as Engeland noted, the intended level of municipal autonomy inherent in the Local Government Act of 1992 (Baldersheim & Ståhlberg, 1994; Larsen & Offerdal, 2000) has *not* been utilized within the policy domain of primary education (Engeland, 2000). Moreover, after the millennium shift, a series of standardized measurement instruments were implemented in order to assess student achievements and the quality of student learning, which we assume will further de-stimulate local policy formation and strategy formation in the municipalities.

The tools in use, and thereby the foundation for quality improvement, are based on premises defined by national authorities (Skedsmo, 2009). This type of central coordination can create a certain dependency, which establishes new patterns of interaction between the national and local authorities (Ogza, 2009). These developments may result in less local autonomy and increased bureaucratization of the school system. At the same time, local autonomy has been emphasized in the national policy discourse. White Paper No. 30 refers to the municipalities as *school owners* and defines broad areas of tasks and responsibilities of municipalities and schools related to quality improvement (Royal Ministry of Education and Research, 2003-2004).

# MEDIATION: SUPERINTENDENTS' LEADERSHIP FUNCTION

Indirect steering through quality indicators, paired with ambiguous and vague policy formation in municipalities, is likely to become a central issue in superintendents' leadership practices. The data in our 2009 study support this notion and illustrate multiple mediation categories: buffering, filtering and translation. Through performing mediation roles as coordinators and gatekeepers (Gould & Fernandez, 1989), a series of national policy initiatives have been filtered out in the superintendents' daily dialogues with the school principals. Moreover, the national quality assurance rhetoric has been translated into softer language when the superintendents meet their school principals through discussions focused on quality issues. Further, current school reform implementation, which in policy documents is infused with managerial rhetoric, has been typically translated into a traditional school development language in the daily leadership discourse. Engeland and Langfeldt (2009) also bring evidence that the current superintendent position is more loosely coupled with the national policy regime and tightly coupled with the top management core of the municipality organization. When this occurs in a situation characterized by a vague and unclear policy regime, it stimulates superintendents to fill the gaps by means of their own preferences.

## THE NORWEGIAN SUPERINTENDENT: MEDIATION ANCHORED IN PROFESSIONAL DEMANDS

The findings presented show that school superintendents are educators with a career path bound to the school institution for a significant amount of time. Moreover, the typical superintendent in our sample is an educated professional teacher with supplemental credentials in educational science. The empirical results are in line with earlier conceptualizations of the superintendent role, with strong emphasis on educator competence, drawn from other national educational systems (Bjørk & Kowalski, 2005). When the superintendents' mediation practices are anchored in dominant norms and ideologies of the teaching profession, an assumption supported by the empirical data, it is fair to interpret this pattern as a case of normative and cultural-cognitive path-dependency (Scott, 1995).

Our findings underscore the hypothesis of a "political vacuum" in Norwegian municipalities when it comes to local school governance evident in local curriculum development, evaluation criteria, implementation strategies, organizational innovation and learning goals. This point makes mediation a central leadership function at this meso-level of the Norwegian educational system, and we see this topic as a promising path for further research and theory development of superintendent leadership.

## APPENDIX 1. SUPERINTENDENTS' RELATIONSHIP WITH THEIR SCHOOL PRINCIPALS: RANKED TASKS

| Task categories | Frequency | Percent |
|---|---|---|
| *QUALITY MANAGEMENT* | | |
| Quality development | 33 | 4.42 |
| Quality system development | 15 | 2.01 |
| Quality control and quality assurance | 12 | 1.61 |
| Control, reporting and follow up of national policy | 29 | 3.88 |
| | *89* | *11.91* |
| *HUMAN RESOURCE MANAGEMENT* | | |
| Competence development of school staff | 88 | 11.78 |
| Recruitment and Human Resource Management | 50 | 6.69 |
| Meetings with school principals | 11 | 1.47 |
| | *149* | *19.95* |

# APPENDIX 1. (Continued)

| Task categories | Frequency | Percent |
|---|---|---|
| FINANCIAL MANAGEMENT | | |
| Budgeting and resource allocation | 33 | 4.42 |
| Financial management | 89 | 11.91 |
| | 122 | 16.33 |
| ADMINISTRATION AND COORDINATION | | |
| Secretary unit for policy board | 2 | 0.27 |
| Coordination, law issues and daily administration | 51 | 6.83 |
| School buildings | 3 | 0.40 |
| Internal and external communication / information | 6 | 0.80 |
| Management by Objectives | 11 | 1.47 |
| | 73 | 9.77 |
| PEDAGOGICAL LEADERSHIP AND SCHOOL DEVELOPMENT | | |
| Supervision, support and guidance of school leaders | 74 | 9.91 |
| Pedagogical leadership | 16 | 2.14 |
| School development | 91 | 12.18 |
| Team development school principals | 5 | 0.67 |
| School leadership development | 37 | 4.95 |
| Developmental projects | 11 | 1.47 |
| Efforts for shared sense of purpose among staff | 4 | 0.54 |
| | 238 | 31.86 |
| STUDENT LEARNING ORIENTATED TASKS | | |
| Adapted learning /children with special needs | 8 | 1.07 |
| Subject issues | 3 | 0.40 |
| Improvement of pupils' learning achievement | 10 | 1.34 |
| School climate and learning environment for pupils | 11 | 1.47 |
| Follow up of national test data | 17 | 2.28 |
| | 49 | 6.56 |
| STRATEGIC LEADERSHIP | | |
| External collaboration with parents and stakeholders | 11 | 1.47 |
| Organizational development | 14 | 1.87 |
| Strategic analysis and forecasting | 2 | 0.27 |
| | 27 | 3.61 |
| N = 747 / 249 | | 100% |

# REFERENCES

Aasen, P., Møller, J., Rye, E., Ottesen, E., Prøitz, T. S., & Hertzberg, F. (2012). Kunnskapsløftet som styringsreform - et løft eller et løfte? Forvaltningsnivåenes og institusjonenes rolle i implementeringen av reformen (Knowledge promotion as governance refrom - a promotion or a promise? *The role of the civil services and the institutions in the implementation of the reform)*. Oslo: NIFU-STEP.

Afsar, A., Skedsmo, G., & Sivesind, K. (2006). Evaluering og kunnskapsutvikling i ledelse av utdanning (Evaluation and knowledge creation in educational leadership). In K. Sivesind, & G. Langfeldt (Eds.), *Utdanningsledelse (Educational leadership)*. Oslo: Cappelen.

Baldersheim, H., & Ståhlberg, K. (1994). From top-down to bottom-up: Free communes and the politics of administrative modernization. In H. Baldersheim, & K. Ståhlberg (Eds.), *Towards the Self-regulating Municipality. Free Communes and Administrative Modernization in Scandinavia.* Aldershot: Darmouth Publishing Company.

Ball, S. J. (1994). *Education reform. A critical and post-structural approach.* Buckingham: Open University Press.

Ball, S. J. (2008). *The Education Debate.* Bristol: The Policy Press.

Bjørk, L., & Kowalski, T. J. (2005). *The Contemporary Superintendent: Preparation, Practice and Development.* Thousand Oaks, CA: Corwin.

Blåka, S., Tjerbo, T., & Zeiner, H. (2012). *Kommunal organisering 2012 (Municipal organization in 2012).* Oslo: NIBR.

Bukve, O. (1997). *Kommunal forvaltning og planlegging (Local administration and planning)* (3 ed.). Oslo: Det Norske Samlaget.

Bæck, U. D. K. (2010a). From a distance- How Norwegian parents experience their encounters with school. *International Journal of Educational Research*, 48, 342-351.

Bæck, U.-D. K. (2010b). "We" are the professionals: A study of teachers' views on parental involvement in school. *British Journal of Sociology of Education*, 31(3), 323-335.

Christensen, T., & Lægreid, P. (2002). *Reformer og lederskap: omstilling i den utøvende makt (Reforms and leadership: change in the governing power).* Oslo: Universitetsforlaget.

Datnow, A. (2002). Can we transplant educational reform, and does it last? *Journal of Educational Change*, 3, 215-239.

Engeland, Ø. (2000). *Skolen i kommunalt eie - politisk styrt eller profesjonell ledet skoleutvikling (The municipal ownership of schools - politically governed or professionally lead school development).* Oslo: University of Oslo.

Engeland, Ø., & Langfeldt, G. (2009). Forholdet mellom stat og kommune i styring av norsk utdanningspolitikk 1970-2008 (The relation between state and municipality in governing Norwegian educational policy 1970-2008). *Acta Didactica Norge*, 3(1), 1-16.

Floyd, S. W., & Wooldridge, B. (1997). Middle management's strategic influence and organizational performance. *The Journal of Management Studies*, 34(3), 465.

Forsell, A. (2001). Reform theory meets new public management. In T. Christensen, & P. Lægreid (Eds.), *In: New Public Management. The transformation of ideas and practice.* Burlington: Ashgate.

Gould, R. V., & Fernandez, R. M. (1989). Structures of mediation: A formal approach to brokerage in transaction networks. *Sociological Methodology*, 19, 89-126.

Helgøy, I., & Homme, A. (2006). Policy tools and institutional change: Comparing education policies in Norway, Sweden and England. *Journal of Public Policy*, 26(2), 141-165.

Hovik, S., & Stigen, I. M. (2004). *Kommunal organisering 2004 (Municipal organization in 2004)*. Oslo: NIBR.

Hovik, S., & Stigen, I. M. (2008). *Kommunal organisering 2008 (Municipal organization in 2008)*. Oslo: NIBR.

Hudson, C. (2007). Gonverning the governance of education: The state strikes back? *European Educational Research Journal*, 6(3), 266-282.

Johansson, O. (2010). Skolchefens funktion och scen (The function and the scene of the school superintendent). In J. Höög, & O. Johansson (Eds.), *Struktur, kultur, ledarkap – förutsättningar för framgångsrika skolor? (Structure, culture, leadership - enabling conditions for progressing schools?)*. Lund: Studentlitteratur.

Johansson, O., Holmgren, M., Nihlfors, E., Moos, L., Skedsmo, G., Paulsen, J. M., & Risku, M. (2013). Local decisions under central watch - A new Nordic quality assurance system. In L. Moos (Ed.), *Transnational influences on values and practices in Nordic educational leadership - Is there a Nordic model?* Dordrecht: Springer.

Johansson, O., Moos, L., Nihlfors, E., Paulsen, J. M., & Risku, M. (2011). The Nordic superintendents' leadership roles: Cross national comparisons. In J. McBeath & T. Townsend (Eds.), *International handbook on leadership for learning*. Dordrecht: Springer.

Karseth, B., & Sivesind, K. (2009). Læreplanstudier - perspektiver og posisjoner (Curriculum studies - perspectives and positions). In E. L. Dale (Ed.), *Læreplan i et forskningsperspektiv (A research perspective on curriculum)*. Oslo: Universitetsforlaget.

Larsen, H. O., & Offerdal, A. (2000). Political implications of the new Norwegian local government act of 1992. In E. Amnå, & S. Montin (Eds.), *Towards a new concept of local self-government*. Bergen: Fagbokforlaget.

Lundgren, U. P. (1990). Educational policymaking, decentralication and evaluation. In M. Granheim, M. Kogan & U. P. Lundgren (Eds.), *Evaluation as policymaking: Introducing evaluation into a national decentralised educational system*. London: Jessica Kingsley.

March, J. G., & Olsen, J. P. (1976). *Ambiguity and choice in organizations*. Oslo: Scandinavian University Press.

March, J. G., & Olsen, J. P. (1984). The new institutionalism: Organizational factors in political life. *American Political Science Review*, 78(3), 734-749.

Meyer, J. W. (1992). Centralization of funding and control in educational governance. In J. W. Meyer & W. R. Scott (Eds.), *Organizational environments. Ritual and rationality. Updated Edition*. Newsbury Park: Sage Publications.

Moos, L. (2006). What kinds of democracy in education are facilitated by supra- and transnational agencies? *European Educational Research Journal*, 5(3 & 4), 160-168.

Moos, L. (2009). Hard and soft governance: The journey from transnational agencies to school leadership. *European Educational Research Journal*, 8(3), 397-406.

Møller, J., & Skedsmo, G. (2013). Centralization and decentralization as twin reform strategies. In L. Moos (Ed.), *Transnational influences on values and practices in Nordic educational leadership - Is there a Nordic model?* Dordrecht: Springer.

Nihlfors, E. (2003). *Scholchefen i skolans styrning og ledning (The superintendent in governance and leadership of the school)*. Uppsala: Uppsala University, Acta Universitatis Upsaliensis. Uppsala Studies in Education, 102.

Nihlfors, E., Johansson, O., Moos, L., Paulsen, J. M., & Risku, M. (2013). The Nordic superintendents' leadership roles: Cross national comparison. In L. Moos (Ed.), *Transnational influences on values and practices in Nordic educational leadership - Is there a Nordic model?* Dordrecht: Springer.

Offerdal, A. (1992). *Den politiske kommunen (The political municipality)*. Oslo: Det Norske Samlaget.

Ogza, J. (2009). Governing education through data in England: From regulation to self-evaluation. *Journal of Education Policy*, 24(2), 149-162.

Paulsen, J. M. (2012). Parental involvement in Norwegian schools. *Journal of School Public Relations*, 33: 29-47.

Rowan, B. (2002). The ecology of school imrpovement: Notes on the school improvement industry in the United States. *Journal of Educational Change*, 3, 283-314.

Røvik, K. A. (1996). Deinstitutionalization and the logic of fashion. In B. Czarniawska & G. Sevón (Eds.), *Translating organizational change*. Berlin: De Gruyter.

Scott, W. R. (1995). *Institutions and organizations*. Thousand Oaks, Calif.: Sage.

Sivesind, K. (2009). JUSS+PED=SANT? Om felles nasjonalt tilsyn i Oslo og Akershus (Law + Pedagogy = True? On national supervision in Oslo and Akershus counties). *Acta Didactica Norge*.

Sivesind, K., & Bachmann, K. (2008). Hva forandres med nye standarder? Krav og utfordringer med Kunnskapsløftets læreplaner (What is changed with new standards? Demands and challenges in the curricula of the knowledge promotion). In G. Langfeldt, E. Elstad, & S. Hoppmann (Eds.), *Ansvarlighet i skolen. Politiske spørsmål og pedagogiske svar (Accountability in schools. Political questions and pedagogical answers)*. Oslo: Cappelen Akademisk.

Skedsmo, G. (2009). *School governing in transition? Perspectives, purposes and perceptions of evaluation policy*. PhD thesis. Department of Teacher Education and School Development, Faculty of Education. University of Oslo, Oslo.

Skedsmo, G., & Hopfenbeck, T. (In progress). *Integrating sustainable school improvement and assessment policies: A study of how local educational authorities and schools respond to new national expecations*.

Thompson, J. D. (1967). *Organizations in action: social science bases of administrative theory*. New York: McGraw-Hill.

Tushman, M. L., & Katz, R. (1980). External communication and project performance: An investigation into the role of gatekeepers. *Management Science*, 26(11), 1071-1085.

Weick, K. E. (1976). Educational organizations as loosely coupled systems. *Administrative Science Quarterly*, 21, 1-19.

Weick, K. E. (1996). Fighting fires in educational administration. *Educational Administration Quarterly*, 32(4): 565.

Weick, K. E. (2001). Management of organizational change among loosely coupled elements. In K. E. Weick (Ed.), *Making sense of the organization*. Malden, Mass.: Blackwell Publishing.

Yan, A., & Louis, M. R. (1999). The migration of organizational functions to the work unit level: Buffering, spanning and bringing up boundaries. *Human Relations*, 52(1), 25-47.

## Policy Documents

White Paper No. 30 (2003-2004). *Kultur for læring (A culture for learning)*: The Royal Ministry of Education and Research.

White Paper No. 31 (2007-2008): *Kvalitet i skolen (Educational Quality)*: The Royal Ministry of Education and Research.

In: The Educational Superintendent
Editor: Adam E. Nir

ISBN: 978-1-62948-972-8
© 2014 Nova Science Publishers, Inc.

*Chapter 4*

# PEDAGOGICAL SUPERVISION AND SUPERINTENDENTS IN POLAND: ON THE WAY TO THE QUALITY OF EDUCATION

## *Joanna Madalińska-Michalak*

University of Lodz, Poland

The purpose of this chapter is to present the current situation of pedagogical supervision and superintendents' role and duties in Poland. The chapter is organized in three main sections. In section 1 the social, political, economic and demographical circumstances of Poland are briefly presented. Section 2 provides both a description of the structure of compulsory education in Poland and patterns of accountability system. It focuses on aims and major challenges of the education in Poland. At the same time it shows achievements in international tests and major change initiatives. In section 3 the description of pedagogical supervision and superintendents' role and duties − in the context of the main reforms of pedagogical supervision that has been implemented over the last decade in Poland − is presented.

In this section, on the basis of the state report prepared by the Supreme Audit Office, I will present some weaknesses of the new system of pedagogical supervision in Poland and recommendations for its improvement. At the end I will formulate some conclusions about the new system of pedagogical supervision in Poland, taking into account the activities that, by definition, should serve the quality of education.

It is worth noting that the different definitions of quality can be classified into two groups: the approaches that pay attention mainly to the quality of outputs and the approaches that focus on the quality of processes in developing, implementing and improving institutional activities.

It is often the case that when speaking of education and its quality, it is easy to revert to such managerial concepts as quality control, quality mechanisms, quality management, etc. These concepts convey a technocratic and top-down approach in the development of "quality assurance movement" in the system of education (Michalak, 2011). The dynamic aspect of quality (in both the outputs and the process perspectives) is a dimension which is pointed out in the new reform of pedagogical supervision in Poland.

## CONTEXTUALIZATION

The year 1989 was a crucial year in the contemporary history of Poland. After the agreements of the so-called "round table" resulting from the negotiations between the representatives of the opposition and the representatives of the ruling government, the first partially free parliamentary elections took place in June 1989. The first totally free and democratic elections were held later, in 1991. A dynamic period of political, social and economic transformation began in Poland. The rebirth of parliamentary democracy led to the creation of many political parties and the development of independent mass media. The decentralization of public authority continued along with the local reform. The introduction of the market economy limited the State intervention in the economy and initiated restructuring and privatization processes (Blok, 2006).

In the 1990s Poland entered the path leading to integration with Western European countries. In 1991 it became a member of the Council of Europe and concluded the Association Agreement with the European Community, which was ratified by the European Community in 1993. Poland became a member of the OECD in 1996 and the North Atlantic Treaty Organization (NATO) in 1999. On 1 May 2004 Poland became a member of the European Union.

The political system in Poland is defined by the Constitution of the Republic of Poland of 2 April 1997. In accordance with the Constitution the legislative power is exercised by a two-chamber Parliament which includes the lower chamber – the Sejm – and the upper chamber – the Senat – both elected for a four-year term. The Sejm consists of 460 members elected according to the proportional election system. It exercises the legislative power and supervises the government. The Senat has 100 members elected according to the majority system. The legislative power of the Senat is limited to the legislative initiative and proposals of amendments to bills passed by the Sejm. The executive power is exercised by the President and the Council of Ministers (*KonstytucjaRzeczypospolitejPolskiej*, 1997).

The territorial organization of the Polish state ensures the decentralization of the public authorities. This territorial division is defined in the Act of 24 July 1998 on the Introduction of the Basic Three-tier Territorial Division: provinces (*województwo*), districts (*powiat*) and communes (*gmina*). Poland is divided into 16 provinces, 379 districts, and 2,478 communes.

As laid down in the Constitution, the commune (*gmina*) is the basic local government body. It is obliged to fulfill the needs of the local community in the following areas: healthcare, welfare, culture and education. It is responsible for administering kindergartens (*przedszkole*), primary schools (*szkołapodstawowa*) and lower secondary schools (*gimnazjum*). This body operates on the basis of the Act of 8 March 1990 on the Commune-level Local Government. The district (*powiat*) was established in 1998 as the second level of local government. The district supports the commune in performing all functions which extend beyond the capacity and purview of the latter. It administers upper secondary schools and hospitals, and manages public roads. It is also responsible for combating unemployment, and for the protection of consumers' rights. It operates on the basis of the Act of 5 June 1998 on the District-level Local Government.

The head of the province (*wojewoda*) represents the Council of Ministers in a given region and he/she supervises the institutions performing the tasks entrusted to the state. Responsibilities of the self-governing province include regional economic and social development as well as the establishment and administration of public initial and in-service teacher training institutions, educational resources centers, and schools and institutions operating at regional and supra-regional levels. Its scope of activities does not interfere with the independence of the district and the commune.

The transformation of the Polish economy involved the transition from the centrally steered economy to a free market one. This transformation included in particular the change in the structure of ownership of economic entities (privatization), the abolishment of State control over foreign trade, liberalization of financial movement between Poland and other countries, the introduction of legislation stimulating development of entrepreneurship and competition on the internal market, liberalization of prices, and the introduction of internal exchange of the Polish zloty and of a uniform rate of currencies.

Poland's accession to the European Union in 2004 began a period of boom in the Polish economy. The growth in exports stimulated a growth in production and employment and, as a result, an increase in internal consumption. At the beginning, the growth of production was achieved with no investment due to some production potential still present in the Polish economy. Further growth of demand resulted in increased investment which contributed to a relatively high economic growth. Due to Poland's strong economic links with other EU Member States (with the EU accounting for 78.9% of the total Polish exports in 2007), the economic situation within the EU has particular importance for the condition of the Polish economy. In 2007 the Polish economy was still growing. The year 2008 saw a gradual economic slowdown in Poland. However, the Polish economy still witnessed a high rate of growth and the global financial crisis had a limited effect on it. According to the Central Statistical Office, the Polish GDP grew by 5.1% in 2008. The economic indicators recorded in 2008 show both certain strength of the Polish economy and some growing difficulties. In 2009, after three years of a high rate of economic growth, a drop was observed. It should be stressed that Poland was the only EU Member State that noted an economic growth in 2009. After a clear slowdown in the first six months of the year, the production growth rate increased in industry, retail sales, transport and communication services, as well as in foreign trade. The years 2010–2011 were a period of a gradual recovery of the economic potential after the slowdown recorded in 2009. In 2011 the Polish GDP was 4.3%. The main driving factor for the economic growth was home demand, but the net contribution of export was +0.9% (GUS, 2012a).

As far as demographic circumstances are concerned, it is worth noting that in Poland 38.1 million people inhabit an area of 312,685 square kilometers. The average density of the population is 122 people per square kilometer. Since 1989 a process of limited turnover of generations has been observed in Poland. In 1999 a real decline in the population was observed for the first time. It was mainly caused by a drop in the number of births and negative net definitive international migration. Currently, the fertility rate is the lowest among the EU countries and one of the lowest in Europe – in 2011 the fertility rate in Poland was 1.3. In December 2011, the number of young people under 29 years of age was 14,150,000 and accounted for 36.7 % of the population (GUS, 2012a,2012b).

According to the long range demographic prognosis for the period up to 2035, the number of Poles will decrease steadily and the rate of this decrease will progressively grow. The process of aging of the Polish society will occur. The proportion of the post-working age population will increase. The so-called demographic burden index (the ratio of the post-working age population to the working age population) will increase from 55 in 2007 to 73 in 2035 (Jóźwiak&Kotowska, 2010).

The Polish language is the official language in Poland, as stated in the Constitution and the Act on the Polish Language. Compared to other European countries, Poland is very homogeneous in terms of ethnicity. It is estimated that no more than 3% of the total population are national minorities. The years since 1989 have seen a rebirth of national and ethnic identity among the minorities.

The network of schools teaching in languages of national minorities or offering additional classes in these languages for pupils from national minorities has been steadily developing – the number of such schools has increased four-fold since 1990 (Bogaj, Kwiatkowski&Szymański, 1998; Szczygielski, 2008). The rights of ethnic and national minorities with respect to learning the minority language or education in the minority language as well as the right to learn about the history and culture of the minority are exercised on the basis of the principles laid down in the amended Education System Act of 7 September 1991.

The freedom of conscience and the freedom of religion are guaranteed by the Constitution. Churches of all denominations and the State are independent and autonomous. There is no official religion in Poland. The Roman Catholic Church is the largest church in Poland (around 87% of the population are Roman-Catholic). The Church has the right to administer educational institutions, i.e., kindergartens schools and schools of all levels, in accordance with the canon law regulations and the relevant Acts of Parliament (e.g., those concerning the school and higher education systems, etc.).

# THE EDUCATIONAL SYSTEM

The period of political transformation has brought about new legislation, which has become the basis for changes in education. The old education system was characterized by the primacy of information (understood as a set of facts) over skills, teaching by academic areas, the reduced educational role of the school and its lack of partnership with the pupils' home, the narrow-specialization and long-duration vocational training, and the primacy of collective education over individual education (Michalak, 2005, p. 141).

The most important reasons underlying the necessity to carry out a comprehensive reform of the education system in Poland included the following six most important ones: (1) the lack of capacity within the education system to adapt to the pace and scope of economic, social and cultural change; (2) the crisis of the educational role of the school resulting from the predominance of the transmission of information over the development of skills, competences and the shaping of personality; (3) the lack of equal opportunities of gaining access to education at all its levels and the low percentage of young people completing secondary and higher education; (4) the necessity to adapt the education system to the provisions of the Constitution and the system reform of the State; (5) the necessity to adapt vocational education to the changing needs of the market economy; and (6)the need to establish closer links between schools at all levels and the family, as well as the local community (Bogaj et al., 1998, pp. 34-35).

The reform of the State administration system and the education reform assume that only the nation educational policy is developed and carried out centrally, while the administration of education and the running of schools, pre-school institutions and other educational establishments are decentralized. The responsibility for the administration of public kindergartens, primary schools and lower secondary schools (gymnasia) was delegated, at the lowest first-level administration, to local authorities (communes). It became the statutory responsibility of the districts − middle, second level administration − to administer upper secondary schools, art schools and special schools. The provinces *(voivodships)*have the coordinating function, supervising the implementation of the policy of the Ministry of National Education and being responsible for pedagogical supervision. The inspection of teaching standards in schools comes directly under the Ministry of National Education and is represented by a regional administrative body, called *"kuratoriumoświaty"* (Regional Education Authorities – REAs). According to the division of the country into 16 autonomous provinces, there are 16 Regional Education Authorities, and the Superintendents *(kuratorzyoświaty)* head the Regional Education Authorities.

The main legal basis for the school education and higher education systems is provided by the Constitution of the Republic of Poland. Its provisions referring to fundamental freedoms and citizens' rights state that every person has the right to education and education is compulsory until the age of 18. Education in public schools is free of charge. Parents are free to choose schools other than public ones for their children. Citizens and institutions have the right to establish primary, lower secondary, upper secondary and post-secondary schools, as well as the Higher Education Institutions and childcare centers.

The Polish school education system is based on such main parliamentary acts as the School Education Act of 7 September 1991 (with further amendments), the Act of 8 January 1999 on the Implementation of the Education System Reform (with further amendments), and the Act of 26 January 1982 Teachers' Charter (with further amendments).

In accordance with the Education System Act of 7 September 1991, the education system comprises kindergartens, primary schools, lower secondary schools (gymnasia), upper secondary and post-secondary schools (see Figure 1). In the light of the existing law, institutions of higher education form a separate higher education system or sector.

Pre-school education is regarded as the first level of the education system in Poland.

Pre-school education for children aged 3–5/6 years is organized in kindergartens *(przedszkola)*, pre-school classes in primary schools *(oddziałyprzedszkolne)* and other pre-school settings, including pre-school units and pre-school centers. For children aged 3−4 pre-school education is voluntary and is subject to parental decision. In 2010/2011 the attendance rate for children aged 3 amounted to 49.8% and those aged 4 to 64.1%. At present, the increase in the participation of children in pre-school education is one of the government's priorities (GUS, 2012d, pp. 58-61).

Since 1999/2000 children between the ages of 6/7 and 13 attend primary schools for a period of six years. Primary education is accessible to and obligatory for all pupils. Children are required to enter primary education when they have reached or will reach the age of 7 in a given school year. Primary education is based on one-year compulsory pre-school preparation for children who will enroll in grade 1 of primary school in the following school year.

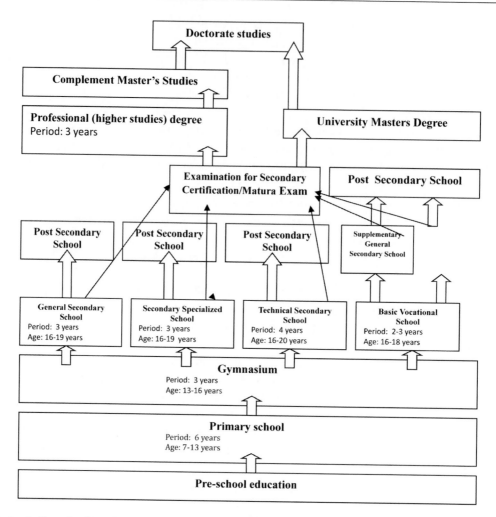

Figure 1. Organization of the education system of in Poland.

The amendment to the School Education Act of 1991 made primary school education compulsory also for 6-year-old children. This change, however, has been implemented gradually, i.e., from 2009 to 2013, and it is still optional, whereas in 2014 it will become compulsory for this age group. General education in primary school is divided into two stages: the first stage of education including grade 1 to 3 of primary school (early school education), and the second stage of education including grades 4 to 6 of primary school.

Before 1999 there was no distinction in the Polish education system between lower and upper secondary schools. The lower secondary level was included in the 8-year single structure school. In the school year 1999/2000 a new type of school, i.e., gymnasium,was established. This school constitutes lower secondary level (ISCED 2).The gymnasium offers three years of full-time general lower secondary education for pupils who have completed the reformed 6-year primary school. It is compulsory for all pupils. Study covers grades 1 to 3 (pupils aged 13 to 16) and it is not divided into stages. The gymnasium is concluded with an external exam giving access to upper secondary education.

Introduction of the lower secondary level resulted in the reform of the upper secondaryschool system (ISCED 3). As a result the following post-gymnasium schools are open to candidates who have successfully graduated from gymnasia: *liceumogólnoksztalcące* (3-year general secondary school); *liceumprofilowane* (3-year specialized secondary school); *technikum* (4-year technical secondary school); *zasadniczaszkołazawodowa* (2- to 3-year basic vocational school).

The Matura examination, necessary for admission to higher education, is held at the end of the 3-year general secondary school or 3-year specialized secondary school and at the end of 4-year technical secondary school.

At the levels of upper secondary/post-secondary education in Poland there are alsothe following types of institutions: *uzupełniająceliceumogólnoksztalcące* (2-year supplementary general secondary school); and *technikumuzupełniające* (3-year supplementary secondary technical school).

General upper secondary schools are non-compulsory and mostly coeducational.The main objective of general upper secondary education is to prepare young people foradmission to higher education establishments of various types.

In line with the Education System Act of 1991, schools can be of two types: public (state) schools, which offer free education within the framework of the core curricula, and non-public schools. Non-public schools can be civic (community), church or private ones. They are financed with fees received from parents. Funds can also come from private enterprises and foundations. Non-public schools are eligible for a grant calculated according to the number of pupils, which equals 100% of the average cost of educating those pupils in a public school. Non-public schools in Poland have the right to issue school certificates that are recognized by all other schools and by the universities. They may be distinguished from public schools by their individualized teaching programs, and by a wider range of curriculum choice.

All pupils attend public schools free of charge. The only admission criterion is the age limit (for pre-school forms – to have reached 6 years of age during the calendar year in which compulsory education starts; for primary schools – to have reached 7 years of age). Parents are obliged to register their children at schools or in kindergartens nearest to their home.

The admission criterion for lower secondary schools is the certificate of primary school completion (to obtain this certificate a pupil needs to sit an external test at the end of primary school education).

The assessment of the knowledge and skills of pupils throughout the school year is not standardized in Poland and remains totally at the discretion of teachers. Assessments are made on the basis of regular written and oral tests.

**Table 1. Public and non-public schools in Poland**

| Sector | Type of school | | | | | |
| --- | --- | --- | --- | --- | --- | --- |
| | Primary schools | | Lower secondary schools Gymnasia | | Upper secondary schools | |
| | N | % | N | % | N | % |
| Public schools | 13,041 | 94.66 | 6,765 | 90.08 | 7,729 | 71.12 |
| Non-public schools | 736 | 5.34 | 745 | 9.92 | 3,139 | 28.88 |
| Grand Total | 13,777 | 100% | 7,510 | 100% | 10,868 | 100% |

Source: GUS, 2012c, p. 167.

The results obtained at the end of each semester must be approved by the teachers' council of each school. Pupils who obtain unsatisfactory results can repeat a year if the teachers' council decides so.

The external evaluation system in compulsory education consists of the two external standardized tests and examinations. At the end of the 6-year primary school (age 13) a general, obligatory test is administered. Completion of this test allows pupils to start education in the lower secondary school (gymnasium), and it provides pupils, parents and both types of schools, i.e., the primary school and the gymnasium, with information about the level of achievements of the pupils. The skills required in the core curricula are examined. It was conducted for the first time in 2002 by the Regional Examination Boards. At the end of the 3-year lower secondary school (gymnasium), at the age of 16, pupils take a general, obligatory examination. This examination tests abilities, skills and knowledge in the field of the humanities and science, as well as a foreign language. The results of the test together with the final assessment of the pupils' performance determine the admission to uppersecondary schools.

The number of credits indicated on the final certificate of lower secondary school (gymnasium) and the test scores in specific subjects determine pupils' admission to an upper secondary school.

The final secondary education certificate (*świadectwomaturalne*) is required by all institutions for admission to the higher education system. The admission is based on the results of final secondary education examination, the Matura examination (*egzaminmaturalny*). Additional admission requirements depend on the type of institution or faculty (e.g., predisposition tests in the field of arts and sports).

The education system in Poland has been able to cope with unprecedentedly and increasingly high educational aspirations of citizens in the last two decades. This results in its outstandingly high levels of participation in education at higher levels, i.e., after the completion of compulsory education, as compared to highly developed countries. Poland has achieved one of the best results in Europe in terms of participation of young people aged 15-24 in education at the ISCED 1−6 levels (from primary education to doctorate programs), the number of young people holding upper secondary qualifications and the reduction in the number of early school leavers, which is one of the measurable objectives of the strategy Europe 2020. Between 2000 and 2011 Poland made the most rapid progress in the EU with regard to increasing the number of young adults holding higher education qualifications in the 30−34 age group.

International education surveys show outstanding progress in learning outcomes at the end of compulsory education: Polish pupils' achievements at this level of education are currently classified in PISA above or at least at the average level among the most developed countries cooperating within the framework of the EU and the OECD. It is worth stressing that Poland's PISA results in 2000 were one of the factors impelling reform in schools and teacher education over the last two decades. Poland spends around US$40,000 in educating each of its school students, less than half of what richer countries like the United States and Norway spend on education, and it now achieves similar results, which can be observed in the PISA 2009 results. In the PISA 2000 examination, Poland's average student score was 479, well below the OECD average of 500 points (OECD, 2001). More than 21% of students reached only Level 1 or below. The PISA 2000 results also showed a real disparity between the educational competencies of students in the general education system and the basic vocational schools. Nearly 70% of the basic vocational school students obtained scores reflecting the lowest literacy level. Thanks to a series of school reforms that began in the late 1990s, Poland has dramatically reduced the numbers of poorly performing students in the last 10 years, and in the PISA 2009 tests is ranked among the top 15 OECD countries (OECD, 2010). The average difference in results, between the top 20% and bottom 20%, is of 97 points, slightly lower than the OECD average of 99 points. This suggests that the school system in Poland provides relatively equal access to high-quality education.

The above-mentioned achievements of Polish education coexist with deep decentralization of the management of the education system. Repressed before the transformation of the political system, the organizational and financial potential was released after 1989. Most of the educational tasks at the pre-school up to upper secondary school levels are currently managed by a local authority. The organizational and financial responsibility of local authorities for the development of education stimulated local educational ambitions, facilitated the rationalization of the school network, and helped to lift the burden of debts regularly incurred to finance educational tasks when these fell within the purview of the governmental administration. At the level of post-secondary education, especially in higher education, the potential of non-public education, supported by considerable private expenditure of learners and their families, was opened up. Decentralization in the management of education has recently been reinforced by steadily increasing autonomy of schools and higher education institutions (HEIs). A policy based on learning outcomes has been introduced in school and higher education in line with the European Qualifications Framework, providing schools, HEIs and teachers with greater autonomy in the organization of the education process. Another major feature of the education system in Poland is the steadily increasing duration of compulsory education. In the late 1990s, the duration of compulsory education, then covering an 8-year primary school, was extended. A new form of compulsory education was introduced by the Constitution of the Republic of Poland of 1997: the obligation to continue education until the age of 18 in school-based or non-school-based settings (part-time compulsory education). Moreover, in 2004 a new form of compulsory education was introduced: one-year obligatory pre-school preparation for 6-year-old children.

## SUPERVISION AND SUPERINTENDENTS

In this section attention will be paid to the main reforms of pedagogical supervision that have been implemented over the last decade in Poland. Firstly, I will describe the assumptions guiding these reforms and focus on the latest one and on the role of superintendents. Secondly, I will present in detail three inter-related forms of supervision that taken together can contribute to the quality of education in a single school, and broadly speaking, in the whole system of education. Finally, on the basis of state report made by the Supreme Audit Office (the top independent state auditing body, whose mission is to safeguard public spending), I will present some weaknesses of the new system of pedagogical supervision in Poland and recommendations for its improvement. In this way I will move from the level of conceptual assumptions that underpin the new reform to the reality of education in Poland and its challenges.

## MAIN REFORMS OF THE PEDAGOGICAL SUPERVISION SYSTEM - SUPERINTENDENTS AND THEIR ROLE

The current arrangements within the pedagogical supervision system were put in place in the school year 2009/10 by the Regulation of the Minister of National Education of 7 October 2009 on pedagogical supervision. The pedagogical supervision system existing before 2009 was modified on the basis of regulations of the minister responsible for school education adopted successively in 1999, 2004 and 2006.

Pursuant to the Regulation of 1999, pedagogical supervision involved mainly two elements: checking the school's compliance with the requirements concerning its statutory tasks and supporting school staff. The 2004 Regulation introduced the concept of evaluation understood as assessing the relevance and effectiveness of educational activities in relation to their stated aims and with regard to potential improvements. Finally, the Regulation of 2006 provided for compulsory evaluation of educational activities undertaken by schools. However, it did not define clearly any specific tasks for pedagogical supervision or rules and tools for quality assurance as part of pedagogical supervision. As a result, external pedagogical supervision consisted mainly of checking schools' compliance with the law. It did not focus sufficiently on the evaluation of the quality of their work and it did not provide them proper support essential for improving the quality of education and for the implementation of improvements and development plans.

The main reasons behind the modernization of the pedagogical supervision system in 2009 included (1) the lack of a uniform, comparable system of the pedagogical supervision across the country, (2) the ineffectiveness and the limited usefulness for improving quality in schoolsof the previous system and its inability to respond to the pace and scope of changes and educational needs of the society, (3) insufficient efforts taken by schools and their managing bodies in order to improve the quality of education (this resulted in educational inequalities related to pupils' or students' background which pose problems in less developed regions of the country), (4) the need to gather reliable information to design the national education policy and education policies at regional and local levels, and (5) the need to provide pupils and teachers with opportunities for comprehensive personal and social development in line with their aspirations and capacities.

The arrangements put in place in 2009 were aimed at establishing a pedagogical supervision system which contributes to better quality of education on the one hand through supporting the development of kindergartens, schools and other educational institutions, and enabling comprehensive development of pupils and teachers, and on the other hand through supporting the national authorities in developing and pursuing an educational policy based on comparable data on the entire education system. The new arrangements make up an integrated system of internal and external quality assurance, covering both early childhood and school education, and both public and non-public schools within these sectors.

The system includes three inter-related elements referred to as forms/mechanisms of supervision:

- *evaluation* based on uniform requirements laid down in the legislation, which focuses on the quality of education and care and other statutory activities undertaken by schools and other educational institutions − the requirements cover four areas:

outcomes of educational activities (performance), processes taking place in a given institution, school environment, and institutional management;

- *legal compliance auditing* which aims to check the compliance of educational, care-related and other statutory activities undertaken by schools, education institutions and teachers with the legislation;
- *support* for schools, education institutions and teachers in their educational, care-related and other statutory activities.

Pedagogical supervision is carried out at the central, regional and institutional levels and all three above-mentioned forms of pedagogical supervision and the tasks connected with them are carried out on an obligatory basis by both external pedagogical supervision bodies vis-á-vis schools (external quality assurance) and by the principal within a given school (internal quality assurance). The results of internal evaluation are taken into consideration in external evaluation. Internal pedagogical supervision is carried out at the institutional level within schools. The principal is responsible for internal pedagogical supervision. He/she works together with other teachers holding management positions.

The external pedagogical supervision bodies include: at the central level – the Minister of National Education (the minister responsible for school education), the Minister of Culture and National Heritage (for art schools), the Minister of Agriculture and Development of Rural Areas (for agricultural schools), the Minister of Environment (for forestry schools) and the Minister of Justice (for youth detention centers, hostels for underage young people, diagnosis and consultation centers, and schools within these institutions); and at the regional level – the heads of the Regional Education Authorities (superintendents – *kuratorzyoświaty*) in given provinces.

Superintendents are appointed and dismissed by province governors (the head of the government administration in the region) upon the consent of the Minister of National Education. Thus, the heads of the REAs are not independent from the national authorities (see: amended Educational System Act of 7 September 1991, article 30). Pursuant to the amended Education System Act of 1991, the heads of the REAs exercise pedagogical supervision over public and non-public schools within their provinces. These tasks are performed in accordance with detailed guidelines laid down in the Regulation of the Minister of National Education of 7 October 2009 on pedagogical supervision, the aims of the national policy in the area of pedagogical supervision and an annual pedagogical supervision plan adopted by the minister.

Conditions of service for the superintendents are regulated by the Civil Service Act of 21 November 2008 as the superintendents, like inspectors and other staff in government administration and the REAs, have the status of civil servants, and by the Act of 26 January 1982, the Teachers' Charter, as they are also considered teachers. The positions of superintendents in the REAs require teaching (pedagogical) qualifications. Therefore, they may be taken by teachers holding a Master's (magister) degree who have at least seven years of teaching experience and who have at least three years of experience in one of the institutions responsible for pedagogical supervision over kindergartens, schools and other educational institutions, or in an institution which is the managing body for kindergartens, schools or other educational institutions.

Article 32 of the amended Education System Act of 1991 states that the superintendent shall perform his/her role through the Regional Education Authorities, which are state budgetary units. Province governor, at the request of the superintendent, can create the delegation of the Regional Education Authorities. The head of delegation of the Regional Education Authorities may, under the authority of the superintendent, lead different matters in the area of the delegation including educational supervision and take administrative decisions. The minister responsible for education, in consultation with the minister responsible for public administration, determines, by regulation, the organization of the Regional Education Authorities and the rules to create their delegations.

The superintendents supervise education within public and non-public schools and institutes and teacher training institutions, including the non-public teacher training institutions nationwide that are in the given province. The areas of responsibilities of the superintendents in the context of pedagogical supervision are in particular connected with the need to carry out an external evaluation, legal compliance auditing and support.

As part of two of the three forms of pedagogical supervision, i.e., external evaluation and control, the superintendents appoint teams to conduct evaluation and compliance audits from among inspectors working in the REAs, and consider any possible objections to their reports raised by the school principals concerned. If an evaluation has shown that a given school meets one of the quality requirements only at the lowest level or, a compliance inspection has revealed any failure to observe the law, the superintendent instructs the school principal to undertake remedial measures. If the principal fails to undertake such measures, the superintendent may dismiss the principal of the public school or close down the non-public school concerned.

As part of support, the tasks of the superintendents involve for example: preparing and publishing the results of pedagogical supervision on the REAs' website, including conclusions from external evaluation and compliance inspections; disseminating good practice examples; promoting the use of evaluation to improve school performance; and organizing conferences and seminars for heads of schools.

The superintendents have to present conclusions from pedagogical supervision in a given school year to the Minister of National Education.

In line with these ideas of pedagogical supervision, the superintendents in performing their roles first and foremost work with the local government authorities on the development and implementation of regional and local education policy in line with the state education policy. At the same time the superintendents interact with the local government authorities in the formulation and development of the material base of schools and institutions.

## QUALITY ASSURANCE AND PEDAGOGICAL SUPERVISION

Quality assurance of school education is based primarily on three elements/mechanisms of pedagogical supervision: evaluation, legal compliance auditing and support. All these elements are discussed below − in the context of the role of the superintendents and their task of pedagogical supervision − because they jointly determine the quality of schools.

It should be noted that the arrangements of qualityassurance are divided into external and internal quality assurance. External quality assurance includes external evaluation and legal compliance auditing of schools and external pupil assessment. Internal quality assurance includes internal evaluation of schools and the appraisal of individual teachers.

# EVALUATION

External evaluation of schools aims to assess the extent to which the school meets quality requirements in the four above-mentioned areas identified in the legislation: outcomes of educational activities (performance), processes taking place in a given institution, school environment, and institutional management. Thus, two types of evaluation are distinguished: overall evaluation covering all four areas and problem-specific evaluation in one or some of the areas. For each of the four areas, the legislation defines specific requirements, which can be regarded as quality criteria or standards, together with a description of these requirements at levels D and B (which are the reference points for the scale of A to E). External evaluation determines the level at which a given school (kindergartens or institution) complies with the requirements.

The legislation distinguishes the following five grades or levels: Grade A – very high level of compliance with a requirement; Grade B – high level of compliance with a requirement; Grade C – medium level of compliance with a requirement; Grade D – basic level of compliance with a requirement; and Grade E – low level of compliance with a requirement.

Levels D and B are the reference points. In case a school does not meet requirements at level D, grade E is given; meeting requirements at a level higher than D but lower than B results in giving grade C. Meeting requirements at a level higher than B results in giving grade A. Where a school is given grade E for at least one of the requirements concerning the first of the four areas listed ("Performance"), the head of the REA instructs its head to develop a program and schedule for improving performance.

The external evaluation of each of the four areas takes into account – as was mentioned above – the results of internal evaluation. An external evaluation team is obliged to analyze results of internal evaluation and compare them with results of its own analysis. The requirements for schools (and kindergartens and institutions) do not include all possible issues related to their responsibilities vis-á-vis pupils and parents. Instead, they point to strategic and priority tasks selected in a way that should enable planning of the school's activities. Thus, the analysis of these requirements would not give a "complete" picture, but rather show the aspects which are considered to be of key importance.

Pursuant to the legislation, external evaluation is conducted on both a regular (scheduled) and ad hoc basis. The legislation does not define the frequency of external evaluation. Scheduled evaluations are carried out in line with the aims of the national policy and a pedagogical supervision plan in which the Minister of National Education defines the scope of evaluations for every school year.

For example, in accordance with the main lines of the education policy for the school year 2011/12, the tasks in the area of evaluation are defined as follows: overall evaluation (25% of all evaluations in this school year), problem-specific evaluation in the area "Performance" (50% of all evaluations), and problem-specific evaluation in an area chosen by the head of the REA on the basis of findings from pedagogical supervision (25%).

The minister's guidelines do not specify the number or proportion of schools (kindergartens or other institutions) undergoing evaluation in a given year. Within the framework set by the minister, the heads of the regional education authorities (REAs) develop more detailed plans for supervision in their provinces. Criteria for the choice of schools (kindergartens or institutions) to be covered by evaluation are determined by superintendents. The head of the REAs may take into consideration criteria such as the date of the previous evaluation in a given school, poor learning achievements of pupils, complaints and irregularities or voluntary applications for evaluation from schools. Ad hoc external evaluations are carried out in case it is necessary to take action which was not envisaged in the pedagogical supervision plan.

The procedure for external evaluation is laid down in the legislation. External evaluation is conducted by an expert or teams of experts set up by superintendents, who appoint experts from among inspectors working in the REAs.

At the end of the evaluation, the inspector or team of inspectors presents the findings and conclusions from the evaluation to the teaching council of the school (kindergartens or institution) (which is a collective body composed of the school/institution's head as its chair and all teachers). Then the inspector/team prepares a report that contains findings and conclusions and assesses the extent to which requirements specified in the legislation have been met. The head of the REAs forwards the report to the school's/institution's head and its managing body. The school's/institution's head may raise objections to the report which are considered by the head of the REAs. If the objections are found justified, changes are made in the report.

The legislation does not identify tools for evaluation. In practice, the evaluation teams use a variety of methods available in social sciences. These include, for example, quantitative methods such as surveys and qualitative methods such as analysis of documents, individual and group interviews among wide circles of respondents (the principal, teachers and other staff, pupils, parents, representatives of the managing body and institutions cooperating with the school, i.e., counseling and guidance services, culture centers and NGOs) as well as observation of classes.

Reports on external evaluation of individual schools are published in the website "Education evaluation system – pedagogical supervision" (http://www.npseo.pl) launched as part of the above-mentioned project: "Enhancing the effectiveness of the pedagogical supervision system and quality evaluation of schools." They provide information for comparative analysis of evaluation results in schools. According to the data published on the pedagogical supervision website, a total number of 2,120 evaluations were carried out in all provinces and types of schools jointly between 1 January 2010 and 30 November 2011. Depending on the area of evaluation, between 53% and over 63% of kindergartens and schools fulfill the quality criteria at level B (see the scale of A to E above), over 15% to 18% at level A, 0% to 0.7% at level E, and the remainder at level C or D.

In addition, the superintendents – as was mentioned above – obligatorily prepare annual reports for the minister which contain findings from pedagogical supervision, including evaluation, in their province and publish summary evaluation reports on the REAs' websites. The conclusions from these reports are used by the superintendents to devise a pedagogical supervision plan for the coming school year, including specific activities aimed at quality improvement in schools. Similar reports are prepared at national level by the Ministry of National Education.

At present, conclusions from regional reports serve as an input to define the main lines of the education policy and the pedagogical supervision plan for the next year at national level, which can be perceived as a positive aspect of new reform of pedagogical supervision in Poland.

# LEGAL COMPLIANCE AUDITING AND SUPPORT

Compliance auditing aims to assess whether and to what extent schools comply with the legislation concerning their educational, care-related and other statutory activities. Compliance auditing is based on the same approach as evaluation. External compliance audits or inspections are conducted on a regular and ad hoc basis, and the frequency of scheduled inspections is not prescribed in the legislation. Inspections are carried out in line with a pedagogical supervision plan for a given school year, prepared by the superintendent on the basis of national educational policy priorities and the national pedagogical supervision plan drawn up by the Minister of National Education. Ad hoc inspections are carried out in response to needs that were not taken into account in the pedagogical supervision plan. The procedure for compliance audits/inspections is laid down in the legislation. Like evaluations, external inspections are conducted by persons or teams appointed by the superintendent from among inspectors working in the REAs. During a compliance inspection, inspectors use standardized audit forms, approved by the minister, which cover issues to be examined. An inspection report is provided to the head of the school concerned. The principal may raise objections to the content of the report which are considered by the superintendents; in justified cases changes are made in the document. Where a compliance audit reveals any failures to observe the regulations by the school, the superintendents instruct the school principal to eliminate the shortcomings. Should the school head fail to do so, the head of a public school is dismissed by its managing body or a non-public school is struck from the register and, consequently, closed down. Audit reports concerning individual schools are not published. Summary results of compliance auditing are presented in annual reports on pedagogical supervision which the superintendents are obliged to prepare for the Minister of National Education. Findings from the inspections are used in pedagogical supervision plans in the next years.

Pursuant to the legislation, the superintendents are obliged to publish findings from pedagogical supervision, including conclusions from external evaluations and legal compliance inspections, on their websites; to disseminate examples of good practice; to promote the use of evaluation results in order to improve the performance of schools and to organize conferences and seminars for the heads of schools.

# STATE AUDIT OF THE FUNCTIONING OF PEDAGOGICAL SUPERVISION

In 2012 the Supreme Audit Office (NIK) undertook the audit of the pedagogical supervision exercised by the superintendents and school principals of public schools. It was a planned control, carried out on the initiative of the Supreme Audit Office.

The purpose of the audit was to assess the functioning of pedagogical supervision in the system of education, implemented by the Ministry of National Education, the school superintendents and the heads of public schools. The audit covered the activities of the Ministry of National Education, nine of the 16 superintendents and heads of 51 public schools (18 primary, 13 secondary schools and 20 secondary schools). The control comprised three school years from 2008/2009 to 2010/2011.

According to the Supreme Audit Office, in spite of educational projects undertaken within the framework: The Operational Program Human Capital (OP HC), called "The high quality of the educational system," which was devoted to enhance the efficiency of the system of pedagogical supervision and evaluation of the quality of schools, and in spite of the introduction in 2009 of new rules of pedagogical supervision, a breakthrough in the effectiveness of pedagogical supervision in the education system was not achieved. The pupils' learning outcomes and the results of the audit uncovered inefficiency and low effectiveness of the new reform of system of pedagogical supervision in Poland.

Some of the main findings of the control by the Supreme Audit Office show that Minister of National Education in the school year 2009/2010 (i.e., in the first year of the regulation on the pedagogical supervision in 2009) did not provide an adequate number of qualified persons to conduct external evaluation. Only 155 inspectors of the Regional Educational Authorities were trained (90 in the school year 2009/2010, and 65 in the school year 2010/2011). The first 90 inspectors received permission to conduct an external evaluation by February 2010, and the further 65 in August 2010, which meant that they could start their activities in this area by the school year 2010/2011.

In the school year 2009/2010 a new form of pedagogical supervision, i.e., external evaluation, comprised only 0.4% of the total number of supervised schools and institutions, and in the school year 2010/2011 – 2.9%.

Superintendents view several organizational factors which adversely affect the performance of tasks in the field of pedagogical supervision. These are: (1) commission by the Ministry of National Education of ad hoc time-consuming tasks, e.g., collecting a variety of information on the issue of education, the distribution of teaching materials, recruitment of participants and information meetings organized in the framework of projects run by the Ministry (such as the project entitled: "Improving learning outcomes of pupils with special educational needs), (2) reduction of the number of inspectors, which resulted in the increase of the workload in fulfilling inspectors' mandatory tasks, (3) inadequate time (too short – only seven days) for communication of the results of evaluation to the school teaching council, particularly in the case of a comprehensive evaluation carried out in large schools, (4) difficulties associated with the interpretation of the control sheets, set by the Ministry of Education, by the inspectors, and (5) limiting the numbers of external pedagogical supervisions carried out in schools only to areas of control specified in the control sheets, which results in a limited ability to identify areas of needed support for school (for example, in helping to solve current legal problems and pedagogical problems).

The Supreme Audit Office invited experts (researchers and practitioners) to share their opinions on the new system of pedagogical supervision and its functioning. The experts pointed to the need for designing the effective educational supervision rules, including the definition of pedagogical supervisions. The experts stressed that it is very important to address a few significant issues in order to improve the quality of pedagogical supervision and the quality of schools. They suggested providing the school superintendents and school principals with the instruments that would allow reliable assessment of the quality of education (there is a conceptual disarray of pedagogical supervision in educational law, especially in defining the tasks and responsibilities of school superintendents and school principals), providing citizens with accurate information about the quality of education and the quality of schools and teachers, as well as following the principle of making a comprehensive assessment of the quality of education in schools through combining data from the external exams with the data from the survey conducted during pedagogical supervision (a methodology for these evaluations must be developed). Furthermore, in their opinion, the detailed rules of pedagogical supervision and school support must be regulated in the system of pedagogical supervision, the tools to study the comparability of test results in subsequent school years must be developed, the quality of evaluation reports, including the description of the reality of the school, must be improved and it is necessary to ensure greater stability of the laws, including the provisions relating to the pedagogical supervision.

In the opinion of the Supreme Audit Office, the Ministry of National Education – in order to improve the efficiency and effectiveness of pedagogical supervision and in order to eliminate identified irregularities in the control – should define the concept of pedagogical supervision and determine the rules of its conduct, including the possibility of an effective impact in case of deviations from the accepted rules. Apart from this, the Ministry of National Education should create greater possibilities for professional development in the field of evaluation for the inspectors, senior inspectors and the chief inspector, who work in the Regional Educational Authorities and are responsible for fulfilling the task of school pedagogical supervision, and should carry out the task of supervision over schools and educational institutions, for which the Minister Education is the lead authority (pursuant to the provisions of Article. 35, paragraph. 1 point 1 Educational System Act of 1991).

In accordance with the Supreme Audit Office's report recommendations, the superintendents should not only comply with the applicable rules of the pedagogical supervision in carrying out audits and external evaluations in schools and educational institutions, but also increase the number of schools and the planned annual external evaluations so as to obtain annual representative data on the level of compliance of the monitored schools and requirements in areas subject to evaluation. The Supreme Audit Office's report also pointed to the importance of increasing the effectiveness of pedagogical supervision through making the decision of removing the discrepancies and deficiencies in the supervised schools and institutions and implementation of special programs of improving the effectiveness of education in the situations of unsatisfactory results of external tests and exams.

According to the assumptions made by the Minister of National Education in Poland, the modernization of pedagogical supervision had two main goals: the development of the education system and improving individual schools and educational institutions. For the purpose of the development of the education system, the unification of the external pedagogical supervision across the country has been accomplished, generally applicable requirements of the State towards schools and institutions have been formulated, the evaluation and control tools have been made uniform, and people responsible for external pedagogical supervision have been trained.

External pedagogical supervision designed in such a way were supposed to allow for obtaining reliable and comparable assessment of schools and institutions and, consequently, for carrying out the analysis and formulation of conclusions and to create short-and long-term development strategy of education at the state/central and regional level.

Improvement of the work of a single school or institution was based mainly on the introduction of internal evaluation and the key requirements in the form of actions that affect the quality of education. All of the regulations that underpinned the new reform of pedagogical supervision seem to be important for improving the quality of education. In particular, creation of the possibilities for schools principals and teachers in making the decisions about the extent and methods of implementation of the conclusions from the internal school evaluation can allow the school to choose its own path of development and enables improvement of schools and educational work resulting from the needs of pupils and the local community.

Taking into account the fact that new reform of pedagogical supervision was introduced in the school year 2009/10, we can state that it is still too early to assess the extent to which it contributes to improving the quality of education. However, the present analysis shows us the discrepancy between the laudable objectives of the latest reform of the system of pedagogical supervision and the realities. On the basis of the report of the Supreme Audit Office, one can conclude that pedagogical supervision exercised through superintendents' visits to schools was not sufficiently efficient and effective. The implementation of new pedagogical supervision rules in 2009was not adequately prepared. As a result, between 2009 and 2012, different forms of supervision were not sufficiently used.

A focus on quality in education should on the one hand always enhance and improve the current status and develop the systems that assure it, and on the other hand perceive the concept of quality of education as an ongoing exercise. It is not a state that is reached once and for all but one that needs to be pursued continuously.

Pedagogical supervision should be one of the most important tools employed by state bodies to influence the quality of education in schools, pupils' learning outcomes and the assessment of the work of school principals and teachers. However, it is important to acknowledge that since 1996, the concept of pedagogical supervision has changed several times. Therefore, none of these forms became established enough to enablethe production of reliable assessments of the efficiency and effectiveness of supervision.

The latest reform seems to have a lot of positive solutions for pedagogical supervision and may lead to a better quality of education in the shortest time, but the conditions for its implementation should have been much betterprepared.

# REFERENCES

Blok, Z. (2006). *Transformacja jako konwersja funkcji wewnątrzsystemowych na przykładzie Polski.* [Transformation as a conversion of intra-systemic functions on the Polish example]. Poznań: Wydawnictwo UAM.

Bogaj, A., Kwiatkowski, S.M.,& Szymański, M.J. (1998). *Edukacja w procesie przemian społecznych.* Warsaw: IBE.

GUS (2012a). *Rocznik Statystyki Międzynarodowej.* [*Yearbook of International Statistics*]. Warsaw: Główny Urząd Statystyczny.

GUS (2012b). *Rocznik Demograficzny.* [*Demographic Yearbook of Poland*]. Warsaw: Główny Urząd Statystyczny.

GUS (2012c). *Oświata i wychowanie w roku szkolnym 2011/20112.* [*Education in school year 2011/12*]. Warsaw: GłównyUrządStatystyczny.

Jóźwiak, J., &Kotowska, I. E. (2010). *Przewidywane zmiany liczby i struktury wieku ludności w Polsce do 2035 r. i ich skutki ekonomiczne* [*The projected changes in the number and age structure of the population in Poland by 2035 and their economic effects*]. Warsaw: Kancelaria Prezydenta Rzeczypospolitej Polskiej.

Karta Nauczyciela [Teacher's Charter], Act of 26 January 1982, *Journal of Law* 1997, No 56, item 357 with further amendments.

Konstytucja Rzeczypospolitej Polskiej z dnia 2 kwietnia 1997 [Constitution of the Republic of Poland of 2 April 1997] (1997). Dz.U. 1997, NR 78 poz. 483.

NIK (2012). *Nadzór Pedagogiczny Sprawowany przez Kuratorów Oświaty i Dyrektorów Szkół Publicznych. [Pedagogical supervision exercised by the superintendents and principals in public schools]*. Warsaw: NajwyższaIzbaKontroli.

Michalak, J. M. (2005). *The priorities of Polish educational policy.Fostering teacher professionalism in schools.*In S. Kiefer & T. Peterseil (Eds.). *Analysis of educational policies in a comparative educational perspective* (pp.141-165).Linz: Pädagogische Hochschule des Bundes Oberösterreich, Institute of Comparative Education.

Michalak, J. (2011). Teacher education in the context of improving quality in higher education in Poland. In E. Eisenschmidt& E. Löfström (Eds.), *Developing quality cultures in teacher education: Expanding horizons in relation to quality assurance* (pp. 35-54). Tallinn: University of Tallinn.

OECD (2001).*Knowledge and Skills for Life. First Results from the OECD Programme for International Students Assessment (PISA 2000)*. Paris: OECD. www.oecd.org.

OECD (2010).*PISA 2009 Results: What Students Know and Can Do: Student Performance in Reading, Mathematics and Science* (Volume I). Paris: OECD.

Rozporządzenie Ministra Edukacji Narodowej w sprawie nadzoru pedagogicznego z dnia 7 października 2009 roku.[Regulation of the Minister of National Education of 7 October 2009 on pedagogical supervision]. *Journal of Law* 2009, No 168, item 1324.

Szczygielski, K. (2008). *Geografia mniejszości narodowych i etnicznych w Polsce. [Geography and ethnic minorities in Poland]*. Opole: Wydawnictwo Instytut Śląski.

Ustawa o systemie oświaty z dnia 7 września 1991 roku z późniejszymi zmianami. [Education System Act of 7 September 1991 with further amendments]. *Journal of Law* 2004, No 256, item 2572.

In: The Educational Superintendent
Editor: Adam E. Nir

ISBN: 978-1-62948-972-8
© 2014 Nova Science Publishers, Inc.

*Chapter 5*

# THE ELUSIVE CHARACTER OF THE SCHOOL SUPERINTENDENT ROLE: THE ISRAELI CASE

### *Ronit Bogler*

The Open University of Israel, Israel

Understanding the role of Israeli school superintendents requires an acquaintance with the social system within which they operate. Hence, I will first present the political, demographic, social and economic circumstances of the country since its establishment, followed by the description of the development and structure of the educational system. School superintendents in the educational system will then be discussed in relation to the transformation from centralized to decentralized system, ending with a discussion about the elusive notion of the superintendent's role in relation to the trust-regulation tension.

The State of Israel, established in 1948 as a representative democracy on the southeastern shore of the Mediterranean Sea, has a parliamentary system with proportional representation and universal suffrage. The Prime Minister is the head of the government, and the 120-member Parliament (the Knesset), representing a large number of political parties, is the state's unicameral legislative body. Israel is considered to be the second smallest nation in the Middle East. In 2013, its population was estimated to be 7,993,100 people, of whom 6,022,800 are Jewish. The second-largest ethnic group in Israel is the Arabs, with 1,651,600 people (including Muslims, Christians, Druze and Bedouin) (Central Bureau of Statistics, 2013).

The natural growth in Israel is among the highest in the world and, in addition, the country absorbs large waves of immigrants (Soffer, 2008). Since the establishment of Israel, Jewish immigration has been diversified and encompasses Jewish diasporas from all over the world. In the last three decades, Israel has absorbed large waves of immigrants mostly from Eastern Europe and from Ethiopia. In recent years, there has been a significant increase of immigration from Western Europe to Israel (particularly from France and Great Britain) (Ministry of Immigrant Absorption, 2013).

Israel is characterized by diverse cultural groups, and as such it is considered to be a highly multicultural (Bar Shalom, 2006) and multilingual society. It represents cultural richness, on the one hand, and a divided society, on the other hand. This cultural diversity provokes a dialogue between many sub-groups and around different issues, for instance the religious and the secular, newcomers and veterans (Kenny-Pas, 1996), and Jews and Arabs (Smooha, 1992).

From an economic point of view, Israel has gone from a centralized and socialist economic system, based on agriculture and some low-tech industries, to a modern, privatized and competitive economy that promotes free market policy and globalization (Shtrasler, 2008). Today, the country's leading export areas are in high-tech, agriculture and diamond cutting. In 2010, Israel was formally invited to accede to the Organisation for Economic Co-operation and Development (OECD, 2010), and recently it moved closer to energy independence as natural gas from a vast offshore field began flowing into the country. This discovery will benefit the country both strategically and economically (*The New York Times*, 2013).

## DEVELOPMENT OF THE EDUCATIONAL SYSTEM

Since the establishment of the State of Israel, the educational system has gone through major development stages. As described by Elboim-Dror (2001), education in Israel has been depicted by "dialectical development, and not by linear evolution. While some features remain constant, radical change is its main characteristic. The education system can be seen to have grown in zigzags, fitfully and discursively, with each period incubating the succeeding contradiction" (p. 90).

In the 1950s, during the period of mass immigration, the country was challenged to provide basic education to a swiftly growing population, while struggling to overcome severe limitations of the educational infrastructure, such as a lack of schools, classrooms and qualified teachers, poorly educated parents and severe economic adversity. These years of mass immigration resulted in a change in the composition of the student population in elementary schools, and the ratio of students from weak populations rose (Ministry of Education, 2012a). The difficulties of a new state, striving to absorb large immigration waves, gave rise to the idea of the "melting pot" – one of the more important declared purposes of the Zionist movement, which should be conceived more as assimilation (Yuchtman-Yaar, 2005).

Two approaches can be used to confront inequalities in a society: centralization or decentralization. In Israel, the first option was favored, and thus a highly centralized system of government took responsibility for regulating the flow of immigration, prioritizing the locations to which the immigrants would move and allocating the economic, educational and organizational resources. Even in the educational realm, the centralized government used its power and authority to control: "...To a large extent the political establishment decided where and under what conditions they [the immigrants] would dwell, how they would earn a living, in which educational system their children would learn..." (Yuchtman-Yaar, 2005, p. 93). Consequently, a top-down structure was established, where the Ministry of Education has an extremely significant impact on most aspects of the educational system. This system has operated in a steady and rigid structure of an organizational hierarchy where the superintendency fills a significant role of controlling and supervising processes to transfer an ideology that attempts to minimize the gaps resulting from ethnic, religious, economic and social conflicts.

The educational system underwent a reform, beginning in the late 1960s (with the establishment of the secondary schools), which led to pluralism in educational frameworks and programs of study, while attempting to take into account the needs of weaker populations. At the end of the 1970s and the beginning of the 1980s there was a sharp and rapid increase in the secondary school attendance rate, and "between 1980-1990, the number of students enrolled in secondary education grew by 55%. In 2008/09, about 71% of students in grades 7-9 were enrolled in lower secondary schools" (Ministry of Education, 2012a, p. 72). Beginning in 1990, a new, sizable wave of immigration came to Israel: from 1990-2002, nearly one million immigrants arrived, increasing Israel's population by around 20%. During these years, the total number of students grew by 28%, where half of the increase was a result of this decade of immigration wave (Ministry of Education, 2012a). The educational system therefore has almost continuously been faced with the immense challenges of integrating large numbers of children from various cultural backgrounds. The immigrants have come from all over the world: In the 1950s, most of them came from post-war Europe and Arab countries, a decade later they immigrated from North Africa, and in the 1970s through the early 2000 from the former Soviet Union and Ethiopia. Throughout the years, newcomers have also arrived from the Americas and other parts of the free world.

The state has had to cope with providing the need for more classrooms and qualified teachers as the number of students increased rapidly, but the educational system has had to develop in a relatively short period of time appropriate methods to help absorb the newcomers. There was an immediate need for teacher training programs oriented towards working with immigrant students who represent different cultures and traditions: preparing special curricular support systems; providing short-term classes to teach immigrant students subjects that they have not been exposed to in their countries of origin, such as the Hebrew language and Jewish history; and retraining immigrant teachers to ease their entry into the educational system.

Education in Israel has been characterized historically by the same social and cultural schisms separating the Orthodox from the secular and the Arabs from the Jews. In addition, because of residential patterns and concentrations – of Sephardic Jews in development towns, for example – or because of "tracking" of one sort or another, critics have charged that education has been functionally divided by an Ashkenazic (referring to Jews from Western, Northern and Eastern Europe) vs. Sephardic (Jews of the Mediterranean, Balkan, Aegean, and Middle Eastern lands) distinction.

The development of the educational systems or "trends" in Israel was mainly supported and used by the political parties that represent different interest groups, according to their religious orientation and ethnic background. Due to political agreements that were aimed at maintaining the pre-state status quo, educational segregation favored by the Orthodox was founded. This segregated system has been a source of intense conflict and competition throughout the years, especially at times of large waves of immigration. The various parties sought to get the votes of the immigrants and to have control over socializing the immigrants' children to secure their own political future. Following political conflicts in the early years of statehood, reform legislation – the 1953 State Education Law – reduced the number of trends from four to two: a state-supported religious trend and a state-supported secular trend. In reality, nonetheless, there were still additional systems beyond the two trends that received state subsidies. Throughout the years and to date, schools are divided into five groups: *State schools*, attended by the majority of the students; *State religious schools*, which emphasize

Jewish studies, tradition and observance; *Independent religious schools,* which focus almost entirely on Talmud Torah; *Independent Private schools,* which reflect the philosophies of specific groups of parents (e.g., Democratic Schools), or are based on a curriculum of a foreign country (e.g., the American School); *Arab schools,* with instruction in Arabic and a focus on Arab history, religions and culture. Below, there is a detailed description of each type.

State schools: The curriculum of the state schools is 75% state-mandated and 25% supplementary that is used mainly to create programs in line with a specific philosophy of the parents. The core curriculum includes mathematics, language skills, science, history, Jewish studies, art and physical education. Jewish studies are given a national, cultural interpretation without any emphasis on the students' religious observance or belief.

State religious schools: The State Religious schools emphasize Jewish and religious studies in the curriculum in addition to adhering to religious norms and daily prayers. They offer very little in terms of secular subjects, and aimed mainly to prepare male students for the yeshiva, an educational framework that follows the primary school. Nevertheless, students in the State Religious schools are taught the core curriculum, which offers a common and equal scholastic basis for students in the education system. Teaching the core curriculum is one of the conditions to gain the budget for students by the Ministry of Education.

Independent religious schools: These Talmud Torah schools place most emphasis on religious studies and observance, and they avoid teaching core curriculum such as math, language skills, history and science. They are named "*independent* religious schools" because the Ministry of Education is not responsible for the curriculum, the hiring and firing of teachers, or for the registration of students, although the schools do receive State support.

Independent private schools: Private schools which are recognized by the Ministry of Education teach the basic state curriculum. Nevertheless, staff and parents are the ones to decide on the instructional and educational norms of each school. This type of school includes, among others, the Democratic schools, where students play an active role in running the school in conjunction with parents and teachers.

Arab schools: The Arab schools in Israel teach in Arabic, and they follow the same curriculum as the Jewish ones. In East Jerusalem and the West Bank, Arab education follows the Jordanian curriculum and students take the Jordanian matriculation examinations. Al-Haj (2005) claims that "[t]he segregated education system that separates Arabs and Jews is also reflected in a segregated curriculum" (p. 52).

The Israeli educational system consists of three levels: primary, middle and high schools. The primary schools include all students up till the six grade, who then move to the middle school for three more grades. In high schools, students attend four grades, and upon completing the twelve grade, they need to take the matriculation exams. The structure of the primary and middle schools has changed during the years, from an 8+4 to a 6+3+3 structure.

Almost all high schools maintain the legal status of independent, recognized schools. They are operated by public bodies (e.g., municipalities, national networks), and receive most of their funding from the Ministry of Education. Some high schools provide a general academic education, while others are devoted to teaching music or arts, and an additional group of schools are oriented toward vocation acquisition in trades and occupations (e.g., practical engineering, electronics). Yeshiva high schools offer general or technical studies with Torah studies. There are also institutions offering day and night courses for preparation exclusively for matriculation exams.

Most of the secondary schools teach academic curricula in science and the humanities to prepare the students to take the matriculation exams. Students choose the level at which they will take the exam (three, four or five units) and take the classes accordingly. These requirements are somewhat parallel to basic, honors or advanced placement classes in the U.S. Some schools offer courses in non-standard subjects, such as Russian, Yiddish, drama, dance, etc. The students are given a class grade, known as an "internal grade," that affects their final scores in the course after completing the matriculation exam.

In the 2011-12 school year, the distribution of students in the educational institutions under supervision was as described below.

### Table 1. Students in educational institutions under supervision

| Educational Institution | 2011-2012 | 2012-13 | (estimate) % (increase) |
|---|---|---|---|
| State schools | 671,748 | 668,692 | -0.45 |
| State religious | 210,368 | 212,379 | 0.96 |
| Independent religious* | 279,039 | 288.640 | 3.33 |
| Arab schools** | 417,214 | 430,518 | 3.19 |

\* The Independent religious schools include the Talmud Torah.
\*\* Arab education includes Muslim, Christian, Bedouin or Druze students.
Source: Ministry of Education, 2013a.

### Table 2. Students, schools, classrooms and teachers

| | 2011/12 | 2012/13 (estimate) | %(increase) |
|---|---|---|---|
| Students | 1,564,742 | 1,586,011 | 1.36 |
| Schools | 4,422 | 4,502 | 1.81 |
| Classrooms | 61,890 | 62,962 | 1.73 |
| Teachers (estimate) | 132,271 | 137,567 | 4.00 |

Source: Ministry of Education, 2012b.

### Table 3. Students by school level

| | 2011/12 | 2012/13 (estimate) | % (increase) |
|---|---|---|---|
| Pre-primary public school | 394,012 | 405,057 | 2.80 |
| Kindergarten | 156,707 | 163,840 | 4.55 |
| Primary education | 922,730 | 942,057 | 2.09 |
| First grade | 145,179 | 145,857 | 0.47 |
| Middle school | 268,651 | 267,944 | -0.26 |
| High school | 374,103 | 376,118 | 0.54 |
| Senior high school | 105,730 | 107,014 | 1.21 |

Source: Ministry of Education, 2012b.

Among the Jewish students, in the 2011-12 academic year, 58% enrolled in state schools, 18% in state religious schools and 24% in the independent religious schools. The 1.5 million students attend over 4,400 schools (pre-primary through high school) in almost 62,000 classrooms with over 130,000 teachers (Ministry of Education, 2013a). The increase in the number of students in the pre-primary and primary education may be attributed to a recent decision of the Israeli government to provide free education to preschoolers (ages 3-4).

In recent years the academic achievements of Israeli students (15-year-olds) in the Programme for International Student Assessment (PISA), based on data collected from more than 400,000 students in 57 countries, have declined (OECD, 2007). In PISA 2006, Israeli students scored below the OECD average, in each of the three scales – science, reading and mathematics. (For a thorough and critical examination of the Israel's low relative standing on various international achievement tests: TIMSS - Trends in International Mathematics and Science Study, PIRLS - Progress in International Reading Literacy Study and PISA, see Cahan, Casali & Herskovitz, 2013.) These relatively low academic achievements in the international tests have caused policy-makers in the top level of the administration to come up with new programs to improve the standing of the Israeli students. As in the case of the high stakes tests, research shows that too often the main goal of the school staff has become to "teach to test" (Smyth & Banks, 2012). Teachers devote more time to exam preparation, thus narrowing the scope of the curriculum and breaking down the knowledge acquired, depending on the subjects that are expected to be included in the exams.

It should be noted that the national expenditure on education is about 8.2% of Israel's GNP, placing Israel among the high investing countries in public education in comparison with OECD countries (Ministry of Education, 2011).

## LANDMARKS IN THE DEVELOPMENT OF THE EDUCATIONAL SYSTEM

The Israeli educational system has gone through a number of changes which can be viewed as a result of the historical events that have taken place (Michalovitz, 2005). As expected, the first phase of changes occurred during the state's establishment, with the mass immigration to Israel, the ingathering of the exiles, a period of austerity and economic distress (the 1950s). At that time, the predominant values emphasized social solidarity and socialism, a "melting pot" policy, equal education for all, and fulfillment of society's needs. As indicated by Volansky (2007, p. 351): "The ethos of equality has been a driving force of Israel's education system since Israel became an independent state in 1948. This deep concern for equality was closely allied to the view that education is the main means of consolidating Israel's largely immigrant population into one nation." These founding principles resulted in the enactment of the first free, compulsory education law from five to fourteen, the establishment of the state education, the discontinuation of educational streams and a general organization of the educational system.

Following an improvement in the economic situation, the Six Day War (1967), and emergence of the problem of the disadvantaged, there was a growing interest in reducing social gaps, encouraging equal opportunity in education, and compensating for social and/or cultural deprivation. These developments gave rise to structural changes such as support for the disadvantaged among the preschool children and extending the free compulsory education law to include the 9th grade while keeping the 10th grade free but not compulsory. During the

1970s, additional developments in the educational system occurred: high school studies were free of charge, and additional plans for the disadvantaged were implemented including the adoption of the integration policy.

The 1980s brought additional changes in the educational system where the $10^{th}$ grade became compulsory and preschool became free as well. At that time, there was also a growing trend toward teaching reading in kindergarten to equip the new generation with language skills. The 1990s brought some economic growth that caused education to be placed high on the agenda as a priority. In addition, the large wave of immigration from the former Soviet Union and the advent of information and communications technology to teaching and learning gave rise to new reforms. There was a growing emphasis toward liberalism and individual freedom, equality and civil rights, and a move toward market economy and privatization. These changes provided a fertile ground for the implementation of a policy that called for school autonomy, accountability, emphasis on science and citizenship education, ongoing professional development programs for teachers, greater support for the Arab sector, and the opening of colleges in Israel (Michalovitz, 2005). At that time, a third of the country's schools became self-managing (Volansky, 2003, 2007).

The first decade of the $21^{st}$ century was characterized by continued reforms that aimed at granting greater autonomy to schools, improving the teacher's status (the "New Horizon" program that was implemented in the elementary and middle school levels; the "Courage to Change" ["Oz LeTmurah"] reform that was implemented at the high school level).

In 2012, the Ministry of Education extended free education to include nursery school children (ages 3-4), thus providing a comprehensive system of 15 years of formal education free of charge. The state is, consequently, responsible for the general educational programs, curricula, quality of teaching and education, teacher training, professional development, and the supervision for training provided in the academic training institutions. This description of the inclusive responsibility of the state highlights the dominant role of the Ministry of Education in spite of the various reforms that continue in the spirit of greater autonomy to the school. The academic year in Israel runs from September through June, six days per week, with about 35 hours per week for teaching. Hebrew is the language of instruction in the Jewish schools, and Arabic is used in the Arab schools. All students start to learn English in the primary school years, either in grade 4 or grade 5. Since 1998 computers have been installed into virtually all primary schools across the country, and a number of strategies have been adopted to encourage computer use.

The Ministry of Education's homepage (2013b) lists a number of objectives defined as top priority. Among them are: A. Reducing gaps and promoting scholastic achievement; B. Fostering Zionist values and instilling cultural heritage; C. Fostering democratic values of equal opportunity for both genders and special needs populations; D. Fostering human values of tolerance and preventing violence; E. Promoting science and technology education; F. Promoting professional empowerment of teachers.

# THE STRUCTURE OF THE EDUCATIONAL SYSTEM

The Israeli educational system is governed by a central authority that has kept the conservative ideology of uniformity throughout the years, although many changes have been undertaken (Pur & Gordon, 1982). As indicated above, the educational system is characterized by "trends" that were established in the State Education Law in 1953, but they continue to exist until today representing different political parties. This characteristic is an example of what Pur and Gordon describe as "centralization for uniformity" (1982, p. 224). The educational system is still highly standardized and centralized, and this reality is clearly shown in the curriculum compulsory for all students, including non-Jewish students, that dominates most of the "trends" today. The Ministry is responsible for all levels of education, including higher education, though the latter is controlled by the Council for Higher Education. The curriculum addresses the diversity of the population in a number of different ways, above and beyond the basic divisions among the state and state-religious schools and private schools. Below is a schema that demonstrates the centralized bureaucratic control of the Israeli educational system.

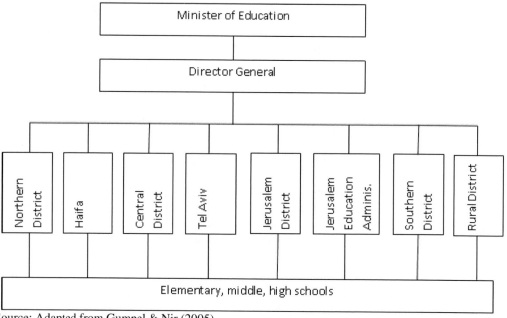

Source: Adapted from Gumpel & Nir (2005).

Figure 1. A schema of the centralized bureaucratic control of the Israeli educational system.

## SUPERINTENDENTS IN THE EDUCATIONAL SYSTEM

The Israeli educational system is headed by the Minister of Education who is appointed by the Prime Minister. After being appointed to the post, the Minister of Education appoints a Director General who is the general manager of the Ministry, a professional rather than a political figure.

The State Educational Regulations (originated in 1956 and updated in 1986) defined the roles of those who act as civil servants based on their professional performance.

District Manager – Manager of the compulsory educational system in the district, and the manager of the district office of the Ministry of Education and Culture.

District Superintendent – Supervisor responsible for the pedagogical areas under the supervision of the District Manager.

Comprehensive Superintendent – the Superintendent who is responsible for the operation of the schools according to the educational regulations defined by the Ministry of Education. The Comprehensive Superintendent's major tasks entail the controlling and supervising of school conduct in line with Ministry regulations, which include the implementing of educational policy, developing school performance and personnel, and enabling local initiatives to take place.

There are eight districts (seven regional urban ones and one rural district), each headed by the District Manager and the District Superintendent. Below is an organizational chart of the superintendency role set vis-à-vis the school principals. Each Comprehensive Superintendent, out of an estimated 150 affiliated with the eight superintendency districts, is responsible for the operation of a number of schools (elementary, middle or high schools). Very often, the superintendents are responsible for the supervision of too many schools, classes and teachers (Lazin, 1982), a reality with which the current superintendents need to cope these days.

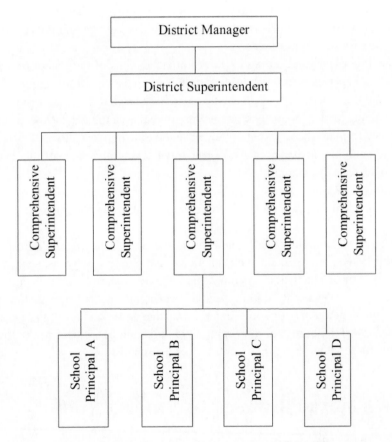

Figure 2. An organizational chart of the comprehensive superintendency in the Israeli educational system.

As indicated by the State Educational Regulations (Supervision orders, 1956, updated in 1996), the main responsibilities of the Comprehensive Superintendent include:

- Representing the Ministry of Education and Culture in reference to the school principal and the contacts between the Central Office and the local educational community;
- Confirming the educational policy and the Central Office guidelines and verifying that they are implemented (this includes dealing with curriculum, extra-curricular programs, allocation of standard hours);
- Evaluating and controlling the educational institutions and providing feedback in areas such as: quality of educational and organizational management, laying down the educational policy of the school, level of perseverance and success of students, the school academic achievements, the school educational and social climate;
- Guiding the school principal in resource planning and budgeting and allocating toward achieving educational and organizational goals;
- Assisting in the developmental processes of the autonomous school principal; assisting the principal in promoting pedagogical initiatives, preparing study programs and implementing innovations, guiding the principal in improving teaching and learning processes;
- Participating in and being involved with recruiting processes of a new school principal, evaluating his/her job performance and preventing his appointment if necessary for pedagogical reasons;
- Evaluating teachers according to the recommendations of the school principal or the Director Superintendent and the approval or disapproval of requests from the principal/the superintendent for the dismissal of a teacher;
- Maintaining office hours and attending to requests related to the district which originate from teachers, parents, students and public representatives;
- Coordinating the activities of the instructional setting and those of other supervisors who operate in the school;
- Fulfilling any other activity according to the instructions of superiors (Director Superintendent, District Manager, Director General or the Minister).

Though there are a number of different roles in the educational hierarchy responsible for various administrative and pedagogical functions that are typically associated with the inspectorate and superintendency system, this chapter focuses on the comprehensive superintendent who serves as the "middle person" between the school principal to whom s/he is inclined to grant autonomy to some extent, and the upper levels of the organizational hierarchy (e.g., local authority or the central administration), which stress the need to establish regulations that will ease their control over the schools.

## MOVING TOWARDS DECENTRALIZATION

Since the 1970s, the Israeli Ministry of Education has introduced a number of restructuring initiatives aimed towards decentralizing the educational system and increasing school control (Nir & Eyal, 2003). Decentralization implies "establishing a somewhat flat organizational configuration" (Kowalski, 2013, p. 94), meaning that schools, principals and teachers are granted some degrees of authority and autonomy to act. However, in the Israeli case, these decentralization policies led to a "paradoxical school autonomy" (Inbar, 1987 in Nir & Eyal, 2003) as they called for increased school autonomy and, at the same time, maintained central regulations and control mechanisms which undermined school autonomy. In 1992, the Minister of Education commissioned a steering committee that aimed at examining the possibility of extending the scope of school autonomy and introducing school-based management (SBM) into the Israeli schooling system. The committee recommended introducing SBM based on a set of guidelines (Volansky & Bar-Elli, 1996): (1) Schools will develop a clear definition of specific goals; (2) Schools will develop a work plan that corresponds with the defined goals; (3) Schools will implement and use extensive monitoring and assessment methods; (4) Schools will be granted full independence in using their budget; (5) Schools' authority to deal with personnel matters will be broadened; (6) There will be a governing body for each school (recommendations 5 and 6 were later on postponed).

The case of the SBM reform, which was aimed at granting greater autonomy and independence to the schools, may serve as a test case for examining the role of the comprehensive superintendent at times when decentralization takes place.

## THE ROLE OF COMPREHENSIVE SUPERINTENDENTS IN SBM SCHOOLS

The introduction of SBM required reconsideration of the role definitions of all officials who were directly influenced by this change initiative, and redefinition of the power relations within which individuals were assumed to act in these newly-created circumstances (Nir & Eyal, 2003). This argument was especially relevant to top hierarchical positions that were formally in charge of controlling and monitoring the educational processes taking place in schools, as in the case of the school superintendent.

The committee, appointed by the Minister of Education, also addressed the issues of supervising SBM schools and recommended that "the superintendent of SBM schools will focus on supporting, counseling and strengthening schools, and will assist schools in achieving their goals as defined by their governing body. This way, the superintendent will ensure that the national educational goals on the one hand and school independence on the other hand are attained" (Ministry of Education, 1993, p. 45 in Nir & Eyal, 2003, p. 551). In reality, however, in spite of extensive efforts that have been made since the 1980s (Yonai, 1999, in Nir & Eyal, 2003), the formal role definition of the superintendent has remained almost the same throughout the years. This may partly be explained by the superintendents' professional union's resistance to narrowing superintendents' authority, but mainly because: ". . . it is believed beyond reasonable doubt that even when increasing the independence of educational institutions, there is a need for the supervision of the superintendent" (Ministry of Education, Culture and Sports, 1984, in Nir & Eyal, 2003, p. 551).

Consequently, the formal role definition of the superintendent has remained unchanged although the introduction of SBM to the educational system took place in 1996. The superintendent has a number of central responsibilities which include, among other things, being the representative of the central office at schools, approving and monitoring the implementation of central regulations by schools, monitoring and evaluating school administration and monitoring students' achievements.

To learn about the current perceptions of the Israeli superintendents of their role, I conducted, with Adam Nir, research in which we collected data through questionnaires from 129 of about 150 comprehensive superintendents in the Israeli educational system. The data were collected in the 2010-2011 school year during superintendents' weekly meetings in 7 of the 8 districts. The superintendents were asked, among other things, about their job description, responsibilities and their impact on policy formation at the district level and their relationships with school principals. The respondents' mean age was 54 (sd=6.5); 66% women; 90% held Master or PhD degree, with 30 years on average of educational experience (sd=6.5) and nine years on average of experience as superintendent (sd=6.6); 83% had previously been teachers and 70% principals. The sample included 74% Jewish and 26% Arab and Bedouin superintendents.

The majority of the superintendents in the study (66%) reported that they experience autonomy at work. When they were asked to describe their role on a 10-point scale, where forming policy appears on the one side and implementing policy on the other, most reported being somewhere in the middle. When asked about their ability to actively influence the formation of educational policy in their district, 70% agreed with this statement. This is an interesting finding which implies that the superintendents perceive themselves as playing an active role in affecting the policy that is determined at the district level. Though in general the superintendents in this study did not characterize themselves as capable of affecting policy formation at the national level, when it comes "close to home," to their actual districts, they value their ability to affect policy formation and thus affect their actual work. When asked about their impact on the selection of school principals, 67% responded that they have much impact on this aspect of their job, thus implying that the superintendents feel that they have an impact on both: the district and the schools.

Another interesting finding refers to the superintendents' self-concept: 88% reported that they are looked at as professionals in their district. This finding, as are some of the findings indicated above (e.g., the superintendents' feeling of autonomy in the job) may imply that the superintendents feel that they are trusted by the administration at the district level. The superintendents can be relied upon because they know what is expected of them and how they need to operate toward their role partners. Nevertheless, the superintendents reported about considerable administrative work that is a result of the control and regulation imposed on them by the central office. Eighty-seven percent of the sampled superintendents agreed with the statement, "the administrative component of my ongoing work is heavy." This seems to be related to the regulations that are imposed by the central office requiring them to spend too much time in filling out forms. This tension between regulation, which is imposed by the central administration, and trust – a feeling that is shared by employees – is not unique to superintendents only. Nor is it unique to the educational realm only. This tension exists in all types of organizations (Levin, 2012). The challenge is to find the balance between the two, trust and regulation. Obviously, this is a challenging task, especially when considering the role duties of the Israeli comprehensive superintendent.

Introducing SBM in centralized systems while maintaining an unchanged superintendents' formal role definition exposes the comprehensive superintendents to role conflict and stress, which encourages them to rationalize their involvement with SBM and/or adopt various resistance behaviors (Nir & Eyal, 2003). This type of ambiguity regarding the external supervision of schools that they are expected to sustain needs to be clarified, and the role of the school superintendent redefined in line with norms and values that the SBM initiative aims to advance.

## BALANCING TRUST AND REGULATION

The description of the centralization and decentralization notions of educational systems represents the essence of the potential problematic and conflictual situations with which superintendents may be confronted in their role. Thus, in countries where the educational systems are decentralized, one may observe different patterns of relationships between superintendents and their role partners, above and below their place in the organizational hierarchy.

Decentralization, in Israel and in other countries, offers new opportunities for local education authorities to redefine their responsibilities towards schools and to extend their influence over schools (Addi-Raccah & Gavish, 2010). It allows superintendents to gain more autonomy in issues such as recruitment of new members, budget planning and decision-making processes. Nevertheless, the central office has not undertaken the decision yet to change the superintendent's role definition while implementing a policy of autonomy. Thus, the centralization-decentralization issue exhibits the dilemma of trust vs. regulation. On the one hand, the decentralization idea calls for granting greater autonomy to comprehensive superintendents, and to school principals so that they will be accountable for what is taking place in their schools. On the other hand, the superintendents are expected to follow the regulations that are determined by the central administration every once in a while and make sure they are implemented in schools. This tension between the call for greater autonomy, on the one hand, and adherence to procedures and regulations, on the other hand, is well reflected in the centralization-decentralization issue.

More than 25 years ago, Inbar (1987) questioned whether autonomy is possible in a centralized educational system. According to his view, the decentralization act was not successful because the top position officials, including inspectors and superintendents, opposed giving up their power and the right to control school administration (policies, plans and activities). Consequently, school autonomy became an abstract notion with no likelihood to be truly implemented. This was also found with regard to providing parents the opportunity to take an active role in school governance. It seems that only in unique schools have they had some impact on school matters (Nir & Bogler, 2012), but the decentralization trend emphasizes the importance of granting some impact in school to interest groups such as the parents.

During the past quarter of a century, additional large-scale reforms have been implemented, calling for granting more autonomy and self-managing practices to schools, with greater accountability of the principals and school personnel, but the role definition of the superintendent has not changed. Superintendents are expected to use their experience and wisdom to juggle effectively between the stated purposes of the administration and the actual situation where they realize that their power is limited and bounded. They are caught in the middle between top level officials who expect them to control and supervise and the school principals and teachers who perceive and anticipate gaining greater responsibility and autonomy to decide about the educational processes and outcomes for which they are accountable. The superintendent's role has, therefore, become an elusive and fluid one, causing a continued feeling of frustration and vulnerability among both the superintendents and their role partners inside and outside of the schools.

To achieve better understanding of the superintendent's role in the transition from centralization to decentralization, the top officials in the Ministry of Education need to create the conditions for compatibility among all the system components involved in the educational process at the macro (state) and the micro (local authority and school) level of management. To ensure an effective educational structure, where the stated goals of decentralization are implemented, a thorough examination of the current hierarchical educational system needs to be taken. To clarify the elusive concept of the superintendent's role, the central office needs to reexamine whether each of the hierarchical levels in the organizational pyramid functions according to its stated goal and incorporate changes wherever needed. Only after the superintendents' roles are defined to suit the current move toward decentralization will one be able to examine what roles they should carry, as depicted by various scholars in Björk and Kowalski's book (2008): the superintendent as teacher-scholar, as manager, as democratic leader, applied social scientist or communicator. What would better describe the nature of the Israeli superintendents' workplace in this era? Possibly they should all be able to demonstrate various facets (those listed above and others), but does each facet have the same degree of importance or weight when considering the superintendents' roles in different working circumstances with assorted role partners? Future research should explore the associations and tensions between the structure of educational systems and the superintendents' role characteristics within them in addition to exploring the optimal balance between trust and regulation.

## REFERENCES

Addi-Raccah, A., & Gavish, Y. (2010). The LEA's role in a decentralized school system: The school principals' view. *Educational Management Administration and Leadership, 38*(2) , pp. 184-201.

Al-Haj, M. (2005). National ethos, multicultural education, and the new history textbooks in Israel. *Curriculum Inquiry, 35*(1), 47-71.

Bar Shalom, Y. (2006). *Educating Israel: Educational entrepreneurship in Israel's multicultural society.* New York: Palgrave/MacMillan.

Björk, L.G., & Kowalski, T.J. (2005). *The contemporary superintendent. Preparation, practice, and development.* Thousand Oaks, Cal.: Corwin Press.

Cahan, S., Casali, N., & Herskovitz, A. (2013). Is Israel's rank on international achievement tests really surprising? http://www.goldfingercom.com/clients/hakoled/Pisa.pdf

Central Bureau of Statistics (2013). *Israel population. Population, by population group.* Retrieved 23 March, 2013. www.cbs.gov.il

Elboim-Dror, R. (2001). Israeli education: Changing perspectives. *Israel Studies, 6*(1), 76-100.

Gumpel, T. P., & Nir A. E. (2005). The Israeli educational system: Blending dreams with constraints In: Kas Mazuerk & Margert A. Winzer (Eds.). *Schooling around the world: Debates, challenges and practices.* N.Y.: Allyn & Bacon, pp. 149 - 167.

Inbar, D. (1987). Is autonomy possible in a centralized education system? In Isaac A. Friedman (Ed.). *Autonomy in education: Conceptual framework and implementation processes*. Jerusalem: The Henrietta Szold Institute. pp. 53-71 (Hebrew).

Kenny-Pas, B. (1996). Israel towards the new millennium. In B. Kenny-Pas & M. Lissak (Eds.). *Israel towards the new millennium: society, politics, culture*. Jerusalem: Magnes Press (Hebrew).

Kowalski, T. J. (2013). *The school superintendent. Theory, practice, and cases*. Thousand Oaks, Cal.: Sage.

Lazin, F. A. (1982). Education policy in Israel: The reality of implementation. In E. Ben-Baruch & Y. Neumann (Eds.). *Educational administration and policy making. The case of Israel*. Herzliya: Ben-Gurion University & Unipress – Academic Pub., pp. 125-137.

Levin, B. (2012). Balance trust and accountability. *Phi Delta Kappan, 94*(1), 74-75.

Michalovitz, R. (2005). The structure of the educational system as an expression of a world view. In Paldi, E. (Ed.). *Education and challenge of time 2*. Tel Aviv: Reches, pp. 598-607 (Hebrew).

Ministry of Education (2011). *The Educational system in the 2010-2011 school year*. Ministry of Education, Department of Economics and Budgets: The Economics and Statistics Wing. Jerusalem, August, 2011.

Ministry of Education (2012a). *Facts and figures*. Section D: Development of education: Facts and figures. Retrieved on March 8, 2013. (http://cms.education.gov.il/ NR/rdonlyres/80371F5E-6AFC-445A-81A5-2DB9EAFC6184/130306/sectionD.pdf )

Ministry of Education (2012b). Retrieved on March 23, 2013. http://cms.education.gov.il/ EducationCMS/Units/Owl/Hebrew/UvdotNetunim/netunim/

Ministry of Education (2013a). Retrieved on March 17, 2013. (http://cms.education.gov.il/ EducationCMS/Units/Owl/Hebrew/UvdotNetunim/netunim/).

Ministry of Education (2013b). Retrieved on April 10, 2013. (http://cms. education.gov.il/EducationCMS/Units/Hofesh/DeenVeHeshbon/2008/2008/MatarotYeadi m.htm )

Ministry of Immigrant Absorption (2013). *Information and advertising – Statistics*. Retrieved 13 March 2013. www.moia.gov.il

Nir, A. E., & Bogler, R. (2012). Parental involvement in school governance and decision making in Israel. *Journal of School Public Relations, 33*(3), 216-236.

Nir, A.E., & Eyal, O. (2003). School-based management and the role conflict of the school superintendent. *Journal of Educational Administration, 41* (4/5), 547-564.

OECD (2010). Decision of the Council to invite the State of Israel to accede to the Convention on the OECD. Retrieved on 2 April, 2013. http://www.oecd. org/newsroom/45167312.pdf

OECD (2007). PISA 2006: Science Competencies for Tomorrow's World Executive Summary. http://www.oecd.org/dataoecd/15/13/39725224.pdf

Pur, D., & Gordon, D. (1982). Conservatism and centralization in school systems – the case of the Israeli high schools. In E. Ben-Baruch & Y. Neumann (Eds.). *Educational administration and policy making. The case of Israel*. Herzliya: Ben-Gurion University & Unipress – Academic Pub., pp. 223-244.

Shtrasler, N. (2008). From kibbutzim and oranges to the silicon valley of the Middle East. In S. Aharoni & M. Aharoni (Eds.). *Israel, economy & society: 60 years*. Kfar Sava: Miksam Press.

Smyth, E., & Banks, J. (2012). High stakes testing and student perspectives on teaching and learning in the Republic of Ireland. *Educational Assessment, Evaluation and Accountability, 24*(4), 283-306.

Smooha, S. (1992). *Arabs and Jews in Israel. Vol. 2: Change and continuity in mutual intolerance.* Boulder and London: Westview Press.

Soffer, A. (2008). Demographic aspects and environmental and political implication. In S. Aharoni & M. Aharoni (Eds.). *Israel, economy & society: 60 Years.* Kfar Sava: Miksam Press.

State Education Regulations (Supervision orders). (1956, updated in 1996). Retrieved 17 April, 2013. http://www.nevo.co.il/law_html/law01/152_031.htm#Seif14

The New York Times (March 31, 2013). Israel taps an offshore natural gas field. Retrieved 2 April, 2013. http://www.nytimes.com/2013/04/01/world/middleeast/israel-turns-on-natural-gas-flow-at-offshore-site.html?_r=0

Volansky, A. (2003). From experiment to educational policy: The transition to school-based management in Israeli schools. In A. Volansky & A. I. Friedman (Eds.). *School-based management – An international perspective.* Ministry of Education, Jerusalem (English/Hebrew), pp. 217-232.

Volansky, A. (2007). School autonomy for school effectiveness and improvement: The case of Israel. In T. Townsend (Ed.). *International handbook on school effectiveness and improvement.* N.Y.: Springer. pp. 351-362.

Volansky, A., & Bar-Elli D. (1996). Moving toward equitable school-based management. *Educational Leadership 53*(4), 60-62.

Yuchtman-Yaar, E. (2005). Continuity and change in Israeli society: The test of the melting pot. *Israel Studies, 10*(2), 91-128.

In: The Educational Superintendent
Editor: Adam E. Nir

ISBN: 978-1-62948-972-8
© 2014 Nova Science Publishers, Inc.

*Chapter 6*

# THE NEW EXECUTIVES IN A LANDSCAPE OF CHANGE: THE EMERGING REALITY OF PLURAL CONTROLLED SCHOOLING IN ENGLAND

### *Philip A. Woods and Amanda Roberts*
University of Hertfordshire, UK

The landscape of leadership of the school system in England is changing. Harris (2012, p. 537), for example, concludes that the days of "local town halls making and implementing policy and shaping and directing the local schools system in furtherance of locally determined priorities seem to be gone." The institutional basis for a role as an executive head within such a process has similarly receded in England. There are still local authority senior executive officers responsible for school education, but their responsibilities and powers have changed and new executive positions are developing in the emerging system. This chapter explores the unfolding new system and the changing roles within it in terms of their complexities, opportunities and challenges.

The UK is made up of four countries: England (population 52 million), Scotland (5 million - which is the subject of another chapter in this volume), Wales (3 million) and Northern Ireland (2 million) (Office for National Statistics, 2011). Constitutional reforms from the 1990s have given the UK a more federalist and devolved character in terms of the relationships between the constituent countries. This makes the UK more of a "dual" or "quasi-federal" state (Bogdanor, 2009, Eymeri-Douzens, 2011, p. 16) in which England lacks its own Parliament but is governed through the UK Parliament where the majority of seats, by virtue of England's size, represent English constituencies. The smaller countries each have their own representative body which decides on devolved matters, including education.

The focus of this chapter is England. While there has been devolution to the countries of the UK, within England the story is one in which the role and influence of local government and local democratic legitimacy have been diminished. This has been part of a long-term policy trend since the 1980s to change the role of the central state. Policy in the UK, and consequently in England, has been at the forefront of reconfiguring the public sector through privatization, public-private partnerships, introduction of market principles and implementation of managerialist reforms (Flinders, 2011). The dominant trend has been towards a market-orientated, performative logic of governance. In this, central government attempts simultaneously to reduce its responsibilities for direct provision of services and to promote a mix of private and public service providers and a more entrepreneurial culture driven by an instrumental rationality in which progress and achievement are measured against performance targets and financial goals (Woods, 2011, 2013). Within this logic, democratic legitimacy through local representative bodies has little value. The principal role of local institutions is to play a part in furthering the market-orientated, performative logic of the central state. Since the 1980s there have been different emphases as governments changed. When elected to government in 1997, for example, New Labour developed a number of initiatives with the aim of encouraging public participation in local government (Newman, 2001, pp. 128-130). The overriding thrust of policy in England, however, continued to be centrally driven, with local authorities being seen increasingly by central government as its agents. This emerging system is explained in more detail in the next section.

## THE EDUCATION SYSTEM

The UK as a whole had 32,500 schools in 2011/12 (Department for Education, 2012a, p. 7). The great majority of these are in England: 24,300 schools serving 8.1 million pupils, which includes 16,800 primary and 3,300 secondary schools in the public sector (pp. 10, 11). Most pupils in England attend state funded schools: 4.2 million primary school pupils and 3.2 million secondary school pupils do so, compared with just over half a million (577,000) who attend privately funded independent schools (Department for Education 2012b, p. 1). In state funded schools, substantial proportions of pupils are entitled to free school meals (18%), have a first language other than English (17% and 13% respectively at primary and secondary levels), and are of ethnic minority origin (28% and 23% respectively at primary and secondary levels) (Department of Education, 2012b, pp. 1, 2).

Responsibility for the school system in England rests with the Department for Education, a department of the UK government. This national level of government has the constitutional capacity to shape the school system through legislation (which it can initiate in Parliament) and government agencies. It has the capacity to determine and influence the content of the educational process in schools. Agencies include Ofsted (the Office for Standards in Education, Children's Services and Skills) which inspects and regulates services (including schools) that care for children and young people and provide education and skills for learners of all ages. It reports to Parliament, rather than the Secretary of State for Education directly, but its statutory powers and duties reflect the policies of central government. Ofsted has a powerful impact on schools and their priorities because its evaluation of individual schools has significant implications for them (Richards, 2012).

A second way that central control is enacted is through structural change (Woods, 2011). In England, new organizational structures have been facilitated by central government. The policy for structural change reflects the drive towards a market-orientated, performative logic of governance referred to above. The intention is to bring new "players" into the field of school education to sponsor or partner new types of school that are independent of local democratic control, so as to promote enterprise, innovation and the dissolution of traditional boundaries which are seen in this logic as obstacles to school improvement. Integral to this process is a radical alteration of the role of the 152 local authorities with a responsibility for school education (National Foundation for Educational Research, 2011). They have lost powers downwards to schools; and they have lost powers upwards to central government. LAs now are left with core responsibilities in their area to ensure a sufficient supply of school places, to tackle "underperformance" in schools and ensure high standards, and to support vulnerable children (Parish, Baxter & Sandals, 2012). They also "retain a duty... to exercise their functions with a view to 'promoting high standards' of education and 'the fulfilment of learning potential'. . . " (Harris, 2012, p. 537). The latter duty, as Harris observes, "clearly lacks real enforceability" since LAs are losing their capacity to manage the local school system.

The consequent trend is towards what can be termed plural controlled schooling, i.e., a system characterized by multiple sources of control and education (Woods, 2011). New players are able to enter the system as sponsors or partners of schools which cease to be the direct responsibility of local authorities. Behind the trend is a growth in both control and autonomy, which sounds paradoxical. Enhancements in autonomy, however, have to be understood in the context of a centralized framework (control by central government) which exerts strong influences (through Ofsted inspections, for example) on what is understood to be good and effective education, and on who is able and given opportunities to become sponsors and partners.

The story of school autonomy begins in the late 1980s. Schools (mostly then within LA control) were given significant devolved responsibilities and powers for decision-making on how they spend their budgets and other matters. Reformed school governing bodies, which include parent, local community and teacher representatives, were and still are integral to the accountability system for schools. A key part of the policy vision, however, was for the school system to become more like a market, with parents having the right to choose schools and school budgets being determined by pupil numbers; and for a national policy framework (through inspections and various interventions emanating from central government) to decisively shape schooling in a certain way, consistent with the market-orientated, performative logic.

More recently, this policy direction has been intensified. Central government has facilitated the creation of different types of "independent" school that are funded by the state, outside the direct responsibility of LAs and exempt from the national curriculum. The main types are[1]:

- *sponsored academies.* The first of these began in 2002 replacing existing schools which were deemed to be "failing." They are sponsored by businesses, faith groups, charities and educational institutions such as universities, further education colleges and "successful" schools (National Audit Office, 2010). Some are new schools such as university technology colleges which specialize in subjects like engineering and construction, and studio schools which are supported by employers and emphasize project-based learning in "realistic situations."

---

[1]  See New Schools Network, "Comparison of Different School Types," accessed at http://newschoolsnetwork.org/sites/default/files/files/pdf/Differences%20across%20school%20types.pdf; see also the government website: https://www.gov.uk/types-of-school/academies; and on studio schools: http://www.education.gov.uk/inthenews/inthenews/a00211924/big-business-backs-new-studio-schools

- *converter academies.* These are existing schools that choose to opt out of LA control and do not have sponsors but are run by their own governing body.
- *free schools.* Technically also academies, these are new schools set up by charities, universities, privately funded independent schools, community and faith groups, teachers, parents, or businesses. They can include privately funded schools that choose to opt for free school status and become state funded.

For the purposes of this chapter, we shall refer to all the above schools as academies. Since the election of the Coalition government in the UK, the numbers of academies have increased sharply as a result of deliberate policies by the government. In other words, the Coalition has intensified and accelerated the structural changes begun under New Labour.[2] From a total of 203 academies in May 2010, the numbers had increased more than tenfold to 2,309 by September 2012[3] and almost 3,000 by April 2013. Most of these are secondary schools, which means that more than half of secondaries in England now have academy status. Further growth in numbers of academies is expected, especially in the primary sector (Hill, Dunford, Parish, Rea & Sandals, 2012).

Publicly-funded schools that do not become academies remain within the responsibility of LAs and are known as maintained schools. These remain the majority at the time of writing because most primary schools to date have not converted to academy status.

Many academies and maintained schools have joined or formed collaborative groups, varying significantly in their characteristics and labels (Simkins & Woods, forthcoming 2014). By September 2012 there were 48 sponsored academy chains with three or more academies in each one, with expectations of substantial growth (Hill et al., 2012, p. 8). Some of the chains are national, with academies from different parts of England; others are comprised of academies from a particular local area. One chain has grown to include at the time of writing 69 academies.[4] In addition to such chains, there are many collaborative groupings of maintained schools, with some including academies. Chains and other collaborative groups vary greatly in their formal arrangements and how closely they work together, ranging across a loose-to-tight spectrum of governance. The more tight-knit academy chains have a shared executive leadership and management, while other chains collaborate but have little or no shared governance arrangement. Most large sponsored academy chains have "either a CEO or a director of education as the key individual" (Hill et al., 2012, p. 51). Looser arrangements are characteristic especially of converter academy chains, where governance "is in its infancy" and "there is in effect little if any formal joint governance at this point" (Hill et al., 2012, p. 49).

Groups of maintained schools also vary, creating a large variety of partnerships, networks and cooperative arrangements. Some groups collaborate through joint committees for example, with each school retaining its own governing body; others have closer working arrangements that could include being a federation under a single governing body for the

---

[2] The sources for figures in this paragraph are DfE (2012d, e) and the government website http://www.education.gov.uk/schools/leadership/typesofschools/academies/b00208569/open-academies (accessed 9 April 2013).

[3] 2,309 academies and 79 free schools.

[4] The Academies Education Trust: http://www.academiesenterprisetrust.org, accessed 24th April 2013.

whole group.[5] One approach is where the collaborative of schools takes the lead responsibility for its running as a whole system and for commissioning services. An example is an authority-wide partnership which is run by its member schools, has an independent chair, "is articulating an educational vision for the City [and is] maintaining a collective and integrated approach, owned by all schools including two academies" (Crossley-Holland, 2012, p. 30). Other collaboratives of maintained schools work more closely with the LA. Examples are given in the section which follows.

It is important to note that many maintained schools, and some academies, are "stand-alone" schools, not part of a formal collaborative group. More than eight out of ten headteachers describe their school as "stand alone" (Earley et al., 2012, p. 80).

The complexity and fluidity of the evolving local system is further illustrated by a key component of central government policy - namely, the creation of teaching schools. Teaching schools have responsibility for providing student teacher education and professional development, developing a "self-sustaining" school system, and leading a "teaching school alliance" which is "a group of schools and other partners that is supported by the leadership of a teaching school" and can work within or across LA boundaries. Around 500 teaching school alliances is the target for 2014.[6]

This section has demonstrated the complex pattern of local leadership of education in England. The diversity of executive leadership roles in a changing national picture has also been indicated and the themes of autonomy and control highlighted. The following section continues to develop these themes, extending understanding of a range of emergent leading executive roles.

## EMERGING EXECUTIVE LEADERSHIP STRUCTURES AND ROLES IN THE MIDDLE TIER

The structure of the leadership of education in England is currently in a state of flux. Central government remains accountable for the performance of its schools. Ofsted continues to have a key role in assuring school success. However, the role of the next, middle tier of educational leadership is undergoing a process of fundamental change, resulting in new patterns of middle-tier, leadership roles (Simkins & Woods, forthcoming 2014). In this emerging national picture it would be difficult, and indeed unwise, to attempt to give a comprehensive overview of the entire new pattern of leadership. This pattern is both difficult to define and constantly evolving. Instead we have chosen to highlight some of the most important new leadership structures and to give an insight into the working lives of new leading executive roles associated with these through a series of vignettes relating to:

- emerging versions of the LA role;
- "hard federations" of schools that have a single governing body;
- sponsored academy chains.

---

[5] http://www.education.gov.uk/schools/leadership/governance/b00218939/maintained-school-coll-fed, accessed 24th April 2013

[6] http://www.education.gov.uk/nationalcollege/index/support-for-schools/teachingschools/teachingschools-background.htm, accessed 24th April 2013.

These vignettes are illustrative. They are not drawn from data but are condensed, fictional, narrative cases. As examples, they should not be viewed as typical, since there are numerous different leadership structures and roles emerging in LAs, federations, academy chains and other collaboratives. The vignettes are offered here as a tool to facilitate insights into the lived experience of leaders and to act as the basis for reflection and discussion.


## LAs and Developing Versions of Their Old Middle Tier Role

Middle tier educational leadership in England has historically been provided by local councils through local education authorities (LEAs). From the early 20th century, LEAs appointed Chief Education Officers to be a manager and educational leader (Gillard, 1987). From 2004,[7] as part of a national policy to integrate children's services, LAs were required to appoint a Director of Children's Services (DCS), tasked with improving the well-being of all children and young people (DCSF, 2009). This role involves leading a wide range of activities, people and agencies, in a joint local effort to improve outcomes for all children and young people. A senior local government officer, the DCS provides a line of accountability for those working with young people, though this accountability is less clear as the local schools system becomes more plural and diverse. A particular focus of the role is to ensure that all children, including the disadvantaged and vulnerable, are championed. Contributing to the achievement of this agenda, the DCS leads LAs' management of central services such as place planning, admissions and school support services. A DCS also holds key roles in relation to the quality of education in their local area, providing both support and challenge for school improvement.

The power of LAs has diminished since the 1980s and some of their middle tier roles are being taken on by other leaders within the system. LAs are dependent much more on building relationships, negotiating, facilitating partnerships, and leading and engaging in local dialogues. As one study concluded, LAs take the view that in the new emerging system "relationships are king" (Parish et al., 2012, p. 5). LAs are involved in something much more like network governance than democratic governance in which they enact and manage change in the local schools system on the basis of local democratic legitimacy.

Despite central government's funding cuts, the academies program and the drive to maximize delegation to schools leading to the shift of some of these traditionally middle tier functions to "groups" of schools, there seems to be little impetus to discard the local authority tier entirely and replace it with direct accountability to Whitehall or a complex pattern of academy chains (Thraves, Fowler & Carr-West, 2012). The Department for Education's formal view of the new role of LAs is summarized in the words of the White Paper, "The Importance of Teaching." They see their approach as being to "give local authorities a strong strategic role as champions for parents, families and vulnerable pupils. They will promote educational excellence by ensuring a good supply of high quality places, coordinating admissions and developing their school improvement strategies to support local schools" (Department for Education, 2010, Para. 16).

---

[7]  http://www.education.gov.uk/aboutdfe/statutory/g00206029/statutory-guidance-on-the-roles-and-responsibilities-of-the-director-of-childrens-services-and-the-lead-member-for-childrens-services/the-director-of-childrens-services-and-lead-member-for-childrens-services, accessed 30th April 2013.

Drawing on this guidance, many local authorities are now developing a new version of their old middle tier role, focusing on the provision of central support services. LAs are adopting new structures to support them in best carrying out their new roles. Many are negotiating partnerships and agreements with schools to provide support services, broker support between schools and work with schools in other ways (ADCS, 2012; Crossley-Holland, 2012). In some cases, this is a realignment of previous organizational arrangements. In others, a more radical restructuring approach has been taken. One LA, for example, has developed a social enterprise company – part owned by schools and part by the local authority – to deliver the school improvement services it formerly provided through the county council structures (Herts for Learning, 2012). The county council retains its responsibility for recruitment, admissions and so on. Another LA has an arrangement whereby it works through eight consortia of schools, each consortia being "responsible for the improvement of all member schools" (Crossley-Holland, 2012, p. 28).

An illustrative vignette of one of the emerging models for those leading children's services in LAs is given below.

---

**Vignette 1: Director of Children's services**

I am the Director of Children's services for a small local education authority in England. I came into education 20 years ago because I believed that all young people deserve the best chance they can get in life and that they are best supported in achieving their potential through a child-centered, creative approach to children's services. My beliefs have not changed over time. However, the structures within which I work to put these views into practice have altered fundamentally.

As a Head of Service I now work with a small team of local authority employees who are directly accountable to me. My actual team is much bigger however as I work in partnership with the heads of five consortia of schools, three secondary and two primary. Our common agenda is school improvement. My particular role, alongside my local authority colleagues, is to monitor the performance of the schools within the county, based largely on data provided by them. We support schools in actioning their improvement agenda based on these data though supporting knowledge-building and the sharing of good practice across schools. We also quality-assure consortia services and act as critical friends to the school leaders.

I have other responsibilities outside of the school improvement agenda, including admissions. Responses of my colleagues to the changing role of local authorities in the school system is interesting. Many rightly point out that we have given much of our power over both to schools and to central government. However, the responsibility of the local authority in some ways remains the same. We are still charged with ensuring that our schools provide a high quality of education and to ensure that children become the best they can be. We now achieve this in a tighter partnership with our colleagues in schools however. From my perspective such partnership working can only be positive, although I do see the challenges which a perceived loss of autonomy brings.

---

## Federations

The 2002 Education Act allowed for a group of two or more schools with a formal agreement to work together to raise standards. Such groups of schools can take the form of "hard federations." Hard federations are legal entities, with a single governing body.

However, there are looser arrangements that give individual schools greater autonomy, known as "soft federations" (Lindsay et al., 2007). The leaders of federations undertake some of the leadership roles traditionally associated with middle tier leadership, though not statutory roles based in a local democratically elected council like the LA. This may include building collegiality across a number of schools, providing strategic leadership and managing cross-phase transition. Interpretation of guidance from central government and support for its implementation are also key roles which complement rather than replace the statutory roles based in local democratically elected councils. The overarching framework of the federation structure also allows federation leaders to put in place structural changes in leadership and management (Lindsay et al., 2007). A version of a federation leadership structures is illustrated by Vignette 2.

---

**Vignette 2: Executive headteacher of a federation**

   I am the Executive headteacher of a formal federation of seven secondary schools and one special school. The secondary schools in my federation cater for students between the ages of 11-18. The special school caters for the needs of students, also between the ages of 11-18, with special educational needs. We share one governing body between all eight schools. We decided to come together as a formal federation in order to allow us to concentrate our efforts on common challenges. My job is to lead a strategic, federation-wide approach to community-development and regeneration. I also manage the financial planning of the federation and its staffing.

   Each school within my federation also has its own headteacher. Their role is to lead teaching and learning and to promote developments which support student attainment. I believe that the federation structure has had huge benefits for staff and students within our schools. We are able now to design and source our own staff development programs in a more cost-effective and tailored way than when we were relying on external providers to single schools. We are still happy to access some consultancy support from the local authority but find that we have a pool of skills across the eight schools which means that we can learn most of the things we need to know from one another.

   I work as a team with the headteachers of all eight schools which means that we all have more time to lead and find we are less exhausted at the end of the working week. Personally I have found this a liberating experience.

---

Despite the fact that in 2011, over 90% of schools still followed a standard model of a single, non-executive headteacher (Department for Education, 2012c), there is evidence of recent growth in the executive headteacher model exemplified in Vignette 2 above. Seven percent of respondents to a survey conducted in 2012 (Earley et al., 2012) reported that they were an executive leading two or more schools.

## Academy Chains

   There are two types of academy chains - sponsored academy chains and converter academy chains.[8] The first academy chain came into being in 2004, since when the number of such chains has risen rapidly. By 2012, 48 sponsored academy chains existed, as noted above,

---

[8] The source for information and figures in this paragraph is Hill et al. (2012).

made up of nearly 350 sponsored academies, while 300 converter academies were part of converter academy chains. A number of chains have chief education officers (CEOs) or executive principals with overall responsibility for leading the chain. As with federations, the leaders of academy chains take on many of the leadership roles traditionally associated with the local education authority, such as identifying appropriate leaders for the academies within their chain. Leaders of larger chains tend to have a more strategic view of their wider role, which can include building and leading the chain as an organization, ensuring quality assurance of the chain's education, developing plans, leading reviews across the academies and managing relations with unions, the media, sponsors and external agencies. Previously centralized local authority services such as human resources, insurance, legal services, audit and ICT services are generally provided independently through the chain. Leaders of chains also take on the quality assurance roles previously undertaken by the local education authority. A fictionalized description of a CEO of a sponsored academy chain is presented as Vignette 3.

---

**Vignette 3: Chief Education Officer of a sponsored academy chain**

I am the Chief Education Officer of a large sponsored academy chain. I do not have an education background. Instead I have run a successful commercial company and was appointed because of my strategic management capacity. Our chain is currently made up of 10 academies, of which seven are secondary schools and three are primary schools. I expect this chain to grow with additional academies joining us from the primary sector.

The impetus for us forming such a large chain came from our sponsors who wished both to create a cost-effective operating model and to extend our school improvement model and expertise to a large number of schools.

Each of the academies within my chain has its own headteacher who reports directly to me. This is a recent change in the structure of the chain however. When we had only four schools in the chain, these were grouped into pairs, with an executive principal leading each pair.

The expansion of our chain has had many advantages. We are now in the position to provide a broader base for developing leaders. We now have greater scope both for sharing our school improvement processes and for building on them through more fluid staff development and promotion processes. I do have a concern that if we take on too many new academies our school improvement model may become dissipated, but we are taking steps to ensure that we are in a good position to continue to support both our existing chain and additions to it.

---

Despite the potential for autonomous working, it is clear that some academies are keen to be part of effective LA school improvement strategies and in many LAs they buy the LA's services (Parish et al., 2012). This reflects a growing pattern across chains where leaders, although fulfilling many traditional middle tier roles, do not necessarily see themselves as replacing the role of independent managers of the school system (Thraves, Fowler & Carr-West, 2012). Moreover, not all academy chains are in a position to take on the full range of middle tier roles.

## CHALLENGES

This snapshot of new leadership structures and roles in the English schools system indicates their complexity. Such system change clearly presents many challenges. The largely positive tone of our fictional vignettes is not meant to suggest that there are no conflicts or systemic problems, which many such as Simkins and Woods (forthcoming 2014) draw attention to. We highlight two of the challenges in this concluding section. The first concerns the importance of challenging assumptions about leadership. The second concerns the gaps that this more plural controlled system potentially creates in the local schools system.

## CHALLENGING ASSUMPTIONS ABOUT LEADERSHIP

A key implication of the new leadership structures and roles is their relationship to and impact on the leadership structures and roles of those within maintained schools and academies - teachers, students and others, as well as headteachers. A discussion of educational leadership which focuses on one key leader in each organization (be it a school, chain, federation or other collaborative group) presents only a partial picture of current trends in educational leadership in England. In English schools, a major leadership imperative is instead towards an acknowledgement of the leadership potential of all stakeholders within a school (e.g., National College for School Leadership, 2007). Thus in some schools all teachers and students are invited to lead change (Frost, Frost, MacBeath & Pedder, 2009). These leadership roles are not positional and hierarchical. Instead, they arise from leadership cultures in which the potential of all to contribute positively to school improvement is acknowledged and facilitated.

The concept of distributed leadership is one way of looking and understanding the spread of this more interactive leadership approach. From this perspective, leadership is seen as a phenomenon that emerges from complex, ongoing interactions within organizations and groups, and across them (Gronn, 2009; Woods, Bennett, Harvey & Wise, 2004). Academy chains and school groups potentially need not be envisaged as top-down hierarchies, but as inclusive, interactive networks of influence contributing to their direction and development. Potentially chains may enable "school leaders, teachers and students in the chain to interact with each other to provide mutual support and joint practice development and to refine the chain's pedagogical model" (Hill et al., 2012, p. 92).

Understanding leadership as distributed highlights important features of leadership in all schools, collaboratives and the local systems of which they are part. Different configurations of leadership are possible, depending on how much emphasis is given to hierarchical leadership and how much value and support is given to its distributed character. Hence configurations vary in the amount of hierarchical control and influence involved and the degrees of effective leadership participation made possible (Gronn, 2009; Woods & Woods, 2013). Recognizing this asks challenging and important questions of the new, emerging senior executive leadership roles in England, summarized here as two questions - one about leadership vision, the second about practice: As these new senior leadership roles develop, are they seen as part of a distributed leadership process that facilitates the active participation of teachers, students and other stakeholders and fully values their positive contribution? And, if they are (on the grounds that this leadership approach is the best way to create the conditions for students' learning), are new participative leadership cultures, structures and roles being co-developed within and between schools in order to put this into practice?

## GAPS IN THE SYSTEM

Local responsibility for the schools systems in England is now less clearly located in the body of the locally elected council and its senior executive. Three concerns arise in the current arrangements. The first is the potential for a "planning gap." How effectively will the need to oversee school places, chart demographic trends and plan responses to change be carried out in the new system? The second is the potential for a "public education gap." This concerns the local role in advancing aims that express important public values and goals. For example, LAs' responsibility to advance equality and equity goals in education may be more difficult in a "fragmented and increasingly privately orientated" system (Harris, 2012, p. 543). And where academies are not working collaboratively with other schools, which is the case with some academies, identifying this as a problem and responding to it is not a role that is necessarily best undertaken from a national perspective (Academies Commission, 2013). Third is the danger of an "accountability gap," including a "local democratic gap." Concern has been expressed by headteachers, school governors and others that public funding for academies should be subject to public scrutiny and accountability. The Charity Commissioner, among others, has expressed concerns that centralization of control in chains can lead to too little emphasis on consulting local stakeholders, such as local communities, staff and students (Academies Commission, 2013). Concerns such as these underpin the argument that a clear line of local democratic accountability is needed through local councils with stronger responsibilities and powers than provided for in the present system. Hence some argue that a revived, more active, democratic LA role is required.

The new landscape of leadership roles and structures in the English schools system is uncharted territory. The questions we pose in this chapter around the impact of the new, emerging structures and roles are yet to be answered in practice. A key test will be the degree to which the emerging system of plural controlled schooling in England supports or works against the active and equitable participation of teachers, students and other stakeholders which we hold as central to a democratic educational process.

## REFERENCES

Academies Commission (2013). *Unleashing greatness: Getting the best from an academised system*. The Report of the Academies Commission.

ADCS (2012). *The missing link: The evolving role of the local authority in school improvement*, Manchester: The Association of Directors of Children's Services (ADCS).

Bogdanor, V. (2009). *The new British constitution*. Oxford: Hart Publishing.

Crossley-Holland, J. (2012). *The future role of the local authority in education*. Manchester: The Association of Directors of Children's Services (ADCS). (Accessed at http://www.adcs.org.uk/download/schoolscausingconcern/Future%20role%20of%20the%

20local%20authority%20in%20school%20improvement%20-%20full%20report.pdf,    14 April 2013)

DCSF (2009). *The roles and responsibilities of the lead member for children's services and the director of children's services*. London: Department for Children, Schools and Families (DCSF).

Department for Education (2010). *The importance of teaching*. The Schools White Paper 2010. London: The Stationary Office.

Department for Education (2012a). *Education and training statistics for the United Kingdom: 2012*. London: Government Statistical Service. (Accessed at: http://www. education.gov.uk/rsgateway/DB/VOL/v001096/v01-2012.pdf)

Department for Education (2012b). *Schools, pupils, and their characteristics*, January 2012. London: Department for Education. (Accessed at http://www.education.gov.uk/ rsgateway/DB/SFR/s001071/sfr10-2012.pdf)

Department for Education (2012c). *Statistical first release: School workforce in England: November 2011*. London: Department for Education. (Accessed at http://www. education.gov.uk/rsgateway/DB/SFR/s001062/index.shtml, 20 April 2013)

Department for Education (2012d). *Huge increase in academies takes total to more than 2,300*. Press Notice 7 September 2012, London: Department for Education. (Accessed at http://www.education.gov.uk/inthenews/inthenews/a00213703/huge-increase-in-academies-takes-total-to-more-than-2300, 9 April 2012)

Department for Education (2012e). *Free schools: 55 to open this month – twice as many as this time last year*. Press Notice 7 September 2012, London: Department for Education. (Accessed at http://www.education.gov.uk/inthenews/inthenews/a00213530/new-free-schools-open , 9 April 2012)

Earley, P., Higham, R., Allen, R., Allen, T., Howson, J., Nelson, R., Rawar, S., Lynch, S., Morton., L, Mehta., P., & Sims, D. (2012). *Review of the school leadership landscape*. Nottingham: National College for School Leadership.

Eymeri-Douzens, J. M. (2011). NPM reforms legacy: A common praxeologic, a variety of acclimatizations, a renewed bureaucratization. In J. M. Eymeri-Douzens & J. Pierre (Eds.). *Administrative reforms and democratic governance*. Abingdon: Routledge.

Flinders, M. (2011). Markets, morality and democratic governance: Insights from the United Kingdom. In J. M. Eymeri-Douzens & J. Pierre (Eds.). *Administrative reforms and democratic governance*. Abingdon: Routledge.

Frost, D., Frost, R., MacBeath, J., & Pedder, D. (2009). *The influence and participation of children and young people in their learning (IPiL) project*. A paper presented at ICSEI 2009, the 22nd annual meeting of the International Congress on School Effectiveness and Improvement, Vancouver, Canada, 4-7 January.

Gillard, D. (1987). *The chief education officer: The real master of local educational provision*. (Accessed at www.educationengland.org.uk/articles/01ceo.html, 9 April 2013)

Gronn, P. (2009). Leadership configurations. *Leadership* 5 (3), 381-394.

Harris, N. (2012). Local authorities and the accountability gap in a fragmenting schools system. *The Modern Law Review*, 75(4), 511-546.

Herts for Learning (2012). *A new schools' company - educational excellence together*. (Accessed at http://www.hertsforlearning.co.uk/news/new-schools'-company-educational-excellence-together, 12 May 2013)

Hill, R., Dunford, J., Parish, N., Rea, S., & Sandals, L. (2012). *The growth of academy chains: Implications for leaders and leadership.* Nottingham: National College for School Leadership.

Lindsay, G., Muijs, D., Harris, A., Chapman, C., Arweck, E., & Goodall, J. (2007). *Schools federations pilot study. 2003-2007.* London: Department for Children, Schools and Families.

National Audit Office (2010). *The Academies Programme.* London: The Stationery Office.

National Foundation for Educational Research (2011). *Overview of education system in England, Slough: NFER.* (Accessed at https://www.nfer.ac.uk/nfer/index.cfm? 9B1817FF-C29E-AD4D-0F94-7C84904BFE2E, 14 May 2013)

Newman, J. (2001). *Modernising governance.* London: Sage.

Parish, N., Baxter, A., & Sandals, L. (2012). *Action research into the evolving role of the local authority in education: The final report for the Ministerial Advisory Group ISOS Partnership,* Research Report DFE-RR224. London: Department for Education.

Office for National Statistics (2011). *Summary: UK population projected toreach 70 million by mid-2027,* Newport: Office for National Statistics. (Accessed at http://www.ons.gov.uk/ons/dcp171780_240701.pdf, 2 April 2013)

Richards, C. (2012). Ofsted inspection inspected: An examination of the 2012 framework for school inspection and its accompanying evaluation schedule. *FORUM,* 54(2), 247-272.

Simkins, T., & Woods, P. A. (2014). Understanding the local: Themes and issues in the experience of structural reform in England. *Educational Leadership Management and Administration* (forthcoming).

Thraves, L., Fowler, J., & Carr-West, J. (2012). *Should we shed the middle tier?* London: Local Government Information Unit. (Accessed at http://www.lgiu.org.uk/wp-content/uploads/2012/09/Should-we-shed-the-middle-tier.pdf, 14 April 2013)

Woods, P. A. (2011). *Transforming education policy: Shaping a democratic future.* Bristol: Policy Press.

Woods, P. A. (2013). Drivers to holistic democracy: Signs and signals of emergent, democratic self-organising systems. In S. M. Weber, M. Göhlich, A. Schröer, H. Macha & C. Fahrenwald (Eds.). *Organisation und Partizipation: Beiträge der Kommission Organisationspädagogik,* Wiesbaden, Germany.

Woods, P. A., & Woods, G. J. (2013). Deepening distributed leadership: A democratic perspective on power, purpose and the concept of the self. *Leadership in Education* (Vodenje v vzgoji in izobraževanju), 2, 17-40.

Woods, P. A., Bennett, N., Harvey, J. A., & Wise, C. (2004). Variabilities and dualities in distributed leadership: Findings from a systematic literature review, *Educational Management Administration and Leadership,* 32 (4), 439-457.

In: The Educational Superintendent
Editor: Adam E. Nir

ISBN: 978-1-62948-972-8
© 2014 Nova Science Publishers, Inc.

*Chapter 7*

# DANISH SUPERINTENDENTS IN A COMPLEX WORLD

## *Lejf Moos*

Aarhus University, Copenhagen, Denmark

Superintendents are difficult to identify because they are in the midst of radical changes of educational politics, structures, purpose and governance. As the Danish state enters into global competition and European collaboration, many changes are being made in the public sector and in governing those sectors. Relations between the state and its institutions are being transformed from democratic, public sector governance to business-like, marketplace relations with decentralized schools and more freestanding, private schools. The public sector is governed directly from the Ministry of Education and not indirectly through municipalities.

New forms of governance are emerging. Most important are tools for strategic planning and accountability: quality reports, national test, national standards and international and national comparisons.

Municipal administration is also changing from broad and flat organizations into steeper hierarchies. Some (Christoffersen & Klausen, 2012) call the most preferred administration model, the three-layer corporate model, a professionalization: While power is made more hierarchical it is made less subject or cause oriented.

Superintendents are middle-level leaders and therefore an important link in the chain of governance between national and local politics and school leadership. They find themselves at the intersection of complex, conflicting and often contradictory demands and expectations. They need to confront tensions and handle dilemmas arising from control and trust, management and leadership. The following chapter will tell the story of the Danish superintendent.

## DENMARK

Some 6.5 million inhabitants live in Denmark. The Danish society used to be characterized by *democracy* and *equality* (a little power-distance) and as open minded and *inclusive* in contrast to other cultures (a little uncertainty-avoidance) (Hofstede, 1980). Over the past decade this may have changed as Denmark has experienced some immigration, so the image of a coherent, one-culture nation is gradually changing. The main sources of income shifted from agriculture to industry fifty years ago and are now changing to information and knowledge production.

Since World War Two, we have seen a change in economy and politics. In the years up until 1990, Danish society was described as a mainly social democratic, Nordic Welfare state with strong, productive relations between the labor market and the state: the "Flexicurity System," as it was called (Pedersen, 2010). There also were strong public institutions like social welfare and education that aimed at social justice, equity and participatory democracy (Pedersen, 2010).

As an effect of the emergence of the competition in the neo-liberal global market place, from 1980 and onwards, efforts directed towards restructuring the economy and governance for a competitive state have been made. Some of the core themes of this restructuring have been to adapt the national economy to international marketplace conditions and global competition. This has brought a shift in the aims of public institutions towards stressing New Public Management technologies like outcomes, accountability, employability and labor market competencies (Moos, 2013; Moos & Kofod, 2012).

The Danes used to call the educational system the "World's Best" until PISA showed a different picture (Eurydice, 2012, p. 37).

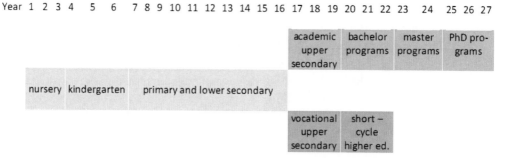

Figure 1. Levels of education in the Danish educational system.

# THE DANISH EDUCATIONAL SYSTEM

*Kindergarten (age 3-6):* The general starting point for most Danish children's educational career is attending kindergarten from age 3-6. Approximately 80% of children of that age attend private day-care or a day-care institution because the number of parents who are active in the labor market is very high: 90% of the fathers and mothers of children attending day-care work (Samspil, 2012).

Prior to kindergarten, most children aged six months through to three years attend day nursery (11,171 children in 2011) or childcare in private homes (56,345 children) out of a total number of 193,000 0-3-year-old children. This means that 35% of the children in this age category attend those nurseries or childcare (Statistikbanken, 2012).

*Folkeskolen (basic school, age 6-16):* The Folkeskole is structured so that there is one year of pre-school class (0), nine years of primary and lower secondary education and a one-year 10th form. Education is compulsory in Denmark for everyone between the ages of 6-7 and 16. Whether the education is received in a publicly provided school, in a private school or at home is a matter of individual, parental choice, as long as accepted standards are met. It is education itself that is compulsory, not school.

The legal frames for basic schooling in Denmark describe the aims. There has been a slide from focusing on participation in a democracy towards educating for employability (the competencies and the willingness to be a part of the labor force).

The Folkeskole has for 20 years been a fully comprehensive school system with no streaming in high and low performing students. Students attend the same schools, but do not necessarily attend the same classes as their peers.

*Immigrant students:* Children of immigrants are called bilingual children. In 2009/10 there were 72,000 bilingual students in the Folkeskole, or 10% of all students (Nyidanmark, 2012).

*Students with special needs:* As was the case in the Salamanca Declaration (UNESCO, 1994), inclusion in the Danish political discussion is argued on two different bases: the social justice perspective and the rising economic difficulties. In 2011, approximately 84,000 students received special needs education, which is 14.3% of all students in the Folkeskole. Expenditures for this are approximately 30% of the overall expenditures for the Folkeskole.

*Restructuring of the school system:* The number of basic schools has been reduced over the past few years, mainly as a consequence of a restructuring of the public sector from 2007 (that will be described in more depth in the next section). By 2011 there were 1,388 public Folkeskoler with 573,393 students, 526 freestanding/private basic schools with 96,071 students, 266 continuation schools (grade 8 or 9) with 24,454 students and 200 special needs schools with 10,040 students (Service, 2012).

Danish society has also undergone demographic changes. Like other European countries, it is now characterized by an increasing number of elderly. This is significant to basic schooling as projections show that the number in the 5-9 age group will decrease by 3.5% in Denmark while it will increase by 5.2% in EU between 2010-2020.

*Freestanding and private basic schools:* By 2009 approximately 13.5% of students attended private schools (Eurydice, 2012, p. 33). The EU average is 18%. A few of those are affiliated with religious groups, but most of them were built on the same values and norms as the Folkeskole. The main purpose of the legislation on private schools is to give parents a choice. The choices, however, are more often led by social rather than educational motives, and recently also geographical motives. When small country schools are closed to keep down public spending, in many cases they are replaced by private schools initiated by resourceful parents. The number of private schools is rising, and so is the number of students attending private schools.

# DECENTRALIZATION OF THE EDUCATIONAL GOVERNANCE SYSTEM

Regulation of the Danish school system has over the last two decades changed in many ways. At the beginning of the 1990s there was a strong, general move to decentralize finances, personnel management and other areas from state level to local (municipal) level and in many cases, later on, to the school level. This was introduced at a time when Denmark like other countries was in a difficult economic situation. At the end of the 1990s a re-centralization of the goal-setting and evaluation of schools was also observed (Tanggaard, 2011).

There are several reasons behind the move to decentralize (Official Journal C 300, 2007). A few examples can illustrate this: the increased influence of parents at school level by organizing school boards and also parents' free choice of schools; the management by objectives and the goal- and result-oriented system gave focus to the professional ability and responsibility on different levels of the steering system, especially on teachers and principals. It was argued that if the state would decentralize tasks to schools, they could cut down on local educational administration staff (Torfing, 2004).

A restructuring of public management was made when 171 municipalities were merged into 98 larger units in 2007, now with at least 30,000 inhabitants (Interiour, 2005). This has brought about new relations and positions as well as new chains of governance: Many municipalities are structured as concerns/groups with a steep hierarchy and a unified pattern of management, often called a "three-layer" structure (i.e., a second administrative layer is inserted between the political boards and schools). Approximately 60% of all municipalities have a mix of traditional, "two-layer" structure, with direct lines between the institutions through the superintendent to the political school board, and the new business-like/enterprise structure: Fewer political boards with their own director are now governing all institutions (Christoffersen & Klausen, 2012). This means that each of them takes care of a broader field of activities. In the superintendent survey[1] we see combinations of school, pre-school, leisure-time institutions, social affairs, Danish education for immigrants, adult education, culture and more (Moos, 2011).

Many large municipalities have also established a new middle-layer between municipal administration and institutions: districts. A superintendent can supervise 4-5 district leaders who take care of 5-6 schools and other institutions each. Within the new municipalities many schools have been shut down or merged into bigger schools.

Whenever the educational system is decentralized, the balance between professional and political power on all levels in the system is changed. The responsibility for and professional ability of principals and teachers are enhanced at the same time as the dual process of setting targets and evaluating the degree to which they are met becomes an important instrument for governing: ... *In using more control and in seeing the educational system as being in a global competition, the politics of education will be more and more reactive in its scope...* (Official Journal C 318, 2008/C 319).

In a period which includes a strong trend of re-centralization of the content of schools (curricula and accountability), the schools find themselves in charge of finances, human resources and day-to-day operations, and at the same time the municipalities have become an important factor in the Ministry's quality assurance system.

Municipalities run their operations based on objectives and frameworks established by Parliament and government. There is discretion in determining how the operation is to be organized in order to achieve the objectives. For example: what resources will be used, how will it be organized, how will the premises be designed and to some extent what staff will be

---

[1] The data presented in the following sections are derived from the Danish part of the Nordic Survey on Superintendents (Moos, 2011) http://pure.au.dk/portal/files/44475188/110808_Danish_Superintendents.pdf.

employed? Regardless of how a municipality decides to organize and run the work, they must guarantee all children and students an equal education.

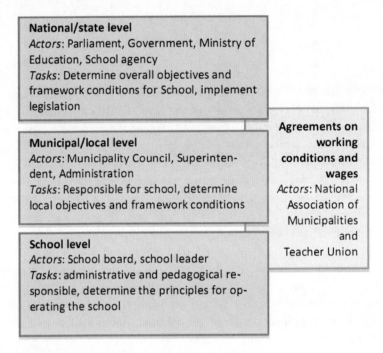

Figure 2. The Danish educational system.

## SUPERINTENDENTS IN THE NEW REALM OF EDUCATIONAL GOVERNANCE

Superintendents used to be positioned in the middle of a parallel chain of governance from national to institutional level: from the political committee (Parliament) and the administrative agency (Ministry) at the national level to two municipal levels. The first level is the political committee (Municipal Council) and administration (Municipal Administration) and the second level is a School Board and Superintendency. Finally at the institutional level there is a School Board with a parental majority for each school and a school leadership. The superintendent is positioned in the middle of this chain at the municipal administration level and thus accountable to municipal principles and national regulations, while servicing and monitoring schools.

The Danish educational system is part of and thus influenced by transnational tendencies but, built on Danish structures and culture, it is also special. Traditionally, municipalities have been important factors in the governance of public sectors, and decentralized educational governance has been a very central part of the Danish educational self-understanding.

Taken together, the present governance model appears to be a joint regulatory enterprise between the state and the municipality sector through a range of "hard" and "soft" steering instruments and quality control. There is a "mixed" mode of regulation that is important for understanding the current context of superintendent leadership in different municipalities in Denmark (Moos, 2009a).


## SUPERINTENDENTS

There are 98 municipalities in Denmark. Each of them is a school district with political boards and administrations with directors. The directors responsible for schools are usually called superintendents. In the survey, however, we find 17 different titles for this position because more than half of the municipalities have allocated more areas to the political board like: day care, leisure time, family matters (Moos, 2011).

"Typical" superintendents are male (only 25% are female), in their mid-fifties and most of them are relatively newly appointed. Superintendents typically studied education and acquired professional experiences within education. They made their career within the municipal educational system. However, with the new, bigger and more overarching administrations, there is a tendency to employ more administrative/management-trained superintendents.

Following public advertisement, the Municipal Board appoints superintendents. Their appointment is typically contract-based, normally lasting 3-5 years.

*The superintendent-board relation*: Superintendents work on a broad range of tasks, being the civil servants positioned between the political, municipal level and the schools. They are responsible for administering the municipal budget for this sector, which includes monitoring how institutions manage their budget. They are responsible for implementing national as well as municipal-political decisions and strategies and monitoring how institutions manage those tasks and are thus an important link in the chain of governance. Superintendents are the contact persons and personnel managers of school leaders. When asked what are their three most important tasks, they list: 1) school and educational development, 2) leading school leaders and their professional development and 3) providing advice to politicians. They are also expected to be active in collaborating with peers and leaders in institutions (Torfing, 2004).

Superintendents feel they are autonomous. Being close to the political decision-making level, they are able to shape decisions. When asked about the expectations of the Chair of the political Board from superintendents, they list the following:

1)  take care of complaints;
2)  give a professional description of issues to the political committee and prepare clear and worked-through descriptions to the agenda of the committee;
3)  provide a good orientation of what is going on in the district and follow up on individual cases;
4)  establish links between the politicians and citizens' needs;
5)  monitor schools; 6) work loyally to implement the political decisions in dialogue with leaders of institutions.

The second and third priorities are important leadership tasks: This is where decisions are made because the *premises* for decision-making are being constructed and it is where it is being decided who may make decisions. The next priorities point to the *connection*-phase of decision-making processes: What is happening to decisions; who is monitoring and leading these processes?

Seen in the light of decision making in a three phase process, we can see that the superintendents consider themselves part, or they are part, of very important functions relating to policy making (Moos, 2009b), the construction of premises closely associated with the preparations of legislation and regulations made in formal and informal networks.

When superintendents refer to people they consult when making decisions, they refer to three priority layers:

- *High priorities*: City Council, chair of committee, school leaders, high level administrators, parents' boards.
- *Middle layer*: parents, teachers, consultants, students, deputy chair of committee, and local professional associations.
- *Low priorities*: citizens, local lobbyists, local trade, and religious groups.

The priorities are clear: The high priority layer includes individuals who hold leading positions within the municipal hierarchy.

Hence, it appears that Danish superintendents are policy makers who are also involved in the implementation of educational processes. They have professional autonomy that enables them to decide with whom to consult. They are civil servants who consider themselves policy makers as well as civil servants: They are centrally positioned when it comes to the construction of premises for decision making, for their implementation and for connecting decisions to practices.

*Superintendent and school leaders:* Superintendents work in multiple fields and with many different stakeholders in a highly political system. The main function is to mediate between political and administrative managers and educational practitioners, especially the school leaders.

When superintendents were asked to describe their most important role tasks, the following emerged:

- Interaction with school leaders
- Interaction with leaders of other institutions that are within the governance of the political board
- Interaction with politicians

Most important stakeholders are the school leaders, the political level, the committee, and the overall municipal level. The mediating role produces a number of dilemmas of choice between what is interesting, meaningful or time-consuming and between different values.

It also produces dilemmas of choice between loyalty towards the political/administrative system and the practitioners, like stretching rules, and ethical dilemmas in the interface between practitioners and governing structures. The image these statements provide indicates that most superintendents do stretch rules and procedure and they question the governing structures. They sometimes experience making decisions that school leaders more readily accept than do politicians. Overall we get an image of a mediator who translates municipal policies and decisions for school leaders. Those activities mean that superintendents influence school leaders to act in line with politics and decisions. That takes place in cross pressures of many kinds and is accompanied – or produces – a number of dilemmas of choice, e.g., between economic responsibilities and educational needs when deciding on class size or on teacher-student ratio.

School leaders are the primary subordinates or collaborators of superintendents. They communicate person to person through mentoring and dialogue. And they support school leaders in thinking strategically. Danish superintendents prioritize face-to-face interaction with school leaders: communication and sparring, but also through work concerning the school and municipal organization and quality reports. When asked to write the three most important tasks in their work with school leaders, superintendents mention communicating with school leaders and advancing their development as the most important function. Superintendents express their interest in leading school leaders and giving them support. The development of the school organization and school district, attitudes and resources is the second priority mentioned, and the third priority is working on quality reports. Relations between superintendents and school leaders are direct, as only 7% said there was another level of leadership – like district leaders – between themselves and school leaders.

## QUALITY ASSURANCE

A major role of superintendents is monitoring and maintaining national quality assurance. Quality assurance and development relations between state, municipalities and schools are pivotal elements of the chain of governance. Parliament legislates and government implements the legislation, issuing regulations and setting the educational agenda. As more tasks and responsibilities have been decentralized from state to municipal and school level over the past 20 years, there has been a need for the legislators and the Ministry to strengthen the couplings between the levels in ways other than the regulatory ones. Thus, new forms and technologies of quality assurances have been developed and implemented in the governance structures, e.g., the quality report.

The next level in the governance chain is the educational administration with the superintendent in the municipalities. This level is responsible for the overall quality of education within the municipality. This includes the monitoring of school outcomes in national tests, arranging and monitoring local, municipal testing and for the work on the Quality Reports. The Quality Report construction is a kind of public governance contract. The national level sets out the frames and aims of education and an overarching template for the Quality Reports. The municipal level – the political board and superintendent - details the frames and aims and also the template for the report in line with local policies. Schools write the reports on a number of issues (the number of sick days reported by the staff, the money used for teachers and other staff, etc.) and they formulate the goals for one or three year within a number of issues. Some of those are laid out by the administration, and some are chosen by the school itself.

Every year the schools evaluate the results for the year and formulate the aims for the next year. The mixture of fixed issues and broader issues of school choice with the self-evaluation procedures aims at producing a strong sense of responsibility and accountability.

The Quality Reports Act (Education, 2007) stipulated that reports from all schools serve as the basis for a dialogue with the administration and as the basis for an annual, municipal report to the Ministry.

The chain of governance is of course built on the premise that all levels are competent in doing their part: schools, administration and Ministry. This part will look into the responses that can be linked to quality assurance and development.

Judging from answers to questions about the number of school administration staff engaged in work on quality assurance, we think the number is very low, in many cases less than one (full-time) position. Other studies are also concerned with the level of quality assurance-expertise in municipal administration: In the EVA study (2009) and studies by Shewbridge and colleagues (2011) as well as Rambøll (2010) there are some concerns as to the strengths of the quality assurance and development competencies in the municipal administrations, even as the superintendents themselves indicate that the Quality Report is seen as by far the most important national reform.

## DISCUSSION

The Danish school system has, as already mentioned, been affected by comprehensive public sector reforms over the last two decades (Moos, 2006). Decentralization of powers, authorities and responsibilities from the state to the municipalities has been a major trend in all Nordic countries (Johansson, Moos, Nihlfors, Paulsen & Risku, 2011), which in theory should lead to higher degrees of freedom and scope for problem-solving and policy making at the local level. On the other hand, it has also been claimed that the state to some extent only has changed the mode of regulation towards more subtle and indirect steering instruments (Moos, 2009b). Municipalities, schools, teachers and pupils are subjected to external evaluation and assessment (Hudson, 2007). Moreover, accountability is strengthened through making results from national tests and evaluations available on special websites, paired with the formation of a ministerial control department where the streams of reports, assessments and performance data are assembled. A mixed mode system of hard and soft governance in the relationship between central agencies and local agents is, thus, evident in the Nordic countries (Moos, 2009b). In theoretical terms, this means the coexistence of loose and tight couplings (Meyer & Scott, 1983; Weick, 2001) between the state and the municipalities.

This shift then contextualizes superintendent leadership at the intersection between accountability, quality control and indirect steering from the state and local government priorities. The present situation gives rise to the following question: Is the Danish superintendent typically a quality control agent on behalf of the state, or a local leadership facilitator who advocates professional school interests? The duality embedded in the school governance context finds resonance in the reported data about the superintendents' individual role interpretation and priorities of leadership tasks. On one hand, the current study portrays a profession oriented learning facilitator as the prototype of the superintendent. Superintendents mention the development and advancement of schools, the leading of school leaders and taking care of their ongoing professional development, and making sure that political goals are implemented as the three most important tasks they fulfill. The monitoring and dialogue on student outcomes is mentioned as the 8th priority.

This image can clearly be interpreted in ways that underscore superintendents' inclination to build on leadership and trust rather than on management and control.

This image is manifested in content and priorities of the superintendents' regular meetings with their school leaders. The data describe frequent discussions around pedagogical "investments" to reach better results for the pupils, paired with discussions on the development of school leaders' competencies. On the other hand, more managerial issues such as economic challenges, financial planning and implementation of strategic decisions are also frequently reported themes with which school principals engage (Johansson, 2010). Taken together, the dominant image of preferred leadership style among superintendents is the one of a professional learning facilitator with focus on pupil orientation.

# REFERENCES

Christoffersen, H., & Klausen, K. K. (2012). *Den danske kommunekonstruktion [The Danish Municipal Construction]*. Odense: Syddansk Universitetsforlag.

Consolidation Act on Quality Report and Action Plans (2007).

Education (2007). Consolidation Act on Quality Report and Action Plans. BEK 167/2007, Ministry of Education, Copenhagen.

Eurydice (2012). *Key Data on Education in Europe 2012*. Brussels: European Commission.

EVA (2009). *Kommunernes arbejde med kvalitetsrapporter.* [Municipal work on Quality Reports]. København: Danmarks Evalueringsinstitut.

Hofstede, G. (1980). *Culture's consequences: International differences in work-related values.* Beverly Hills: Sage.

Hudson, C. (2007). Governing the governance of education: The state strikes back? *European Educationa Research Journal, 6*(3), 266-282.

Interiour, M. f. H. a. t. (2005). *Kommunalreformen - kort fortalt [The Municipal Reform - in short]*. Retrieved from http://www.sm.dk/data/Lists/Publikationer/Attachments/271/kommunalreformen_kort_fortalt.pdf. Retrieved on June 16th, 2013.

Johansson, O. (2010). Skolchefens funktion och scen. In J. Höög & O. Johansson (Eds.), *Struktur, kultur, ledarkap – förutsättningar för framgångsrika skolor? [Structure, culture. leadership - preconditions for successful schools?]*. Lund: Studentlitteratur.

Johansson, O., Moos, L., Nihlfors, E., Paulsen, J. M., & Risku, M. (2011). The Nordic superintendents' leadership roles: Cross national comparisons. In T. Townsend & J. MacBeath (Eds.), *The international handbook of leadership for learning*. Dordrecht: Springer.

Meyer, J. W., & Scott, W. R. (1983). *Organizational environments. Ritual and rationality.* London: Sage.

Moos, L. (2006 ). What kinds of democracy in education are facilitated by supra- and transnational agencies? *European Educational Research Journal, 5*(3 & 4), 160-168.

Moos, L. (2009a). Hard and soft governance: The journey from transnational agencies to school leadership. *European Educationa Research Journal, 8*(3), 397-406.

Moos, L. (2009b). A general context for new social technologies. *Nordic Educational Research, 29*(1), 79-92.

Moos, L. (2011). *Superintendent leadership in Danish municipalities*. Copenhagen: Aarhus University.

Moos, L. (2013). Prelude: Tuning the instrument. In L. Moos (Ed.), *Transnational influences on values and practices in Nordic educational leadership - is there a Nordic model?* Dordrecht: Springer

Moos, L., & Kofod, K. K. (2012). Denmark: Bildung in a competitive state? In K. S. Louis & B. v. Velzen (Eds.), *Educational policy in an international context - Political culture and its effects*. New York: Palgrave Macmillan

Nyidanmark (2012). http://www.nyidanmark.dk/NR/rdonlyres/B15D7142-1B3F-4C40-B245-47C12F6D7A5F/0/tal_fakta_sep_2010.pdf.

Official Journal C 300 (2007). *Conclusions of the Council and the Representatives of the Governments of the Member States, meeting within the Council, on improving the quality of teacher education.*

Official Journal C 318 (2008/C 319). *Conclusions of the Council and the Representatives of the Governments of the Member States, meeting within the Council of 21 November 2008 on preparing young people for the 21st century: An agenda for European Cooperaton on schools.*

Pedersen, O. K. (2010). *Konkurrencestaten [The Competitive State]*. Copenhagen: Hans Reitzels Forlag.

Rambøll (2010). *Country Background report*. Denmark for: OECD Review on Evaluation and Assessment Framework for Improving School outcomes. Copenhagen: Rambøll.

Samspil (2012). http://www.samspil.info/files/PDF Artikler/2010/Samspil_nr23_dec_2009.pdf. Retrieved June 16, 2013

Service (2012). http://www.uvm.dk/Service/Statistik/Statistik-om-folkeskolen-og-frie-skoler/Statistik-om-elever-i-folkeskolen-og-frie-skoler/Elevtal-i-folkeskolen-og-frie-skoler.

Shewbridge, C., Jang, E., Matthews, P., & Santiago, P. (2011). *OECD Reviews of Evaluation and Assessment in Education*. Denmark, 143. Paris: OECD.

Statistikbanken (2012). http://www.statistikbanken.dk/statbank5a/default.asp?w=1920, 2012 #808.

Tanggaard, L. (2011). *Innovativ evaluering i uddannelse [Innovative evaluation in education]*. In K. Andreasen, NannaFriche & A. Rasmussen (Eds.), *Målt & vejet* (pp. 237-254). Aalborg: Aalborg Universitetsforlag.

Torfing, J. (2004). *Det stille sporskifte i velfærdsstaten [The silent switch]*. Aarhus: Aarhus Universitetsforlag.

UNESCO (1994). *Final Report: World conference on special needs education: Access and quality.*

Weick, K. E. (2001). *Making sense of the organization*. Malden: Blackwell.

In: The Educational Superintendent
Editor: Adam E. Nir

ISBN: 978-1-62948-972-8
© 2014 Nova Science Publishers, Inc.

*Chapter 8*

# LOOKING FOR SUPERINTENDENTS IN AUSTRALIA: THE CASES OF VICTORIA AND WESTERN AUSTRALIA

*David Gurr[1], Simon Clarke[2], Lawrie Drysdale[1]*
*and Helen Wildy[2]*
[1]The University of Melbourne, Australia
[2]The University of Western Australia

## INTRODUCTION

Australia has a Commonwealth government that oversees six State and two Territory governments. Education in Australia is a complex interplay between these different levels of government, and between government and non-government schools. There are almost 9,500 schools serving 3.5 million students in Australia. Two-thirds of students attend a government school, 20% a Catholic school, and 14% attend a range of independent schools (Australian Government, 2011). The responsibility for the provision of government schooling constitutionally rests with the State and Territory governments, but increasingly there has been Commonwealth government influence especially in terms of significant grants to both government and non-government schools, the development of a national curriculum, the creation of a national accountability system through the development by the Australian Curriculum, Assessment and Reporting Authority (ACARA) of a national assessment program in literacy and numeracy at years 3, 5, 7 and 9, and a national data collection and reporting program through the My School website (www.myschool.edu.au), and in the provision of means-tested living allowances for students aged 16 and over. The non-government sector is dominated by the large system of Catholic schools coordinated through various Dioceses that serve approximately 20% of all school age children. Apart from the Catholic emphasis and a higher proportion of private income funding the schools, the Catholic system is similar to that of the government, typically adopting similar approaches to curriculum, pedagogy and assessment. Independent schools include a range of religious (e.g., Anglican, Coptic Orthodox, Greek Orthodox, Islamic, Jewish, Lutheran and Seventh Day Adventist) and non-religious (e.g., Montessori and Steiner) schools. The proportion of students attending non-government schools has increased, rising from about 4% of students in 1970 to 14% in 2010 (Australian Government, 2011). In some jurisdictions the proportion attending non-government schools is particularly high, with, for example, the proportion of students attending non-government secondary schools in Victoria standing at 43% in 2012 (Department of Education and Early Childhood Development, 2012a).

The educational landscape is complex, for example, in a recent paper Gurr and Drysdale (2012) highlighted tensions and dilemmas principals face that are related to teaching and learning (education trends such as personalization, the construction of new learning environments and the implication of these for more collaborative teaching, and consideration of the type of leadership needed for contemporary schools), developing people (teacher quality, rewarding teacher, and leadership preparation), and external pressures (the introduction of a national curriculum, and increasing accountability through initiatives such as the public reporting of school performance data). An area of complexity, however, that has received minimal research or commentary is the supervision of schools. Gurr (1999, 2003, 2007), has commented on accountability systems used in Australian education systems, and Gurr, Drysdale and Walkley (2012), Walkley (2012 a, b, c), Anderson (2006), Mulford, Hogan and Lamb (2001) and Gammage (1996 a, b; Gamage, Sipple & Partridge, 1995, 1996) have commented on school governance. Yet, there is no literature that we know of that has attempted to investigate the role of the superintendent in the contemporary Australian setting. In this chapter we do this by taking the cases of the State of Victoria and the State of Western Australia to show how complex and difficult it is to describe the role of school superintendents in the Australian context.

## THE CASE OF VICTORIA

School education is provided in Victoria through 1,537 government schools (68% of all schools), 486 Catholic schools (22%) and 215 independent schools (10%) (DEECD, 2012a). The Department of Education and Early Childhood Development (DEECD) provides policy and frameworks that seek to deliver high quality education in all school sectors. In addition, Catholic schools are governed by one of four Catholic dioceses in Victoria (Melbourne, Ballarat, Sale and Sandhurst; Melbourne is the largest diocese with 329 schools), while independent schools have various governance arrangements (Gurr, Drysdale & Walkley, 2012). Within the government sector, which is the subject of this section, there are 1,137 primary, 75 primary/secondary, 245 secondary, 76 special and 4 language schools (DEECD, 2012a).

In the 100 years that ensued after the establishment of the government school system of education in Victoria through the Education Act of 1872, Victoria operated a highly centralized and bureaucratic inspection process that focused on individual teacher and school performance. Inspectors acted on behalf of the education system and were accountable to the director general of education. These inspectors, in many ways, acted like superintendents through their monitoring of teacher and school performance. However, they were not involved in policy development and had no financial controls. Since the 1970s, under threat by the teacher unions (Nash & Spaull, 1986; Spaull & Hince, 1986), the inspection system was abandoned and replaced by school improvement plans (Macpherson, 1982; Victorian

Education Department, 1982) and the establishment of school councils that included elected members of the school community (State of Victoria, 1975). Councils became responsible for policy development, maintenance of buildings, and aspects of finance, as outlined in "Ministerial Paper 4: School Councils" (State of Victoria, 1983). This was the beginning of a move to school self-management that continues in the present, although its zenith was possibly when self-governing schools were created briefly in 1998 and 1999 before a change of government occurred. These schools received a single-line budget and were free to spend this (including hiring appropriate staff) provided they met the terms of agreement signed between the school and the government (Self-Governing Schools program expanded, *News Release,* Office of the Minister for Education, May 16, 1999).

By the 1990s there was concern that without inspection, or some type of external supervision, there was no way of knowing how successful schools were. In response an accountability framework was established to monitor and make schools more accountable for their performance. This was in response to a new shift toward self-management with the Schools of the Future initiative (Caldwell, Gurr, Hill & Rowe, 1997). The government school system introduced school reviews in 1998 that were a combination of internal and external review processes (Gurr, 2003). Every three years, schools conducted a self-evaluation of their performance based on a number of performance indicators, which an external reviewer verified. In 2005 as a result of the *Blueprint for Government Schools* (State of Victoria, 2003), the accountability framework was modified, differentiated reviews were introduced based on performance, and school reviews conducted every four years. The role of the external reviewer changed from that of a verifier to a critical friend and school improvement advisor. In December 2011, the then newly elected Liberal-National Party Coalition government developed a new policy and direction for state education: "Victoria as a Learning Community" (Dixon, 2011; also see DEECD, 2011). This marks a new emphasis toward school autonomy, focusing on choice, local decision making, and school–community integration. In July 2012, the DEECD produced its draft strategic plan for 2012–2016, which focused on "lifting the state's education and development outcomes into the global top tier over the next ten years" (DEECD, 2012b, p. 3). The document emphasizes four key outcomes: achievement, engagement, well-being and productivity. Furthering the push towards school autonomy, at the time of writing this chapter, the DEECD produced a policy document, *The Compact: Roles and responsibilities in Victorian government school education* (DEECD, 2013a), which outlines the key accountability arrangements of principals and schools. These include the requirement for schools to meet legislative and regulatory requirements and guidelines outlined in various Acts of Parliament, adhere to minimum performance standards and curriculum polices and guidelines, follow contract accountabilities, and meet responsibilities and guidelines for governance arrangements, school accountability, human resources, teacher registration and student engagement. The government has made clear its intention to update and modify these accountabilities over time (DEECD 2013a), and, for example, is proposing to eliminate the role of the external reviewer and replace it with a system of peer review. Currently, models of peer review are being evaluated.

At the same time as the school accountability process has undergone review, so too has the administrative structure of the Victorian Education Department. In the 1990s, regions were an important element, but by 1999 there was discussion that regions might be removed. A change of government in 1999 meant that this did not happen, and over the next decade the role of regions in supervising schools became more important. With the current government, regions have been reduced from eight to four, regional staff have been reduced, and there is a renewed emphasis on school self-management, with schools being encouraged to form networks to support each other as part of a "schools as learning communities" focus (DEECD, 2011) mentioned above.

The Independent Public Schools described in the Western Australian section are perhaps the closest example to self-governing schools that currently exists in Australian government school systems, although proposed changes to the Victorian government system are moving towards the self-governing model. As was mentioned above, at the time of writing this chapter the Victorian government outlined the introduction of a school compact (DEECD, 2013a), which sets out shared understanding between Victorian government schools and the government regarding their respective roles and responsibilities. It is an agreement between Victorian government schools and the Department and it seeks to improve the learning and development of children and young people by:

- clarifying the accountabilities of schools to their community and the system, and minimizing compliance requirements;
- clarifying existing responsibilities of schools and the Department;
- describing existing flexibility available to schools in the management of resources and operations;
- outlining the role of the Department in providing support, resources and guidance.

(DEECD, 2013a, p. 1)

The document underpins the government ethos towards increased autonomy and professional trust. The Compact delineates the school and department responsibilities under five key principles (DEECD, 2013a, pp. 3-8):

1. All students can exercise education choices that meet their learning needs, aspirations and interests, and will be supported to reach their full potential.
2. Schools and the Department share a professional commitment to continual, evidence-based improvement in teaching and learning and to improving student outcomes.
3. Schools provide inclusive, safe and orderly environments for all members of the school community.
4. Resources are managed effectively, efficiently and fairly to deliver the best possible education experiences for all students.
5. Schools and the Department are open and responsive to our communities, and are held accountable for outcomes.

Furthering the push to school autonomy, there is currently a review of governance in Victorian government schools that foreshadows school governing bodies employing principals, managing principal performance, and the granting of more flexibility in determining teacher career structure within the school. The terms of reference also included consideration of corporate approaches to governance, including expert membership on councils or partnerships with non-school organizations (DEECD, 2013b).

Clearly we have struggled to locate the superintendent in the recent history of Victorian education. The current reform in Victoria questions the whole concept of the superintendent as many of the functions and responsibilities that are typically associated with the school superintendent are now delegated to the school. The review by Nir (2014) that opens this book indicates the immense variety in what constitutes the work of superintendents. Without reciting the references Nir has used, the description included: acting as a mediator between competing stakeholder demands; educational, instructional, political and managerial leaders; working in schools with principals and teachers to improve instruction, provide direction, and assist with or control human and financial resources; executive officer of a school board overseeing a school system; acting as a system leader; and so forth. It is this last aspect, system leadership, that is perhaps most pertinent to the Victorian context in the wake of recent research that explores system leadership in Victorian government schools during 2010 and 2011 (Butler, 2014); the reader should note that, as described above, the system has changed yet again, but that this research provides some empirical evidence of how the role of superintendent might be perceived in Victoria.

Butler's research used interviews with four central senior managers (including the public service head of the DEECD, the Secretary, and members of the senior management team of the Office of Government School Education), three regional directors, 14 regional network leaders (RNL) and 23 principals to examine system leadership within the Victorian government education system. The construction of the RNL role was announced late in 2008 (Pike, 2008), with the first commencing in 2009. RNLs were located in one of seven regions, and had responsibility for 20 to 30 schools, supporting principals and the school communities and also acting in a line management role for system initiatives and processes (such as supporting the school accountability process). Butler (2011, p. 1) described this as regulatory action "to deliberately construct a narrowly but explicitly defined system leader role within education." The concept of system leadership explored by Butler is focused on building capacity for improvement in more than one school, and to generate change through system connections. From his research, Butler (2014) arrived at the following definition of system leadership:

> System leadership is the ability to generate change across a system or nested system where this involves creating, utilizing or exploiting connections within the system.

It is a modest definition in many respects. While it captures the core focus of the superintendent role, and that is, to improve a system of schools, it lacks mention of the typical control/power mechanisms attributed to the superintendency, such as governance, fiscal and human resource management, direction setting, accountability and so forth. It is, however, an inclusive definition in that it allows many managers at different levels to demonstrate system leadership. In Butler's research, senior managers were clearly viewed as system leaders. There were expectations and indications that RNLs could also be system leaders, but many also viewed their role as being more concerned with line management and compliance. Principals were not generally seen to be system leaders, primarily because of their focus on their school, and also because of competitive pressures not to support the work of other schools.

So, if we were going to locate superintendents in the Victorian system, they would most easily be found within the senior management roles, especially that of Secretary of the

DEECD, the Deputy Secretary Office of Government School Education, and the four regional directors. They all have budgetary controls, and are involved in setting system directions, monitoring accountability, supporting building improvement and so forth. They are also heavily involved in policy and process developments that lead to change "across a system or nested system where this involves creating, utilizing or exploiting connections within the system." It should be noted that in Victoria, school employment has long been devolved to the school level, including the appointment of a principal. These senior managers are all somewhat removed from schools, and none would work directly with schools on a regular basis. The work undertaken by RNLs in the former manifestation of their role prior to the recent change of government and policy did typically engage them with schools on an almost daily basis, often focused on work that directly impacts on the work of teachers. Many also were involved in promoting change among the schools in their network, and all would have been involved in principal performance appraisal and school accountability. However, RNLs were not involved in setting system directions, and they had no direct fiscal, building or human resource control (other than principal appraisal). RNL's work relied more on the trust dimension of superintendent work described by Nir (2014); they did not have sufficient power to engage much with the control aspect. Conversely, senior department managers rely more on control than trust, as they are too removed from schools to establish the type of relationships needed to promote trust. The exception is that of the regional director role. Some of these directors have in the past established strong, positive relations with schools and so can use both the trust and control dimensions of the superintendent role described by Nir (2014).

Indeed, it may be this role that most closely approximates superintendents in other jurisdictions; they have sufficient influence in aspects such as direction, budgets, buildings and accountability to exert control over schools, while they are close enough to schools to establish positive relationships that lead to using trust for influencing schools. For readers seeking more information on this role, Hopkins, Munro and Craig (2011) describe the school improvement journey of the former Northern Metropolitan Region led by Wayne Craig as the Regional Director. This book tells the story of how Craig led the improvement of this region through the development of a school improvement framework, Powerful Learning, the use of experts in literacy, numeracy and student welfare, and the support of RNLs, principals and teachers in a collective effort to improve student learning. The current regional directors include three males and one female, selected by the DEECD through an open advertisement process, appointed with five-year contracts, and responsible to the Secretary of the DEECD and Deputy Secretary Office for Government School Education (DEECD). While there are no publicly available job descriptions, regions are designed to implement department policy, and regional directors are the leaders of the region. Any of the aforementioned may make claim to the role of superintendent, with the regional director being the most likely candidate. The recent introduction of *The Compact* (DEECD, 2013a) makes this less clear. Far more responsibility is being placed in the hands of schools. The senior bureaucrats are becoming more removed from school operations. It can be argued that the role and function of the superintendent as one person or position in a system is now redundant in such a devolved system where self-governance is the new frontier. In the next section we move to another example of a relatively devolved Australian government education system, and again try to locate the role of superintendent.

# THE CASE OF WESTERN AUSTRALIA

Before the case of the "superintendent" in the state of Western Australia (WA) is presented, it is useful to provide contextual information on the geography and demography of the region, both of which play a part in shaping the role of the "superintendent." Australia is a large land mass, similar in size to China. Western Australia, with an area of 2.6 million square kilometers, makes up one third of the country. At 3.5 times the area of Texas, WA is the second largest state/province in the world. However, its population is sparse. Compared with China with a population of 1.4 billion, and the U.S.A. with a population of 315.4 million, Australia's population in 2011 was only 22.9 million, of whom 2.3 million are found in WA and most of these people reside in the metropolitan area of its capital city, Perth. The 2010 World Bank Annual Report indicates the population density of China to be 142.43 persons per square kilometer, and U.S.A. to be 33.83 persons per square kilometer. Australia has 3.0 persons per square kilometer, making it one of the most sparsely populated land masses on the planet. Western Australia is even more sparsely populated, with only 0.9 persons per square kilometer. The challenge for a centralized education authority is to provide equitably for its small population concentrated in cities and regional centers in the south west corner of the vast state, hugging its coast line and sprinkled lightly across its farming, mining and desert center.

At the time of writing, the state education authority consists of 765 schools catering for 267,643 students aged from 5 to 17 years (Kindergarten to Year 12), in Primary schools (K – 7), Secondary schools (8 – 12), District High schools (K – 10) and Senior Colleges (11 – 12). These schools are currently supported by eight regional education directors, the evolution of which is chronicled in the next section of the chapter. Of these only two are female. Given the evolving nature of the role, it is not surprising that the positions are not tenured; they are selected from within the employees of the education department through an application and interview process for a five year contract. The role is considered critical in delivering a public school system that empowers school communities, according to the rhetoric of the education department. Operationally, the role provides a high degree of administrative and managerial support to the schools in its region. For example, the regional education director deals with complaints, disputes and crises that escalate beyond the school level, a function that consumes at least half the time of the director, according to feedback from its incumbents. The director also monitors each school's performance, through a series of routinely and automatically collated and generated indicators as well as responding with support for schools designated to be "underperforming." The role comprises support for Network Principals, interagency collaboration, and compliance with systemic policies, programs and initiatives. The regional education director is the line manager for school principals, except principals of Independent Public Schools who answer directly to the Director General. Regional education directors represent the Education Department in the local public arena and may be called to resolve local community issues that relate to the school. In terms of accountability upwards, the regional education director contributes to policy and program development by the Corporative Executive and is accountable to the Director General.

The role is challenging, embracing both judge and jury dimensions in relation to its schools. However, the greatest challenge for the role is its vast spread of geographic coverage. For example, the largest district is the size of Turkey, with 54 schools, and 60,000 inhabitants, of whom one tenth are of Aboriginal descent. Two districts are the size of France, one with 55 schools, the other with 31 schools. On the other hand, of the two geographically small regions, those closest to the capital city, each comprises more than 230 schools.

The following section of the chapter chronicles the journey from school inspector to regional education director, through more than half a century of change within the Education Department. The scope and complexity of this task means that our commentary is necessarily selective and spans the period from the 1950s to the present. Indeed, we would argue that this period marks a transformation in the ways in which the functions of the "inspector" have been understood and performed.

The transformation that occurred at least into the 1970s is described cogently by Clyde Bant, a longstanding district superintendent at that time (2005, cited in Berson, 2006, pp.167-168). Bant suggests that the main role of the school inspectors in Western Australia during the 1950s and 1960s was to ensure that schools were complying with the centrally prescribed curriculum and that students were achieving acceptable results at each "standard" as they progressed through their schooling. For this purpose, teachers were visited in their classrooms for inspection once a year. The initial visit was followed up by an additional visit shortly afterwards to ensure that any recommendations for improving practice had been implemented. Bant goes on to suggest that a discernible change to this arrangement occurred in the mid-seventies when teachers were no longer required to be formally assessed and principals were no longer expected to be experts in the finer detail of the curriculum. This change he attributed to a growing recognition within the education community that effective human resource management depended more on cooperation between inspectors, principals and their staff rather than on the traditional domination of the inspector. Hence, it might be argued that the mid-seventies marked a shift in understanding of the superintendent's role from that of being an absolute authority vis-à-vis the principal to one of supporting principals in the supervision and professional development of their staff.

More dramatic in its implications for the schools' "inspectorate" was the reform that occurred in the 1980s affecting the very infrastructure of the state's education system. Until this time public schools in Western Australia had been organized according to a large, bureaucratic system with a high degree of centralized control designed to promote equitable treatment of members of the teaching service as well as equitable distribution of resources to schools. This bureaucratic model of a school system began to be dismantled with the release in 1984 of the *Better Schools in Western Australia* report, which was instrumental in defining the parameters of reform within this context. As such, a plan was established for a more devolved, school-based management system with the main intention of maximizing effectiveness as indicated by the achievement of goals and the economic use of resources. These reforms were to be accomplished by means of school-based decision-making groups, performance monitoring and school development planning, determining that the school rather than the system was the primary unit of change. New terminology was also introduced: significantly for this discussion, "superintendents" were replaced by "district directors." The commitment to this process of devolution of the system has been maintained by the Department up to the present day including, among other priorities, an emphasis on assuring quality in education.

It may be argued that the quest to assure quality in education was exemplified by the School Accountability Framework of 2002, which established the requirements for all schools in relation to accountability and review. According to these requirements, it was the responsibility of district directors to ensure that schools conducted appropriate self-assessments, reported the outcomes of their self-assessment in their school reports and responded with well-considered improvement plans. For this purpose, district directors conducted reviews of schools in order to "validate" the efficacy of the self-assessment. In doing so, and in line with Leithwood's (2010) observation on similar developments in North America, the role of district directors seemed to be shifting from being an organizational manager to being an "instructional" leader. Indeed, we have illustrated in our previous work how, in one of the 14 education districts that existed at that time in Western Australia, directors approached their objective of enabling principals and teachers to become powerful instructional leaders (Clarke & Wildy, 2011).

This shift seemed to gather further momentum in the wake of a review of the school accountability framework that was conducted in 2006. As a consequence of this review, two key modifications were made to the framework that, once again, served to shape the function of the director schools (as the position was now called). First was the introduction of "standards reviews" which replaced the previous school reviews. The emphasis of the new version of the review was to establish whether students were achieving and progressing in their schooling as expected. This arrangement, it was anticipated, would mean that directors schools would now be less involved in reviewing schools and more oriented towards providing support and intervention, especially for schools in which performance was deemed to be unsatisfactory. The second modification that was made to the framework was the creation of an expert review group. The ERG, as it became known, was designed to undertake full reviews of schools adjudged not to be performing to an acceptable standard according to their standards review administered by directors schools. The strategies prescribed by the ERG would then be used by the principal of the school to devise an improvement plan for lifting performance and enhancing school effectiveness. The development and implementation of this plan are assisted by the director schools.

It should also be mentioned that 2009 witnessed the establishment of the first cohort of so-called Independent Public Schools. These schools have more flexibility to set their own strategic direction and authority for day-to-day decisions than other public schools, but they remain part of the Western Australian public school system. At the time of writing there are 255 Independent Public Schools located throughout the state. For these schools an independent review is conducted under the aegis of the Department of Education Services (DES, 2002) in the final year of the school's delivery and performance agreement. The independent review is overseen by consultants recruited by DES who are expected to work collaboratively with schools to provide an objective, independent verification of each school's self-review of its performance in relation to its Delivery and Performance Agreement and Business Plan.

The most recent development occurring within the Department of Education that has, once again, encroached on the role of the director is a new school support model that was implemented throughout the State in mid-2011 (Education Department of Western Australia, 2010). According to this model up to 75 school networks have been created in eight education regions, each headed by a regional executive director, across Western Australia. These networks, as well as eight regional education offices and seven local education offices, have replaced the 14 district education offices. Each network comprises up to 20 schools led by a "network principal." This is a new position created to enable what are described as the "best" principals to extend their influence and knowledge. Network principals still manage their own schools, but are released to assist other principals in the network. In more remote areas, geographical isolation might determine that principals are employed on a full-time basis to support schools in networks across a region headed by a regional executive director, rather than being attached to a particular school.

The Department of Education's rationale for this change lies in the belief that there are several benefits to be derived from the new model of delivery of school support services. First, locating the resources in schools or networks of schools allows principals to determine how support services are used. Secondly, the new school network structure emphasizes and encourages a practitioner approach to support, providing flexibility to schools and networks enabling highly competent principals and teachers to help and support other staff. Thirdly, the reduction in bureaucracy associated with this new structure purportedly enables schools to respond more quickly and in more creative ways to future changes and opportunities in their local environments. Placing greater control of support services in the hands of principals and teachers is intended to ensure that support is better aligned to the specific needs of students and staff. Taking into consideration the previous case in this chapter, it is interesting to note that the structure and rationale for this new arrangement seem to be similar to that of the Victorian model, in which the state was organized into nine regions and 70 networks of schools in 2008. According to Caldwell (2009, p. 21), the intention of this model was to augment traditional vertical top-down or bottom-up lines of authority, responsibility and accountability with lateral arrangements. Whatever its intention, however, the model was abandoned in 2012 in Victoria.

In the context of this chapter, the role of the regional executive director is most pertinent, especially as it intertwines in complex ways with the functions of network principals within the respective region. In this respect the new role has yet to be clearly defined. In the next section we consider the two states together to argue that in the Australian setting, the role of superintendent is not clearly evident and, perhaps, not important.

## DISCUSSION

The question remains as to whom, or what position, in Australian education might be the equivalent of the school superintendent, especially since the term "superintendent" is seldom used and there are few positions within the educational context where it is applied. It is clear that the superintendent as described by Nir (2014) has no direct equivalent in the Australian educational context, but rather the role and functions are carried out at various levels within the government educational systems (and similarly within the Catholic school system). In the independent system the roles and functions tend to be carried out at the local school board level, although all the schools operate with an accountability environment as they are subject to various legislative Acts, and the requirements of government authorities and regulatory bodies (Gurr, Drysdale & Walkley, 2012). In the cases of Victoria and Western Australia, various reform agendas have resulted in further structural and functional changes that make it more difficult to identify a superintendent.

The case studies of the two states presented in this chapter show the diversity of systems, governance arrangements and structures within the education sector in Australia. Yet the majority of the states also show a common trend, particularly in the government systems,, in their tendency to have moved from central bureaucratic control to local support and school autonomy, notwithstanding the numerous manifestations of this trend in recent years.

Within the systems described in this paper, we suggest that the "superintendent" is like a chameleon in that the person and/or position that best encompasses the functions associated with Nir's (2014) definition keep changing depending on the latest restructure and government approach to administering education. In the past in both Victoria and Western Australia, the candidate most likely to be identified as the superintendent was the school inspector. School inspectors had extensive authority and responsibility for education at a district (primary schools) or subject discipline level (secondary schools). Yet even the inspectors were merely line managers within a highly bureaucratic organization. Significant changes in the 1970s and 1980s in both states witnessed the dismantling of the inspectorial system in favor of new reform agenda that promoted school autonomy and changes in system structures and functions. For example regions replaced districts and Senior Education Officers replaced inspectors. In Western Australia during the most recent reform, it appears that the regional executive director has become the person most likely to approximate the superintendent. In Victoria it is less clear, but we have also identified the regional director as the prime candidate, particularly since the role of the RNL as it was conceived under the previous government has vanished. In Victoria and Western Australia, new government reform is creating new relationships between departments and schools. For example, the introduction in Victoria of a *Compact* (DEECD, 2013a), together with proposed changes to governance and accountability, questions the notion that the superintendent role could be encapsulated in one position or person. The shift towards greater school autonomy through clearly delineated responsibilities between schools and the department eliminates roles close to schools, such as that of RNLs, while the senior managers are too removed from schools to be described as superintendents.

Our review of two Australian States suggests that there is no one person, or position, that could be identified as a superintendent. This reflects the complex nature of Australian education, the recent history of continuous and major change that has occurred, and the emphasis on devolving authority and responsibility to the school level. It also suggests that as school systems move to more devolved systems, the need for superintendents may be lessened, and/or it becomes more difficult to identify superintendency as a distinct role. While the roles, responsibilities and functions associated with the superintendent are still important, within the Australian school education context these roles, responsibilities and functions are distributed. This chapter has not presented a full historical analysis, but the recent history of two States indicates these large government systems have operated without a person who is resembles the superintendent as described by Nir (2014). The movement to further school autonomy in these two Australian States suggests that it is unlikely that the superintendent role will be important for the future of these systems. Indeed, it may be that the cases described in this chapter point the way to a new form of school supervision, one that relies more on light-touch administration from the system, and greater school autonomy.

## REFERENCES

Anderson, M. (2006). *Being a school councillor in a government secondary college inVictoria, Australia: constructions of role and meaning.* Doctoral thesis, The University of Melbourne.

Australian Government (2011). Review of funding for schooling — Final report. Canberra: Department of Education, Employment and Workplace Relations.

Berson, M. (2006). *A fair chance in life.* Perth, WA: Scot Print.

Butler, S. (2011) Networks and "system leadership" in Victorian education: Developments in systemic organisation. Paper presented at the ECER conference, Berlin, September 13-16, 2011.

Butler, S. (2014) *System Leadership in Victoria, Australia.* Doctoral thesis, University of Melbourne.

Caldwell, B.J., Gurr, D., Hill, P.W., & Rowe, K.J. (1997). *The schools of the future programme in Victoria, Australia: The principal perspective.* Paper presented at the American Educational Research Association Annual Meeting, Chicago, March 1997.

Caldwell, B. J. (2009). *The power of networks to transform education: An international perspective.* London: Specialist Schools and Academies Trust.

Clarke, S., & Wildy, H. (2011). Improving the small rural/remote school: The role of the district. *The Australian Journal of Education, 55*(1), pp. 24-36.

Department of Education (2002). *The school accountability framework.* Perth, WA: Western Australia Government.

Department of Education and Early Childhood Development (DEECD), (2011). *Towards Victoria as a learning community.* Melbourne: Department of Education and Early Childhood Development.

Department of Education and Early Childhood Development (DEECD), (2012a). *Summary statistics for Victorian schools, July 2012.* Melbourne: Department of Education and Early Childhood Development.

Department of Education and Early Childhood Development (DEECD), (2012b). *DEECD 2012-2016 strategic plan: Consultation draft July 2012.* Melbourne: Communications Division for the Office of the Secretary Department of Education and Early Childhood Development.

Department of Education and Early Childhood Development (DEECD), (2013a). *The Compact: Roles and responsibilities in Victorian government school education.* Melbourne: Department of Education and Early Childhood Development.

Department of Education and Early Childhood Development (DEECD), (2013b). Review of Governance in Victorian Government Schools, retrieved April 9, 2013 from: http://www.education.vic.gov.au/about/department/Pages/governancereview.aspx

Dixon, M. (2011). *Victoria as a learning community: Extended special lecture Melbourne Graduate School of Education.* Melbourne: Communications Division for Department of Education and Early Childhood Development.

Education Department of Western Australia (2010). *Education networks and regions: New ways of supporting schools.* Perth, WA: Education Department of Western Australia.

Gamage, D. T. (1996a). *School-based management: Theory, research and practice.* Colombo, Sri Lanka: Karunaratke.

Gamage, D. T. (1996b). School councils and community participation in Australia and overseas. *Education, Research and Perspectives, 23*(1), 46-60.

Gamage, D. T., Sipple, P., & Partridge, P. (1995). Effectiveness of school boards in the Australian capital territory: Two decades of experience. *Leading and Managing, 1*(4), pp. 277-291.

Gamage, D. T., Sipple, P., & Partridge, P. (1996). Research on school based management in Victoria. *Journal of Educational Administration, 34*(1), pp. 24-40.

Gurr, D. (1999). *Reforms in school supervision and quality control: The case of the state of Victoria.* Paris: International Institute for Educational Planning.

Gurr, D. (2003). Self-directed school reviews. *Leading and Managing, (2003), 9*(2), pp. 169-172.

Gurr, D. (2007). Diversity and progress in school accountability systems in Australia. *Educational Research for Policy and Practice, 6*(3), 165-186.

Gurr, D., & Drysdale, L. (2012) Tensions and dilemmas in leading Australia's schools. *School Leadership and Management, 32*(5), pp. 403-420.

Gurr, D., Drysdale, L., & Walkley, D. (2012) School-parent relations in Victorian schools. *Journal of School Public Relations, 33*(3), pp. 172-198.

Hopkins D., Munro, J., & Craig, W. (2011). *Powerful learning: A strategy for system reform.* Melbourne, Victoria: ACER Press.

Leithwood, K. (2010). Characteristics of school districts that are exceptionally effective in closing the gap. *Leadership and Policy in Schools, 19*(3), pp. 245-291.

Macpherson, R. J. S. (1982). The school improvement program in Victoria, or, how to play the new game. Opinion Papers, ERIC document, ED22983.

Mulford, B., Hogan, D., & Lamb, S. (2001). Professional and lay person's views on school councils in Tasmania. *Leading & Managing, 7*(2), 109-130.

Nash, K., & Spaull, A.D. (1986). Victoria's teacher unions. In A.D. Spaull (Ed.), *Teacher unionism in the 1980s: Four perspectives.* Melbourne: Australian Council for Educational Research, Hawthorn, Victoria.

Nir, A. (2014). Blending trust and control: A challenge for school superintendents. In A. Nir (Ed.), *The educational superintendent: A cross-cultural perspective.* New York: Nova Science Publishers.

Pike, B. (2008). *New leaders for local school networks.* Victorian Minister for Education media release, September 11.

Spaull, A.D., & Hince, K. (1986). *Industrial relations and state education in Australia.* Melbourne: AE Press.

State of Victoria (1975). Education (School Councils) Act of 1975. Retrieved from http://www.austlii.edu.au/au/legis/vic/hist_act/ eca1957258.

State of Victoria (1983). Education (School Councils) Amendment Act of 1983. Retrieved from http://www.austlii.edu.au/au/ legis/vic/bill_em/eb1983194.pdf.

State of Victoria (2003). Blueprint for government schools. Melbourne, Australia: Communications Division of the Department of Education and Training. Retrieved from http://www.education .vic.gov.au/about/publications/policy/blueprint.htm.

Victorian Education Department (1982). The school improvement plan. Ministerial paper no. 2. Melbourne: Publications and Information Branch, Education Department of Victoria.

Walkley, D. (2012a). *The school board and the principal,* Part 1: Is the governance relationship working well for you? *The Australian Educational Leader, 33*(4), pp 25-27.

Walkley, D. (2012b). The school board and the principal, Part 2: The school board and right processes. *The Australian Educational Leader, 34*(1), pp 26-28.

Walkley, D. (2012c). The school board and the principal, Part 3: The school board and right content. *The Australian Educational Leader, 34*(2), pp 41-42.

World Bank (2010). *Annual Report 2010.* Washington, DC: The World Bank.

In: The Educational Superintendent
Editor: Adam E. Nir

ISBN: 978-1-62948-972-8
© 2014 Nova Science Publishers, Inc.

*Chapter 9*

# MAPPING THE TERRAIN OF SUPERINTENDENCY IN TURKEY: STRUCTURAL, INSTITUTIONAL AND NORMATIVE FEATURES

*Kadir Beycioglu[1], Mehmet Sincar[2], Niyazi Özer[3], Celal Teyyar Uğurlu[4] and Cevat Yıldırım[5]*

[1]Dokuz Eylul University, Turkey
[2]University of Gaziantep, Turkey
[3]Inonu University, Turkey
[4]Cumhuriyet University, Turkey
[5]Mardin Artuklu University, Turkey

## INTRODUCTION

Research in the field of educational administration in Turkey has mainly focused on the way principals manage their schools. Superintendents or vice-principals are, in a sense, forgotten in Turkish literature on educational administration (Beycioglu, Ozer & Ugurlu, 2012). This is in contrast to other national contexts where there is extensive research on superintendents' leadership (Bird, 2010; Horsford, 2011; Orr, 2007), their actions, beliefs and experiences (Björk & Lindle, 2001; Brunner, 2000; Fusarelli, 2006; Kamler, 2009; Nestor-Baker & Hoy, 2001; Pijanowski, Hewitt & Brady, 2009), and their affects on schools and student success (Fossey, 2011; Hackman, 2012; Horsford, 2010). There are also other studies expressing the opinions of various stakeholders regarding superintendents and superintendency (Grissom & Andersen, 2012; Mountford, 2004; Petersen, 2001; Petersen & Short, 2001).

There is not a single, "unique" (Nir & Eyal, 2003) professional position labeled "superintendent" in the Turkish educational system as superintendency is an ambiguous concept extending to other roles such as principals, supervisors, coordinators, etc.

In this chapter, we aim to present substantial evidence regarding mechanisms and processes of control characterizing the Turkish educational system using the superintendent's role as a lens. This will follow a description of the Turkish context and educational system.

## THE CONTEXT

Turkey has a population of 75 million which is estimated to rise to 82 million by 2015 (Akşit, 2007). It has been rated an economically developing country, with its $10,500 GDP (rated 65th in the UN list), and has been taken off the underdeveloped countries list for the last 10 years or so. As an EU candidate nation, changes in social, political and economic conditions and many other factors drive the country's centralized public management system.

As a public service, the country's state supervised/managed educational system has to cope with the pressures of "endless and relentless change" (Hargreaves, 2002), and it is also obliged to reshape its structure. As Grossman, Onkol and Sands (2007) stated, "Turkey is seeking to improve its schools to better respond to higher social and economic expectations" (p. 140). Therefore, its educational system has been continuously struggling to reach the level of the developed European countries. The new and advocated method of public management, in a sense, is *decentralization,* a significant issue in Turkey's political arena of today. Although the current government favors decentralization, some have come out against it.

While the Turkish educational system continues to operate within a strictly centralized system, the system has been involved in preparations for decentralization.

## TURKISH EDUCATIONAL SYSTEM

In this very centralized system the Ministry of National Education (MoNE), situated in the capital city of Ankara, has the authority to decide and implement educational policy with the minister at the top of a structure of undersecretaries, boards, consultants, etc. Provincial organizations implement and control the policies designated by the MoNE. Figure 1 presents a brief chart of the structure of the system.

## OVERALL STRUCTURE OF THE SYSTEM

The Turkish educational system has democratic, modern and secular characteristics. The aims of the system are to increase prosperity and welfare of Turkish citizens and society, to support and accelerate economic, social and cultural development in accordance with national unity and integrity, and to make the Turkish nation constructive and creative.

The basic duties of the state have been determined in accordance with the Constitution of the Turkish Republic, the Basic Law of National Education no. 1739, the Law for Unification of Education and the Law for Eight-year Compulsory and Uninterrupted Education no. 4306. The national education system, determined by National Basic Education Act no. 1739, consists of two main parts, namely formal education and non-formal education.

*Formal Education*: Formal education includes pre-primary education, primary education, secondary education and higher educational institutions.

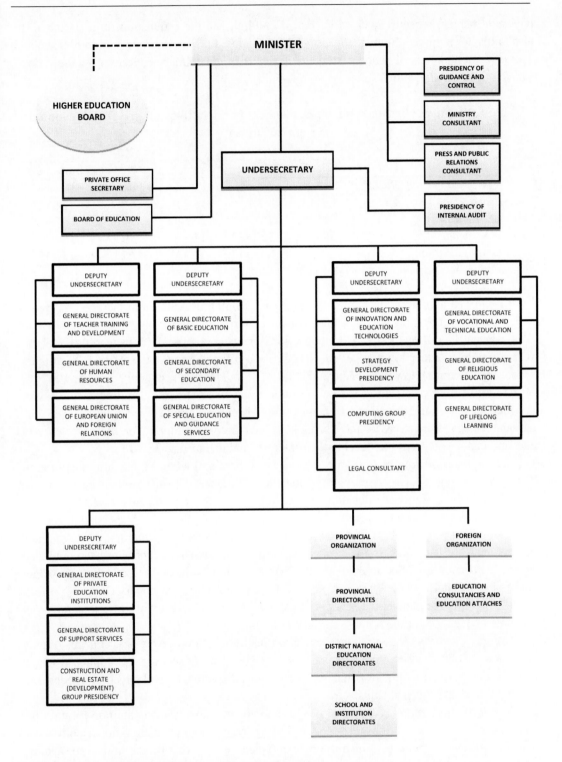

Figure 1. Structure of Turkish Ministry of National Education.

*Pre-primary education* includes optional education of children aged 36-72 months, under the age of compulsory primary education. The purpose of pre-primary education is to ensure physical, mental and sensory development of children and the acquisition of good habits. It also aims to prepare children for primary education and to improve children's spoken Turkish. The numbers of schools, students, teachers in pre-primary education for the school year 2011/12 are shown in Table 1.

**Table 1. Numbers of schools, students, teachers in the public and private educational system in Turkey**

| Type | Number of Schools | | Number of Teachers | | Number of Students | |
|------|--------|---------|--------|---------|---------|---------|
| | Public | Private | Public | Private | Public | Private |
| *Pre-Primary* | 23,556 | 3,641 | 47,712 | 15,221 | 953,209 | 124,724 |
| *Primary Education* | 28,177 | 992 | 261,497 | 20,546 | 5,426,529 | 167,381 |
| *Lower Secondary* | 16,082 | 904 | 250,833 | 18,926 | 5,035,415 | 164,294 |
| *Secondary Education* | 9,384 | 1,033 | 232,517 | 22,378 | 3,824,549 | 156,665 |

Source: National Education Statistics (MoNE, 2013: 51-118).

*Primary education* involves the education and training of children in the age group of 6 to 13. Primary education is compulsory for all children and is free in state schools. As of September 2012, 12-year compulsory education has become a standard. Instead of the eight-year compulsory education, the period of 12 years is divided into three main phases: primary school ($1^{st}$-$4^{th}$ grade), lower secondary school ($5^{th}$-$8^{th}$ grade), high school ($9^{th}$-$12^{th}$ grade). The objective of primary education is to ensure that every Turkish child acquires the necessary knowledge, skills and habits that enable the child to become a good citizen in accordance with national values. Moreover, primary schools should prepare children for the next level of education and enable them to develop their interests and talents (see Table 1).

*Secondary education* includes all general, vocational and technical teaching institutions. The aims and duties of secondary education, in accordance with the general purposes and basic principles of National Education, are as follows: to develop students' awareness of the problems of people and society; to look for solutions and to contribute to the economic, social and cultural development of the country; to prepare students for higher education and professional life according to their interests and abilities. Each student who has completed primary education qualified to enter secondary education has the right to continue his or her studies in secondary education and make use of the opportunities secondary education offers. Table 1 presents the numbers of schools, students, teachers in secondary education and lower secondary education for the school year 2012/13.

*Higher education*: Among higher education institutions are universities, colleges, higher education schools, conservatories, vocational higher education schools and applied research centers. The purpose of higher education is to offer professional development to students in line with their interests and skills.

*Non-formal education*: Parallel to the formal educational system is the non-formal one. This system provides various services including continuing education opportunities for students allowing them to finish their incomplete education; opportunities to acquire professions in line with economic development and employment policies; and teaching people from various professions the knowledge and skills they need for self-improvement.

# THE ORGANIZATIONAL STRUCTURE OF THE MINISTRY

According to Law no. 3797 on the organization and duties of the MoNE, the Ministry today consists of three divisions: central, provincial and overseas organization. It has provincial branches in 81 cities and 850 towns, 58 of them in central towns located close to metropolitan cities. The Ministry has offices in 22 countries with 21 educational undersecretaries and 17 educational attachés.

The MoNE is responsible for the centrally coordinated educational activities in the Republic of Turkey. Each level of education is organized according to its General Directorate. Pre-school education is provided in kindergartens. Primary and lower secondary education consists of eight years of compulsory education. Upper secondary education is also compulsory, and a vast majority of the population participates and has various alternatives such as vocational and art schools. Higher education is provided by state and private universities. The Higher Education Council is responsible for the organization and management of higher education institutions. Adult education is a priority and takes many forms, ranging from formal class-based learning to self-directed and e-learning.

# CENTRAL ORGANIZATION

The central organization of the Ministry comprises the ministerial office where the minister, the undersecretary and deputy undersecretaries sit, the Board of Education and Discipline, Basic Service Units, Advisory and Supervisory Units, and various Auxiliary Units.

The Board of National Education is a scientific consultation and decision-making body directly subordinated to the minister. It helps the minister in almost every education-related matter such as to develop aims/visions, to undertake research, to develop the educational system and to produce educational plans, programs and educational materials. It prepares and submits programs and decisions for implementation upon the approval of the minister, it follows domestic and international educational developments and it takes measures to strengthen national education and training in schools. It also makes decisions regarding the development of the quality of teaching and the proficiency of educational administrative professionals.

The Basic Service Units are comprised of various sub-units such as the General Directorate of Pre-primary Education, the General Directorate of Primary Education, and the General Directorate of Secondary Education to name a few.

Consultancy and Supervisory Units include among others the Board of Inspection and the Board of Research, Planning and Coordination.

And finally, the Auxiliary Units are responsible for a wide range of issues and include the General Directorate of Personnel, the Department of Publications, the Department of In-service Training, the Department of Administrative and Financial Affairs and many other units.

## PROVINCIAL ORGANIZATION

The Ministry of National Education has provincial offices in 81 cities and 850 districts. There is a directorate of national education in each province and district. These directorates in the districts are responsible for the provincial directorates in terms of duties and services. They provide educational services on the basis of province and district. Provincial and district directorates consist of branches, bureaus, permanent boards and commissions according to the characteristics of the service.

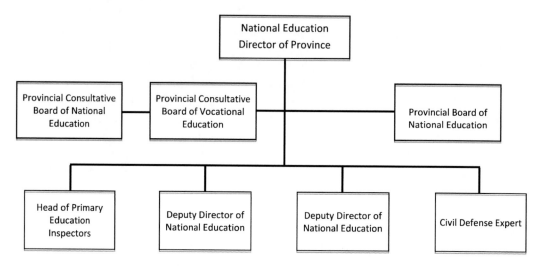

Figure 2. Chart of Provincial Organization.

*Overseas Organization*: The overseas organization of the MoNE was set up to organize educational activities for the protection, presentation and spread of Turkish national culture. Twenty educational counselors and 18 educational attachés serve in various countries to track international educational developments in the fields of general, vocational and technical education, to transfer information about these developments to Turkey and to present abroad the educational and scientific activities conducted in Turkey. The current organizational structure of the Ministry of National Education has reached a rather substantial size. Initiatives have been launched to renew the organizational structure of education and strengthen the effectiveness of the organization. The Law on the Organization and Duties of the MoNE is going to be amended to re-determine the duties of the central organization of the MoNE and make it more functional. These changes are foreseen in the 8th Five-Year Development Plan (2001-2005), the Government Program and Urgent Action Plan which was implemented by the 58th government and is now being implemented by the 59th government, in parallel with the EU legislation.

## DUTIES OF THE MoNE

According to the Unification of Education Law no. 430 issued in 1924, the Ministry is charged with the duty of reaching the goals set for Turkish National Education on behalf of the state. As stated in Law no. 3797 issued in 1992, the duties of the MoNE are: to plan, implement, monitor and control education and training services targeted at teachers and students in the educational institutions at all levels affiliated with the Ministry. The main objectives are to nurture individuals who are committed to Atatürk's principles and reforms, and to Atatürk nationalism defined in the Constitution of the Republic of Turkey; to provide pre-primary, primary, secondary and all other kinds of formal and non-formal education, and to authorize educational institutions, with the exclusion of higher education institutions which are provided by other ministries or institutions. The MoNE is also responsible for an additional wide array of issues such as the organization and implementation of educational training services, the definition of the equivalency of diplomas and certificates of formal and non-formal education institutions, for the articulation of the curricula, regulations and degrees of educational equivalency in secondary education with institutions affiliated to the Turkish Armed Forces and to many additional issues.

## INSPECTION OF EDUCATION IN TURKEY

The Turkish national educational system is based on the Basic Law of National Education. According to this law, the general purpose of the national educational system is to raise good citizens, who may serve as qualified workers in the workforce. All related educational activities conducted by each organization are subject to supervision by the MoNE in terms of their compliance with the goals set by the system. The Ministry is responsible for the inspection of education and teaching services (Basic Law of National Education [BLNE], 1973). This is generally realized by national education inspectors and provincial education inspectors (Decree Law Concerning the Organization and Duties of National Education Ministry [DLCODNEM], 2011). In addition, provincial and district national education directorates and school principals are also responsible for the inspection of their institutions.

## NATIONAL EDUCATION INSPECTORS

National education inspectors work within the MoNE in the Department of Guidance and Inspection. The duties of this body include: (1) guiding Ministry personnel, Ministry schools and institutions and private education institutions in areas that fall under the responsibility of the Ministry; (2) conducting inspections, guidance and preventing irregularities in all areas of activity which are in the area of responsibility of the Ministry; (3) inspecting administrative, financial and juridical acts or transactions of the Ministry organization and its personnel. To realize these duties, 325 (http://rdb.meb.gov.tr) national education inspectors and assistant inspectors are employed (DLCODNEM, 2011) by the Department of Guidance and Inspection, located in Ankara (Ministry of National Education Regulation on Supervisory Board [MNERSB], 1993). The Department has also two extensions located in İstanbul and İzmir, with two national education inspectors working in each (http://rdb.meb.gov.tr).

There is also the Department of Internal Audit Unit which evaluates whether sources are managed and used efficiently. The purpose of this unit is to ensure that activities of the Ministry are managed in accordance with the goals and policies, and that sources are maintained in effective, economical and productive ways (National Education Ministry Internal Audit Unit Presidency Directive [NEMIAUPD], 2008). One Department and eight internal auditors serve in this unit (http://icden.meb.gov.tr/www/teskilat_semasi.php).

To be assigned as national education assistant inspector, individuals must have at least a four-year degree in one the following: science and literature, law, political science, economics and administrative sciences, economics and business administration. They must pass the national education inspector competitive examination. To serve as national education assistant inspectors, individuals must have worked at least three years, write a thesis in relevant fields, succeed in proficiency examination and score a minimum of 70 in foreign language proficiency examination for state employees (DLCODNEM, 2011; Ministry of National Education Bylaw on Supervisory Board [MNEBSB], 1993).

Among the duties performed by the national education inspectors are: (1) inspecting all activities and processes related to institutions working under the jurisdiction of the Ministry, (2) initiating research on issues falling within the area of responsibility of the Ministry, and (3) providing on-the-job training to employees who work in the inspected institutions (MNEBSB, 1993).

## PROVINCIAL EDUCATION INSPECTORS

Some 2,875 provincial education inspectors and assistant inspectors are employed by the Department of Education Inspectors within the provincial national education directorates (DLCODNEM, 2011) of the Ministry (Ministry of National Education [MoNE], 2012). Among their duties they: determine research topics in search for solutions, detect problems and improve the quality in education; present evaluation reports to the provincial national education director; establish guidelines and criteria for various educational processes (Regulations for the Department of Education Inspectors of the Ministry of National Education [RPEIMNE], 2011); provide counseling services and monitor the work of managers, teachers and other employees; provide teachers' and directors' training and professional development; and act to improve the field of education training and management (Regulations for Provincial and District National Education Directorates of the Ministry of National Education [RPDNEDMFE], 2012).

Assistant provincial education inspectors must have a bachelor's degree and eight or more years of experience in teaching and are hired based on their results in a proficiency examination. They are hired for a period of three years. Provincial education inspectors are expected to work in a particular area for a certain time determined by the Ministry, a duration which is not less than two years (DLCODNEM, 2011). Provincial education inspectors and assistant inspectors may inspect formal and non-formal educational institutions of all types (DLCODNEM, 2011) in the province.

While national education inspectors are responsible for the inspection of central organizations of the Ministry and institutions in provincial organization, similar duties in provincial organizations are fulfilled by provincial education inspectors. National education inspectors are involved with inspection, examination and investigation of all institutions that fall within the area of responsibility of the Ministry throughout Turkey. Therefore, contrary to provincial education inspectors responsible for the inspection of institutions only in their provinces, national education inspectors have the authority to inspect both central and provincial organizations. Some of the areas of responsibility of inspectors in the central organization clash with those of provincial inspectors, leading to some conflict, a situation that negatively affects inspector-teacher communication (Yıldırım, 2009; Yıldırım, Beycioğlu, Uğurlu & Sincar, 2012).

Inspection of institutions also includes transmitting innovations from one institution to another, determining reasons that hinder or weaken the institutions, taking relevant measures in time and right place, ensuring effective use of human and physical resources to realize goals of the institution by considering the utilization level of these sources, developing teaching methods and management activities, observing and controlling educational instruction and management processes through objective data and legislation to render them effective and developing these processes by evaluating them according to criteria (DLCODNEM, 2011). Following the inspection, two reports are prepared of which one is given to the institution and the other to the Department of Education Inspectors. This report includes the evaluation of physical conditions, educational and instructional qualities, student achievements, personnel and office workers, and financial issues. Statements concerning the achievements of personnel working in school are also provided (Ministry of National Education Primary Education Inspectors and Inspection Directive [MNEPEIID], 2001).

The inspection of managers, teachers and other personnel is done as part of the inspection of the institution. Managers are evaluated using a "manager evaluation form." Managers' success is evaluated according to the level of the physical conditions of the school, level of instruction, quality of relations, etc. Teachers are evaluated based on the "teacher evaluation form." Teachers' success is assessed based on their level of instruction, classroom management capabilities, quality of relations, etc. The need for teachers' in-service training is also evaluated (MNEPEIID, 2001). Provincial education inspectors determine the shortcomings and areas that need to be developed in addition to pointing out positive and strong aspects of institutions.

In order to obtain a closer look at the mechanisms and processes of control characterizing in the Turkish educational system, semi-structured interviews were conducted with seven male superintendents. These interviews detected several main issues which allow a better description of role challenges of Turkish superintendents.

## JOB QUALITIES

Statements concerning job qualities varied as interviewees emphasized different issues. Two superintendents stated that their role mainly focuses on "planning and mediating." One, for example, emphasized that *"we made plans to repair schools and create a healthy educational environment. We transported nearly three thousand students from villages to schools. All that required good planning and coordination."* Another superintendent referred to mediation as the major quality of his job: *"It is all about the school. We are mediators and function as a bridge. We are the first address of any official dealings of the ministry and also the addressees of the schools. So, we function as a bridge between the schools and the ministry."* Another superintendent described his role as a facilitator: *"My job has no particular function. In other words, I help to make the job of the district national education directorate easier in relation to the distribution of teachers. I assist in coping with the shortages of teachers in schools and report to the district national education directorate."*

Collaboration was another issue that was mentioned by the superintendents. One of the superintendents stated that it was quite difficult to establish relationships with the school community: *"We have poor relationships and communications with the municipality. Our mayor, for example, prioritizes his own political views. At first, we tried to establish good relationships; we visited the mayor several times. However, he considers us unimportant, regardless of whether he rejects or partly accepts our demands."*

Another major theme that some superintendents mentioned is inspection and transparency on the job: *"I share everything with my staff to enable transparency. However, there is no serious supervision. As a matter of fact, there is no control system which inspects, for instance, the inspectors."* However, this is not always the case, as noted by another superintendent: *"The work we do is easily monitored. For example, when a student breaks the rules, I have to assemble the committee and make a decision. I cannot postpone."*

In addition, some of the superintendents referred to the rewards and penalties related to their job: *"I have been working in this profession for ten years. I have seven certificates of achievement and seven certificates of appreciation. Two of these certificates are from the Ministry of National Education. There are only a few people who have a certificate from the Ministry of National Education. However, I have had two reprimands and one warning penalty. Now, I am on trial for malpractice. I have a legal case. What I am trying to say is that when you are not reported to a legal authority, you receive a prize in some cases; while sometimes when you are reported on the same issue - in spite of being innocent - you are punished."*

## DIFFICULTIES ON THE JOB

Holding the position of superintendent exposes individuals to various job difficulties. Most of the interviewees stated that they are exposed to difficulties from within the system as well as from external sources. One superintendent mentioned the lack of safety on the job referring to superintendents' isolation: *"In our region, people who are engaged in purchasing/tender processes have money and so they have influence. These people use the media and spread baseless rumors about us to wear us down when they cannot get what they want.... for example, rivals bid on the school bus franchise to hire school buses: one of them wins the contract, but the one who did not win complained and made threats immediately. This situation and these threats do not affect me personally, because this is my hometown. However, no governmental institution protects me. Rather, the prosecutor treats me unfairly. Our laws are in accordance with European standards, but it is as if we are living in lawless land."*

An additional main difficulty on the job is role conflict. One of the superintendents stated that, *"In our country, the mentality of the 'aggressive manager' is predominant. I am mostly criticized for my not being aggressive. I never get annoyed over this situation. In this respect, when our point of view differs from that of the management, it is seen that we differ in our opinions from both our superiors and our colleagues."* Another superintendent pointed out that the unfair distribution of tasks causes conflict with his/her colleagues and superiors, although they were in the same position: *"The aim of my job is to serve people. However, the department chief thinks that the less he/she works, the more he/she is advantaged. For example, yesterday a document came from the ministry. It was addressed to the department chief. The district director of national education sent this document to the department chief. I came to work and saw the document on my desk. However, the content of the document was not part of my tasks. I gave the document to the district director of national education. He sent the document to the relevant department chief. However, for a while, the department chief said that he would not sign it. So, the district director of national education sent the document back to me. The lot fell to me and I was offended, annoyed and angry."*

Superintendents reported that they often find themselves in conflict with colleagues who are too hasty in fulfilling their tasks: *"While I am fulfilling my tasks, sometimes I am in conflict with my group of colleagues. This is especially so during the supervisions and audits when some friends hurry and want to go home quickly. Normally, it is required that a supervision should last at least two hours. Some of our colleagues are only supervised for a one hour period, and sometimes they demand a quick supervision from the institution. I am not satisfied with the jobs I have carried out over such short periods of time; such supervisions may not be adequate."*

Finally, superintendents complained about work overload and bureaucracy which seems to prevent them from carrying out their jobs properly and undermines the quality of their professional performance. One superintendent said that the bureaucratic structure caused task complications and made it difficult to fulfill the tasks: *"Last year, one of the ministers at a ceremony saw that the flagpoles of some schools were made of wood, while in some other schools they are made of metal. The governor reported this to the director general of national education and the director general reported back to the district director of national education. It is worth noting that ceremony conformity depends on the provincial directorate of national education. They should deal with such issues. Instead, they may say, "You change these flagpoles" to us. This is the case in provincial organizations. Especially in the provinces in metropolitan regions task complications unavoidably arise."*

## CONCLUSION

Superintendency is not confined to a single role in the Turkish educational context. Rather, it includes several ones.

School coordinators are responsible for determining teacher shortages or surpluses in schools and are the ones who appeal to the district directorate with requests for new teachers. Aside from that, they have no other responsibilities. In addition, district directors make decisions regarding all educational services, draw and apply plans and are involved in the monitoring of applications if required. The Department of the District Directorate serves as a bridge between schools and the district national education directorate. It is also responsible to ensure that formally articulated tasks are carried out. Inspectors are mostly responsible to fulfill the tasks of supervision and guidance and are involved in several commissions, although this is not a formal part of their job descriptions.

It appears that Turkish superintendents face several role challenges. They are involved in various tasks such as planning and mediating, inspection, making school processes transparent to senior level officials in the hierarchy, and providing rewards or sanctions to individuals or schools. They perform their jobs although they frequently encounter lack of safety on the job, role conflict and work overload.

It is possible, therefore, to conclude that these unique professional challenges and the strong centralized nature of the Turkish education system make the role of Turkish superintendents a complicated and, at the same time, a challenging one.

# REFERENCES

Akşit, N. (2007). Educational reform in Turkey. *International Journal of Educational Development, 27*(2), 129-137.

Basic Law of National Education [BLNE]. (1973). *ResmiGazete [Official Gazette of the Republic of Turkey]*, 14573, 14 June 1973.

Beycioglu, K., Ozer, N., & Ugurlu, C.T. (2012).The facets of job satisfaction among vice-principals in elementary schools. *Journal of Management Development, 31*(7), 636-647.

Bird, J. J. (2010). Building budgets and trust through the alchemy of superintendent leadership. *Management in Education, 24*(2), 46-50.

Björk, L., & Lindle, J. C. (2001). Superintendents and interest groups. *Educational Policy, 15*(1), 76-91.

Brunner, C. C. (2000). Unsettled moments in settled discourse: Women superintendents' experiences of inequality. *Educational Administration Quarterly, 36*(1), 76-116.

Decree Law Concerning the Organization and Duties of National Education Ministry [DLCODNEM] (2011). *ResmiGazete [Official Gazette of the Republic of Turkey]*, 28054, 14 September, 2011.

Fossey, R. (2011). A sacrificial lamb: A divided school board, a beleaguered superintendent, and an urgent need to improve student achievement. *Journal of Cases in Educational Leadership, 14*(3), 11-29.

Fusarelli, B. C. (2006). School board and superintendent relations issues of continuity, conflict and community. *Journal of Cases in Educational Leadership, 9*(1), 44-57.

Grissom, J. A., & Andersen, S. (2012). Why superintendents turn over. *American Educational Research Journal, 49*(6), 146-180.

Grossman, G. M., Onkol, P. E., & Sands, M. (2007). Curriculum reform in Turkish teacher education: Attitudes of teacher educators towards change in an EU candidate nation. *International Journal of Educational Development, 27*(2), 138-150.

Hackman, D. G. (2012). It's a different world at the high school: A new superintendent discovers competing cultures within the district. *Journal of Cases in Educational Leadership, 15*(4), 22-31.

Hargreaves, A. (2002). Sustainability of educational change: The role of social geographies. *Journal of Educational Change, 3*, 189-214.

Horsford, S. D. (2010). Mixed feelings about mixed schools: Superintendents on the complex legacy of school desegregation. *Educational Administration Quarterly, 46*(3) 287-321.

Horsford, S. D. (2011). Vestiges of desegregation: Superintendent perspectives on educational inequality and (dis)integration in the Post-Civil Rights Era. *Urban Education, 46*(1), 34-54.

Kamler, E. (2009). Decade of difference (1995–2005): An examination of the superintendent search consultants' process on Long Island. *Educational Administration Quarterly*, 45(1), 115-144.

Ministry of National Education - MoNE (2013). *National Education Statistics, formal education 2012-2013.* Ankara: Ministry of National Education Strategy Development Presidency.

Ministry of National Education [MoNE] (2012). *İl eğitimdenetmenlerininyerdeğiştir mekılavuzu [Relocation guide for provincial education inspectors].* Retrieved March 9, 2013, from http://ikgm.meb.gov.tr/kilavuz/ 2012/ 2012%20KILAVUZ %2013%2004 %20-%201033.pdf

Ministry of National Education Bylaw on Supervisory Board [MNEBSB] (1993). *Resmi Gazete [Official Gazette of the Republic of Turkey], 21501,* 19 February 1993.

Ministry of National Education Primary Education Inspectors and Inspection Directive [MNEPEIID] (2001). *Tebliğler Dergisi [Notification Bulletin of the Ministry of National Education], 2521,* February 2008.

Ministry of National Education Regulation on Supervisory Board [MNERSB] (1993). *Resmi Gazete [Official Gazette of the Republic of Turkey],* 21717, 3 October 1993.

Mountford, M. (2004). Motives and power of school board members: Implications for schoolboard–superintendent relationships. *Educational Administration Quarterly,* 40(5), 704-741.

National Education Ministry Internal Audit Unit Presidency Directive [NEMIAUPD] (2008). *Tebliğler Dergisi [Notification Bulletin of the Ministry of National Education],* 2604, January 2008.

Nestor-Baker, N. S., & Hoy, W. K. (2001). Tacit knowledge of school superintendents: Its nature, meaning, and content. *Educational Administration Quarterly,* 37(1), 86-129.

Nir, A., & Eyal, O. (2003). School-based management and the role conflict of the school superintendent. *Journal of Educational Administration,* 41(5), 547-564.

Orr, M. T. (2007). Learning advanced leadership: Findings from a leadership development programme for new superintendents. *Educational Management Administration & Leadership,* 35(3) 327-347.

Petersen, G. J. (2001). Singing the same tune: Principals' and school board members' ;perceptions of the superintendents' role as instructional leader. *Journal of Educational Administration,* 40(2), 158-171.

Petersen, G. J., & Short, P. M. (2001). The school board president's perception of the district superintendent: Applying the lenses of local influence and social style. *Educational Administration Quarterly,* 37(4), *533-570.*

Pijanowski J. C., Hewitt, P. M., & Brady, K.P. (2009). Superintendents' perceptions of the Principal shortage. *NASSP Bulletin*, 93(2), 85-95.

Regulations for Presidency of Education Inspectors of the Ministry of National Education [RPEIMNE]. (2011). *Resmi Gazete [Official Gazette of the Republic of Turkey],* 27974, 24 June 2011.

Regulations for Provincial and District National Education Directorates of the Ministry of National Education [RPDNEDMFE] (2012). *Resmi Gazete [Official Gazette of the Republic of Turkey],* 28471, 18 November 2012.

Yıldırım, M. C. (2009). *Evaluating the instructional supervision practices at primary schools in terms of constructivist learning paradigm principles.* Unpublished doctoral dissertation, Inonu University, Institute of Social Sciences, Malatya, Turkey.

Yıldırım, M. C., Beycioğlu, K., Uğurlu, C. T., & Sincar, M. (2012). The problems thateducational supervisors face in terms of the assigned positions. *Inonu University Journal of the Faculty of Education*, 13 (1), 1-21.

In: The Educational Superintendent

Editor: Adam E. Nir

ISBN: 978-1-62948-972-8

© 2014 Nova Science Publishers, Inc.

*Chapter 10*

# DISTRICT EDUCATION OFFICERS (DEOS) IN INDIA: BETWEEN BUREAUCRACY AND DEMOCRATIZATION

## *Rc Saravanabhavan[1], N. Muthaiah[2] and Sheila Saravanabhavan[3]*

[1]Howard University, US
[2]Sri Ramakrishna MissionVidyalaya College of Education, India
[3]Virginia State University, US

This chapter describes the position and characteristics of a district education officer in India. Before going into a detailed analysis of this lynchpin position, we will set a historic, cultural and political backdrop to fully understand this office. The chapter will also include a discussion of current Right of Children to Free and Compulsory Education (RTE) policies that impact the functions of the District Education Officers (DEO) and how they might drive some changes in the fundamental way a DEO leads schools in the future.

## HISTORY OF EDUCATION IN INDIA

India has had a long history of formal education since prehistoric times. Even before the birth of a written language there, the Vedas in Sanskrit language were imparted strictly in an oral format for at least 800 years beginning 2000 BC. During 1200 BC the verses from the Rig Veda were first believed to have been transcribed into a written form (Altekar, 2009). Typically, a monastic form of education was dominant during this period (Blackwell, 2004). In the later periods, another system of schooling called Gurukul (boarding and learning at the home of the teacher) came into existence. Male children from noble and upper-caste families stayed and learned at the homes of sages. They were taught a variety of subjects from religious to science education (Prabhu, 2006). It is also important to note that, until the era of colonialism, education catered to the dominant religion of the period (i.e., Hinduism, Buddhism, Jainism, and Islam). The advent of the written alphabet spread the opportunity for education to a greater segment of the population. Palm leaves and barks were the main parchments used for writing. Buddhism increased the number of people who had access to receive an education. During this period, between the first century and 800 CE, Buddhist education imparted religion and secular subjects such as science and mathematics. The Buddhists built renowned universities including the Nalanda University in the area now known as Bihar.

The next significant change in education occurred during the Mughal period that began in early 15th century and continued until early 18th century. The Mughal kings established primary and secondary schools around their empire. They also created universities in major cities such as Delhi and Lucknow. These universities paved a way for the fusion of Islamic and Indian thoughts in religion as well as improving existing knowledge in mathematics and science (Altekar, 2009).

With the establishment of British rule in India, Great Britain needed to train Indians to become government workers. English language and a new system of education, that came to be known as the Macaulay system (Thirumalai, 2003), were promoted in the early 1800s, and subsequently institutes of higher education were also established in the mid-1800s. English became the dominant language of professionals in all fields. "It was a new education, characterized by technology, by a philosophy of the relationships between students and teacher, and by politics of control" (Kumar, 2007). It was the 19th century Indian intelligentsia who became the main recipients of this new model of education. They lived in three main cities of the Indian part of the British Empire — Mumbai, Delhi and Kolkata. Families of the intelligentsia still considered their mother tongues to be important, so they also taught their children their native languages. English as the language for career mobility was an important element of the Indian educational system. Thus, there was greater importance placed on being proficient in English and one's native language to engender professional and social success, respectively. This emphasis has continued on even after the political independence in 1947.

Indian scholars who received training in the British educational system exercised a distinct influence over how the Indian educational system evolved during postcolonial period (Choudry, 2008). It was mostly an adoption of the British model with national themes. Remnants of the Macaulay era governance structure, curricula, teaching, learning and testing methods are in existence even in the $21^{st}$ century Indian educational system. After independence in 1947, each of the 14 states and six union territories became responsible for educating its students at the primary and secondary level. The central government coordinated higher education by creating standards for tertiary education. This relationship between central government and the states changed in 1964 when a new national system of education was initiated based on the recommendations of a 16-member education commission. Education became the joint responsibility of the state and central governments through a constitutional amendment.

Since then, Indian polity has had a federal structure, with education in the concurrent list of the constitutional responsibilities. The agency for education at the central government level is the Ministry of Human Resources Development, with its two major wings: the Department of School Education and Literacy and the Department of Higher Education (see Figure 1).

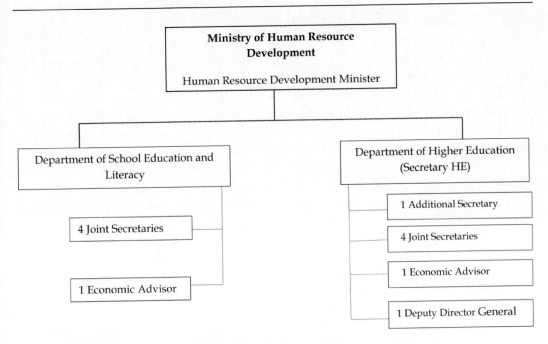

Figure 1. Central Government Organizational Chart – Education.

The Department of School Education and Literacy focuses on primary, secondary and adult education. The Ministry is responsible for creating the schemes for education and broad national goals (e.g., increasing the number of girls in school, universal elementary education and the like).

## CURRENT DEMOGRAPHIC AND EDUCATION STATISTICS

Few countries can compare to India in its sheer size of the school-going population and vastness of diversity. About 360 million among 1.21 billion persons in India were under 15 years in 2011 (U.S. Central Intelligence Agency, 2012). Nearly 264 million children attend (National University for Educational Planning and Administration, 2012) one of the 1.3 million schools that include 785,000 elementary schools and 172,000 secondary or higher secondary schools (Ministry of Human Resource Development, 2012). With its 28 states and seven union territories, each created within its predominant linguistic and cultural boundaries, India exhibits an enormous diversity. Economic disparity has remained part of this diversity and has hindered opportunities for all children to go to school.

Since independence, India has strived to implement educational policies to accomplish its national goals and to meet regional or local needs at the same time. In addition, the central government and the states have struggled to close the gap among children who are able to get an education and those who are not. A significant effort in this regard is the recent law, the Right of Children to Free and Compulsory Education (RTE) Act of 2009, which was ratified by all states (India Development Gateway, 2010). The new law embraces the principles of an existing scheme Sarva Shiksya Abhiyan (SSA) that aims to provide useful and relevant primary education for all children in the 6 to 14 age group and to bridge social, regional and gender gaps through active participation of the community in the management of schools. Since 2009, the central government has expanded the policies for free and compulsory education to secondary school levels as well. This project, entitled Rastria Madyamik Shiksha Abhiyan, has been embraced and implemented by states across the country.

Present-day India is witnessing a phenomenal surge at all levels of education, from primary to university education. The government has allocated thus far the highest portion of its budget to education (4.5% of its GDP) and has encouraged the exponential growth of the private school sector (World Bank, 2009). About 60% of the schools in India are government-run, while the remaining ones are private-aided (PA) or private-unaided (PUA). The state governments manage and finance government-run schools, which must follow the academic regulations of the state board of education. PA schools are privately managed, but the respective state government finances 90% of their budget and requires them to follow state board regulations. PUA schools are the newest and fastest growing ones that do not receive government funds.

The Indian government's interest in expanding more and more primary and secondary schools resulted in the proliferation of private universities. Entrepreneurs took advantage of this area of need and they were allowed to establish colleges and universities. When India embraced the market-oriented economy of the West in the 1990s, there was further escalation of private universities. Since 2008, tertiary education has become a priority for the Indian government. Currently, India has the largest population of college-bound students in the world, but it does not have the accommodations for all these students. There are 611 universities and 33,032 colleges in India with a total enrollment of about 20 million including 5.5 million in online open-university programs. However, this represents only just below 19% in Gross Enrollment Ratio (GER) for people in 18 to 24 years age group (Ministry of Human Resource Development, 2012).

In India, there are 2,572 (not including private institutions) teacher training centers that educate 198,010 future teachers. In the 11th five-year plan, the government was to open five more Institutes of Science, Education, and Research (IISER). [These schools focus on promoting research and education in the sciences.] Ninety percent of the teachers employed in state funded schools are reported to have had some form of teacher training. Teacher training can be categorized into (a) primary/secondary teacher training certificate, (b) bachelor of education and (c) master of education degrees.

## EDUCATIONAL SYSTEMS IN STATES/UNION TERRITORIES

Since 1968, the central government has stressed the need for uniform structure of schooling across the country. The most common format that exists is: 10+2+3, that is: 10 years of primary, upper primary, and high school; two years of higher secondary and three years of college education (Tiyagi, 2009). Table 1 below describes enrollment of students from lower primary up to higher secondary schools in the 28 states and the seven union territories.

**Table 1. Country Data: Distribution and Number of Students**

| Sl No. | State/ Union Territory | No of Revenue Districts | No of Educational Districts | No of Students in LP (I - V) | No of Students in UP (VI - VIII) | No of Students in Sec. (IX - X) | No of Students in Sen. Sec. (XI - XII) | Total |
|---|---|---|---|---|---|---|---|---|
| 1 | Andhra Pradesh | 23 | 23 | 7,540,821 | 3,731,242 | 3,234,073 | 712,194 | 15,218,330 |
| 2 | Arunachal Pradesh | 17 | 17 | 244,488 | 87,577 | 48,849 | 25,864 | 406,778 |
| 3 | Assam | 27 | 27 | 4,070,490 | 1,751,673 | 1,210,282 | 251,526 | 7,283,971 |
| 4 | Bihar | 38 | 38 | 15,646,438 | 4,328,264 | 1,917,731 | 124,458 | 22,016,891 |
| 5 | Chhattisgarh | 27 | 27 | 3,158,200 | 1,479,244 | 814,622 | 392,584 | 5,844,650 |
| 6 | Goa | 2 | 2 | 111,330 | 70,593 | 56,649 | 28,377 | 266,949 |
| 7 | Gujarat | 26 | 26 | 5,888,892 | 2,258,132 | 2,334,305 | 788,158 | 11,269,487 |
| 8 | Haryana | 21 | 21 | 2,291,835 | 1,184,011 | 735,354 | 569,529 | 4,780,729 |
| 9 | Himachal Pradesh | 12 | 12 | 625,518 | 410,109 | 249,453 | 1,047,710 | 2,332,790 |
| 10 | Jammu and Kashmir | 22 | 22 | 1,310,212 | 2,258,132 | 375,109 | 201,570 | 4,145,023 |
| 11 | Jharkhand | 24 | 24 | 5,017,173 | 1,823,571 | 999,136 | 356,205 | 8,196,085 |
| 12 | Karnataka | 30 | 30 | 5,410,240 | 2,260,252 | 2,525,200 | 2,525,200 | 12,720,892 |
| 13 | Kerala | 14 | 38 | 2,016,955 | 1,421,950 | 1,345,699 | 512,363 | 5,296,967 |
| 14 | Madhya Pradesh | 50 | 54 | 10,712,010 | 4,681,679 | 11,879,513 | 911,658 | 28,184,860 |
| 15 | Maharashtra | 35 | 35 | 10,384,478 | 5,697,291 | 5,137,156 | 1,901,136 | 23,120,061 |
| 16 | Manipur | 9 | 9 | 363,833 | 139,849 | 105,115 | 48,334 | 657,131 |
| 17 | Meghalaya | 7 | 7 | 507,945 | 152,184 | 115,585 | 17,462 | 793,176 |
| 18 | Mizoram | 8 | 4 | 174,025 | 61,302 | 49,501 | 19,647 | 304,475 |
| 19 | Nagaland | 11 | 8 | 287,726 | 123,657 | 58,066 | 23,170 | 492,619 |
| 20 | Odisha | 30 | 30 | 4,467,851 | 2,088,574 | 1,675,074 | 1,675,074 | 9,906,573 |
| 21 | Punjab | 22 | 22 | 2,563,140 | 1,401,287 | 682,471 | 495,915 | 5,142,813 |
| 22 | Rajasthan | 33 | 33 | 8,432,836 | 3,570,991 | 2,646,140 | 1,228,078 | 15,878,045 |
| 23 | Sikim | 4 | 4 | 89,837 | 36,705 | 21,128 | 8,775 | 156,445 |

**Table 1. (Continued)**

| Sl No. | State/ Union Territory | No of Revenue Districts | No of Educational Districts | No of Students in LP (I - V) | No of Students in UP (VI - VIII) | No of Students in Sec. (IX - X) | No of Students in Sen. Sec. (XI - XII) | Total |
|---|---|---|---|---|---|---|---|---|
| 24 | Tamil Nadu | 32 | 32 | 6,110,219 | 3,687,045 | 2,308,530 | 1,503,033 | 13,608,827 |
| 25 | Tripura | 8 | 4 | 394,418 | 215,680 | 133,382 | 44,444 | 787,924 |
| 26 | Uttar Pradesh | 75 | 75 | 24,043,102 | 7,975,985 | 4,997,383 | 2,846,347 | 39,862,817 |
| 27 | Uttarakhand | 13 | 13 | 1,084,260 | 554,232 | 469,755 | 267,144 | 2,375,391 |
| 28 | West Bengal | 19 | 19 | 10,231,570 | 4,700,195 | 2,206,419 | 1,231,958 | 18,370,142 |
| A. | Andaman Nicobar | 3 | 3 | 32,224 | 21,129 | 18,863 | 8,369 | 80,585 |
| B. | Chandigarh | 1 | 1 | 93,786 | 55,216 | 31,433 | 28,645 | 209,080 |
| C. | Dadra and Nagar Haveli | 1 | 1 | 39,896 | 19,168 | 8,313 | 3,416 | 70,793 |
| D. | Daman and Diu | 2 | 2 | 17,026 | 9,117 | 6,966 | 3,177 | 36,286 |
| E. | Laksha dweep | 1 | 1 | 6,119 | 4,166 | 3,003 | 2,095 | 15383 |
| F. | Delhi -National capital territorry | 9 | 12 | 1,727,698 | 982,785 | 940,059 | 423,361 | 4,073,903 |
| G. | Puducherry | 4 | 4 | 110,466 | 7,2161 | 58,700 | 23,250 | 264,577 |
| | TOTAL | 660 | 680 | 135,207,057 | 59,315,148 | 49,399,017 | 20,250,226 | 264,171,448 |

Source: Adapted from NUEPA School Report Card 2010-11. http://schoolreportcards.in/SRC-New/Links/DISEPublication.aspx.

Educational governance structures vary among the states and union territories that exist today. Although there are differences in the policy formulations, planning, administration and management, all states and union territories have a department of education (see Figure 2). Fifteen states have one department of education that handles primary, secondary, higher and adult education together, whereas 13 states have separate departments of education for each sector of education (Tiyagi, 2009). Subsequently, there is at least one minister of education, who is usually an elected member of the state legislative assembly, in each state. Under the control of this minister, there are minimally three divisions: (a) secretariat, (b) directorate, and (c) inspectorate, which are responsible for policies, budget, administration and supervision of education from primary up to higher secondary levels. Figure 2 below presents an organizational chart for the Department of Education in the state of Tamil Nadu.

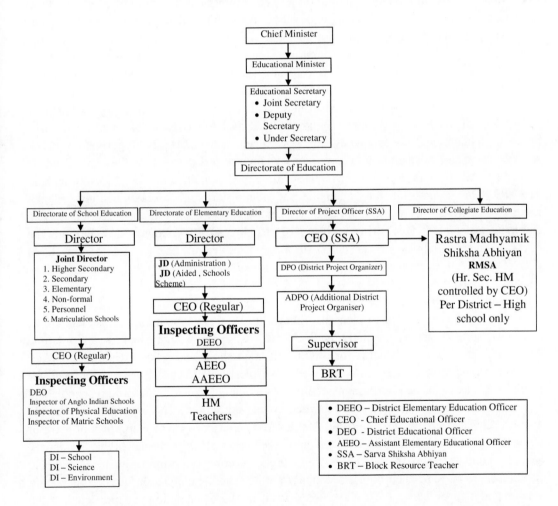

Source: www.prajnya.in/eprs.pdf. Topic: Mapping educational policy structures and processes in Tamilnadu. April 2009, p. 26 and p. 30. retrieved 22October 2013.

Department of school education: http://www.tn.gov.in/schooleducation/contact.htm. Retrieved 22October 2013.

Figure 2. Hierarchy of Educational Administration (State Level – Tamil Nadu).

# THE DISTRICT EDUCATION OFFICER

It is important to note that the position of district education officer (DEO) is embedded in the inspectorate division housed at the district/block level. Depending on the state, the DEO is responsible for either all grades from primary to $12^{th}$ grade or, as in some states, they are given responsibility for one level such as primary, upper primary and secondary grades. The DEO is the government supervisor who directly oversees all schools under his/her jurisdiction. Typically, one becomes a DEO through promotion from lower educational administrative positions such as school headmasters or assistant district education officers. Also, a percentage of the DEO positions are kept open for candidates who successfully complete a state civil service examination and interview. It is likely some of the DEOs who have come directly through the state public service commission may not have had any direct educational administration or teaching experience. The DEOs stay in their positions until they are either promoted to a higher position or they retire from civil service. (Each state has a fixed age for superannuation of its employees and it varies from mid-50s to 60 years.) However, they are likely to be transferred to other school districts or similar positions with different special assignments. In contrast to the school superintendents in the western nations, a DEO in India does not have significant executive powers such as control of budget, recruitment of teachers or principals, and the like. A DEO is more of an inspector who monitors functioning of schools as per government guidelines and reports to regional supervisors (Chief Education Officer or Deputy Director of Education as they are called) in each state. All states in India organize state-wide public examinations for grades 10 and 12. The DEOs are responsible for organizing and administering these examinations for their respective districts. Given the number of students in these grades in each district, it is an enormous task and the DEO office prepares for this all year. The following description of the role and responsibilities of the DEO in one state, Tamil Nadu, captures the basic characteristics of this position in general (K. Devarajan, Director of School Education, Chennai, personal communication, April 23, 2013): Visit and inspect all schools up to high school level and assist the chief education officer/deputy director of education in academic inspection of higher secondary schools (grades 11 & 12); appoint and supervise office assistants, security personnel, clerks including typists; approve salary increase or one-time incentives and retirement benefits for office staff cited above and school headmasters; chair the educational district subcommittee, serve as secretary of the district committee for continuing education; make recommendation to upgrade middle schools to high schools and high schools to higher secondary levels; determine and approve appropriate staff strength, appointments and salaries for all positions in aided high schools; oversee approval of leave of absences utilized by administrative staff and teachers in aided high and higher secondary schools; conduct SSLC/Matric/Oriental and higher secondary examination in March and September every year; keep higher secondary public school examination question papers in safe custody; supervise as the camp officer of all public examinations administered in the district; supervise the compilation of educational statistics relative to the district; and be responsible for all state welfare schemes for school students (examples from the state of Tamil Nadu: free bus passes, free school uniforms, free textbooks, and free bicycles).

The following section presents findings from a recent survey conducted, by the authors, among DEOs in the state of Kerala. This state is considered a model for educational advancement; it boasts of 100% literacy rate and it is in the forefront of implementing more democratized leadership of schools. There are 14 revenue districts and 38 educational districts within this state and there are approximately 52 DEOs responsible for primary through higher secondary education. Of these 52, 14 who are designated as District Project Officers (DPOs) served on special projects in the revenue districts. Out of 38 DEOs in the school districts, 25 (69%) responded to the survey; they represented broader geographic sections of the state. Gender-wise, the respondents were 40% (n=10) female and 60% (n=15) male. While one respondent did not have any prior experience in education, others (n=24) reported a median 25 years of teaching experience (range=2-33 years). Only 20 of the respondents reported having served as headmasters for an average of 4 years. Also, all of them (n=25) had served only a few years (median=2.0 years) in the current position as DEOs (see Table 2).

### Table 2. District Educational Officer's Characteristics - Kerala

| | Age | Years in current position | Years as Teacher | Years as Headmasters | No. of schools and school heads under supervision | Staff members supervised | Number of Schools overseen |
|---|---|---|---|---|---|---|---|
| Valid n | 25 | 25 | 24 | 20 | 25 | 25 | 25 |
| Missing n | 0 | 0 | 1 | 5 | 0 | 0 | 0 |
| Mean | 51.12 | 1.74 | 21.63 | 5.15 | 84.36 | 21.60 | 78.68 |
| Median | 55.00 | 2.00 | 25.00 | 4.50 | 77.00 | 22.00 | 73.00 |
| Mode | 55[a] | 2.00 | 25.00[a] | 4.00 | 70.00 | 25.00 | 70 |
| Std. Deviation | 7.34 | 1.05 | 9.29 | 2.66 | 32.32 | 3.61 | 30.64 |

[a.] Multiple modes exist.

The state of Kerala has a policy of recruiting 40% of its DEOs directly through the public service commission. The sample showed a distribution of 56% of the DEOs who reached their position through promotion within the field of education and the remaining DEOs (44%) were selected directly. Regarding their academic preparation, all respondents had teaching degrees: 88% of them with a B.Ed., and 12% of them with an M.Ed. In addition, 52% (n=13) of the DEOs had a B.A./B.Sc., 44% (n=11) had either an M.A. or M.Sc. degree and one of them had a Ph.D. Also, relevant is the information that 80% (n=20) of these DEOs received short trainings, following their appointment, provided either by a state or the central government agency. A plurality (60%) of all respondents "strongly agreed" or "agreed" that future DEOs should have a master of education degree in administration/leadership. While 20% (n=5) "somewhat agreed" with this idea, the remaining 20% did not support the pre-training. Other salient characteristics of this respondent group were: (a) each of the DEOs supervised a median number of 25 staff members in their respective offices and oversaw a median of 70 schools and school-heads; (b) met with their immediate supervisors on a weekly (24%) or monthly (56%) basis; (c) only 36% were able to report their respective budgets for their school districts; and (d) 68% of them were in the age group closer to retirement (state employees are retired at the age of 56 years in Kerala). It was evident that almost all DEOs who reached this position through promotion, having served as headmasters of schools and/or assistant superintendents for more than two decades, were over the age of 50 and they had only a few years left before superannuation.

The survey elicited information related to various duties and responsibilities of the DEOs. Respondents were asked to indicate a number between 1 and 10 on a Likert scale and pinpoint the professional time and energy each category of duties and responsibilities consumed (1 represented the lowest and 10 the highest amount of professional time and energy). We had listed 21 such categories identified in earlier research (Tyagi, 2009) and left blank spaces for the DEOs to add any duty/responsibility that we might not have included in the list. The following areas were ranked as the top 10 duties/responsibilities that the DEOs spent most time and energy on (numbers in parenthesis show ranking order): inspection and supervision of schools, and preparation of inspection reports (1); preparation for and administration of public examinations (2); provision of feedback to schools on administrative and academic areas (3); coordination with local bodies (3); monitoring scoring of public examinations and report/publish examination results (4); focusing on rules, regulations, acts, statutes of state and central governments (5); provision/monitoring of grants/aid to government-aided schools (5); monitoring of progress of education (pass rates of students, etc.) (5); management and mobilization of resources (6); monitoring of enrollment, retention, achievement and incentives available to under-served groups such as girls, "scheduled castes, scheduled tribes, and other backward caste students" and students with disabilities (7); formulation and implementation of various education programs such as SSA (universal and compulsory education) (8); interactions with local communities (8); collection, collation and dissemination of data and information periodically (9); management of litigation cases of teaching and non-teaching staff in courts (9); and management of programs for adult and non/formal education (10).

An examination of these tasks that take priority in a DEO's daily work reveals the managerial role he or she plays in the school district. The DEOs embody the inspectorate principles and exhibit the "top-down" model of governance. There is little evidence for any contribution they directly make to the formulation or improvement of their respective state educational policies. Neither is there any indication that they engage in a consultative process with parents in terms of improving teaching and learning in schools. The DEO's role is still deeply rooted in the bureaucratic model that was created during the colonial period. While this pattern of administration is acceptable in a system where there has been a strong attachment to centralized governance and a public acceptance of bureaucracy, it stands in contrast to the emerging national and state policies that envision a democratized form of educational governance that is expected to empower local communities to engage in every aspect of running their schools. The following section presents a description of a pivotal law that aims to gradually democratize educational governance and the current status of these democratization efforts. This background is provided to highlight the strategic position in which DEOs operate and to emphasize how a new and improved mode of their recruitment, training, roles and responsibilities will enhance the realization of the spirit of this law.

The central government law, Right of Children to Free and Compulsory Education, passed in 2009, represents the world's largest basic education program that makes the central and state governments concurrently responsible for providing access, facilities, faculty, and all educational tools for children from 6-14 years of age. This law, in alignment with the 2001 Sarva Shiksya Abhiyan (SSA) program for universalization of elementary education, has been adopted in all states and union territories, except in the state of Jammu and Kashmir. Highlights of the RTE provisions are: (a) mandatory free education including midday meals (for qualifying students), books, uniforms, etc., by the state for every child between the ages of 6-14; (b) private educational institutions and schools must admit (starting 2011) at least 25% of children belonging to disadvantaged groups from the neighborhood; (c) strict criteria for the qualification of teachers; and (d) requirement of a teacher student ratio of 1:30 at each of these schools. RTE also envisions the concept of neighborhood schools, an elementary school within one kilometer and a middle school within three kilometer radius. Another important provision in this law is the school management committees. RTE mandates formation and operation of a school management committee in each school. Seventy-five percent of this committee must comprise parents/guardians with appropriate representation from the disadvantaged groups. Also, the committee has to include elected representatives from the local government bodies. The school management committee should have at least 50% women. The school management committee is to (a) monitor the operation of the school, (b) prepare and recommend school development plans and (c) monitor the utilization of grants received from the government, local authorities as well as from any other sources (Ministry of Law and Justice, 2009).

Based on the recent report from the Ministry of Human Resources Development (2012), universalization of elementary and middle school education is the aim. According to this report, as of 2010, 99% of all rural children had a school within a one kilometer radius; during 2008-2009 academic year the dropout rates were contained below 25% with the dropout rate for girls under 17%; and student-teacher ratios were 44:1 at the elementary and 34:1 at the middle-school levels. Although this report highlighted several indicators of achievement in meeting the RTE objectives, there was no reference made with regard to the establishment and operations of village/school management committees.

In the context of democratization of educational governance, village/school management committees are intended to create community level participation and decision making relative to local education. Although there have not been large-scale studies on this topic, the few that have been conducted in a specific state or in a cluster of villages in one district have identified emerging issues. A doctoral research study from the University of Minnesota (Sanchez, 2011) examined the extent of parent/family involvement in the state of Uttar Pradesh and concluded that, although families/parents devoted time and resources toward their wards' education, their participation in terms of school visits and in school activities was limited. Another study sponsored by the National Bureau of Economic Research in Cambridge, Massachusetts (Banerjee, Banerjee, Dufto, Glennerster & Khemani, 2008) conducted a randomized survey among 1,029 village education committee members in 280 villages in Uttar Pradesh. This study revealed that parents faced substantial constraints in participating in the village/school education committees; there was apathy and pessimism about improving their local educational system; many of them did not even know that they were members of the village/school education committee and they did not know the role and responsibilities of this committee. A third study that was conducted in two villages in the state of Haryana (Narwana, 2011) found the reasons for the apathy and pessimism among members of the village/school management committees. At the village level, it appeared that social status, caste barriers, local politics and lack of mobilization impeded the effective participation of all members in these committees. These sample findings illustrated a critical disconnect between the national aspiration and the local competency to fulfill the mandate (Mukundan & Bray, 2004). Almost 80% of these schools are in rural areas and the relevance of community ownership of local education is lost among poor families and parents who lack access, resources, information or organizational skills to influence decisions (Narwana, 2011).

Currently, DEOs specifically assigned to promote SSA mandates, particularly in rural districts across the country, shoulder the responsibility to bridge the gap between local communities and schools. Current emphasis on the DEO's role to facilitate the community participation in school management points to a shift from the traditional inspectorate role this office has been playing so far. As the local parents and other members of the public get more and more involved in the management of schools, it is foreseeable that school and district administrators will need to exercise a more participatory form of governance and minimize their unilateral decision-making and blind monitoring for compliance with rules and regulations. Little information exists on whether DEOs are prepared for these changes and whether the national and local policies are realigned to change how DEOs are recruited, trained and retained to effectively meet the objectives of the RTE.

In recent years, there has been an increase in professional training for these DEOs and they are mostly provided by the state sponsored District Institutes of Education and Training (DIET) and the National University for Educational Planning and Administration (NUEPA), an entity directly under the central government. Very little research data exist to illustrate the quality of these trainings, their impact on DEO's performance, and follow-up measures. Also, these professional trainings are mostly not mandatory for DEOs and it is likely that those who are close to their retirement might be less interested in participating. Given the emerging context of the localized participatory format for school control and administration, the current and future DEOs need to be prepared accordingly. Serious discussions are underway to envision specific qualifications, models of pre- and in-service training. Furthermore, it is necessary to configure a new DEO who plays a transformational leadership role instead of a bureaucrat. The current Indian DEO has little fiscal and executive authority, compared with counterparts in the western countries where educational governance is more decentralized. The Indian DEO does not have so much direct influence on school personnel, or rapport with parents or the immediate community. It is imperative that the pivotal role and characteristics of the DEO undergo fundamental changes to align with the new national aspirations to empower local communities and reform schools for fostering a better learning climate and student success.

## ACKNOWLEDGEMENTS

Grateful acknowledgement is made to the following full-time Ph.D. students at Sri Ramakrishna Mission Vidyalaya College of Education, Coimbatore: K.N. Rathi, P.S. Sabeena, Suprabha Kumar and V. Resmi, for their diligent and scholarly work in the collection of data among DEOs in Kerala. Mr. R. Prabhu, an instructor at the above college, is also recognized with appreciation for data analysis and the production of tables and figures.

# REFERENCES

Altekar, A. S. (2009). *Education in ancient India*. Varanashi, India: Nand Kishore.

Banerjee, A., Banerjee, R., Dufto, E., Glennerster, R., & Khemani, S. (2008). *Pitfalls of participatory programs: Evidence from a randomized evaluation in education in India*. Retrieved from http://www.nber.org/papers/w14311

Blackwell, F. (2004). *India: A global studies handbook*. New York, N.Y.: ABC-CLIO.

Choudry, S. K. (2008). Higher education in India: A socio-historical journey from ancient period to 2006-2007. *The Journal of Educational Equity*, 8(1), 50-72.

India Development Gateway (2010). *Right of children to free and compulsory education*. Kukatpally, Hyderabad: Jawaharlal Nehru Technological University. Retrieved from http://www.indg.in/india/indg-newsletter/gateway-to-indias-development-vol-3-issue1-feb-2010/view

Kumar, N. (2007). *The politics of gender, community, and modernity*. New Delhi, India: Oxford University Press.

Ministry of Human Resource Development (2012). *Report to the people on education 2010-2011*. New Delhi: Government of India.

Ministry of Law (2009, August, 26). Gazette of India: Right of children to free and compulsory education, No. 35 of 2009. Delhi, India: Author.

Mukundan, M., & Bray, M. (2004). The decentralization of education in Kerala state, India: Rhetoric and reality. *International Review of Education*, 50, 223-243.

Narwana, K. (2011). Locating community in school education: A study of village education committees in Haryana, India. *The International Journal of Interdisciplinary Social Sciences*, 5(5), 373-386.

National University for Educational Planning and Administration (2012). Report 2010-11. Retrieved from http://schoolreportcards.in/SRC-NEW/Links?DISEPublication.aspx

Prabu, J. (2006). Educational institutions and philosophies, traditional and modern. In: S. Wolpert (Ed.), *Encyclopedia of India* (Vol. 2, p. 23-28). New York, N.Y.: Thompson Gale.

Sanchez, A. (2011). *Family engagement in education in Uttar Pradesh, India: Factors associated with the involvement of families in their children's education* (Doctoral dissertation). Retrieved from Dissertations & Theses: Full Text (Publication No. AAT 3478508).

Thirumalai, M. S. (2003, April 4). Lord Macaulay: The man who started it all and his minute. *Language of India*, *3*. Retrieved from http://www.languageinindia.com/april2003/macaulay.html

Tiyagi, R. S. (2009). *Administration and management in school education*. New Delhi, India: Shipra.

U. S. Central Intelligence Agency. (2012). *The world factbook: India*. Washington, DC: Author. Retrieved from https://www.cia.gov/library/publications/the-world-factbook/geos/in.html

World Bank (2009). *Education at a glance: India*. Washington, DC: Author. Retrieved from http://siteresources.worldbank.org/EXTEDSTATS/Resources/3232763-1171296190619/3445877-1172014191219/IND.pdf. retrieved 12/10/2013

In: The Educational Superintendent
Editor: Adam E. Nir

ISBN: 978-1-62948-972-8
© 2014 Nova Science Publishers, Inc.

*Chapter 11*

# THE FINNISH SUPERINTENDENT

## *Mika Risku and Pekka Kanervio*

University of Jyväskylä, Finland

## INTRODUCTION

The present chapter attempts to examine superintendence in Finland. It comprises four main sections. It begins with a brief description of Finnish society. The description explores both the present and the past, and includes an attempt to locate superintendence in the development of Finnish society. The second section concentrates on the Finnish educational system. The third section looks at municipalities and local provisions of education, which compose the fundamental operational environment for superintendents. In the fourth and last section, the focus is on the superintendents themselves. This section is based on the first national study (Kanervio & Risku, 2009) on superintendence in Finland. It looks at the demographics, role, position and views, and future of superintendents in Finland.

## FINNISH SOCIETY

Finnish society comprises the overall context for Finnish superintendence, so this chapter will begin with a brief description of it. The description will give both a general presentation of Finnish society today and a concise insight into the history of Finland. The historical insight will focus on positioning superintendence in Finland looking at the development of Finnish society, the educational system and municipalities.

Finland is located in Northern Europe bordering Sweden and Norway to the west, and Russia to the east. Finland is a modern Nordic welfare state with a fairly homogeneous population of 5.4 million people. There are two official languages. Finnish is spoken by the majority (90%), while Swedish is the mother tongue of a smaller minority (6%). Most (76%) are members of the National Lutheran Church. At present the mean age is 42, but the mean age will be rising in the future because the population is aging. Finland is divided into 320 municipalities, of which 57 are urban, 65 semi-urban and 198 rural. The size of municipalities varies significantly (Statistics Finland, 2013a).

Finland is a parliamentary republic. The 200-member Parliament, which represents the power of the people, is elected every four years. Executive power is vested in the President and the Government (Constitution of Finland, 1999). Usually the Government is made up of a coalition with ministers representing various political parties (Finnish Government, 2013). The main goal of the current Government is to develop Finland as a caring and successful country based on a competitive Nordic welfare state model (Valtioneuvosto, 2011). Finland has been a member of the European Union since 1995 (European Union, 2013).

Finnish society has ranked high in several international surveys in the 2000s. In a study by *Newsweek* (2010) in 2010, Finland was selected as the best country in the world, with the Finnish education system excelling in the study. Two years later, the International Transparency (2012) regarded Finland as the least corrupt country in the world, the Finnish people were ranked as the second happiest by the Earth Institute (2012), the World Economic Forum (2012) considered Finland as the third most competitive economy, and the Legatum Institution (2012) evaluated Finland to be the seventh most prosperous nation. Finland has currently been seen to possess the fourth best child welfare system (UNICEF, 2013).

It is essential to note that the development of Finland resembles that of many developing countries of today, and that the present status of Finnish society is very recent (Risku, 2011). Finland was first ruled by Sweden from the 12th century until 1809, and then until 1917 by Russia as an autonomous grand duchy (Jussila, 2007; Lehtonen, 2004). Like in many other countries, the Church had for a long time a decisive role in secular as well as in religious matters. The Church defined Finland as an administrative area (Kuikka, 1992), established the educational system (Lappalainen, 1991; Tähtinen & Hovi, 2007) as well as determined the territorial, administrative and legislative structures of municipalities (Pihlajanniemi, 2006).

Municipalities obtained their own local governments with the 1865 and 1872 Acts (Kuikka, 1992; Pihlajanniemi, 2006). The 1866 Basic Education Act (Peltonen 2002; Sarjala, 1982) and 1898 School District Act (Halila, 1949a; Peltonen, 2002; Salmela, 1946; Sarjala, 1982) mandated the local governments to provide basic education and gave them the right to obtain State aid for it. The above acts may be considered as the starting points for local authorities and local provisions of education in Finland.

After gaining independence in 1917, Finland developed its national governance in a sovereign manner without external powers confining its development. The sovereignty enabled the State to consistently make the effort to extend basic public education to reach every child (Kuikka, 1992; Sarjala, 1982). There was every reason for the aspiration, too. At the end of the 19th century, only 20% of 7-12-year-old children attended basic education schools. There was a significant inequity between the countryside and towns. Only 8% received basic education in the countryside, while in towns in practice everybody did (Kivinen, 1988; Peltonen 2002).

The 1921 Basic Education Act made basic education compulsory for all school-aged children. The State both strongly subsidized local authorities financially and gave them ample time to reach the goals (Halila, 1950; Kivinen, 1988; Lappalainen, 1991; Peltonen, 2002). By 1944 practically all local authorities had succeeded in constructing the school districts and basic education schools that legislation required (Kivinen, 1988; Kuikka, 1992).

Although basic education in the mid-1940s reached almost all school-aged children, educational inequity continued, because the parallel educational system of basic education and grammar schools was maintained (Kivinen, 1988; Kuikka 1992; Peltonen 2002). Local school administration concentrated on basic education and was both limited and weak

(Salmela, 1946; Somerkivi & Laine, 1959). There was neither the space nor the resources for the superintendent, especially in rural areas. The State, on the other hand, had an extensive and strong central administration, which governed society, the educational system and local authorities in a firm manner (Halila, 1949b; Isosomppi, 1996; Nikki, 2001; Sarjala, 1982).

After the Second World War, public debate on the societal role of education intensified. One result was that municipalities obtained the right to establish grammar schools with subsidies from the State (Sarjala, 2008). The 1945 School Board Act obligated every municipality to establish a local school board. The act also decreed that every local school board should include a teachers' representative to act both as the secretary for the board and as the executive manager for the local provision of basic education (Salmela, 1946). This teachers' representative may be regarded as the predecessor of the superintendent in Finland.

The parallel educational system was abolished with the 1968 Basic Education Act, which introduced the nine-year comprehensive school. Again, the State gave local authorities both a lot of financial support and time for implementation (Aho, Pitkänen & Sahlberg, 2006; Isosomppi, 1996; Kupiainen, Hautamäki & Karjalainen, 2009; Sarjala, 1982 & 2008; Varjo, 2007). To ensure implementation, educational administration was notably strengthened at all levels of society (Isosomppi, 1996; Kivinen, 1988; Lapiolahti, 2007; Lyytinen & Lukkarinen, 2010; Nikki, 2001; Sarjala, 1982 & 2008; Varjo, 2007).

Most grammar schools were merged in the local provisions of education (Sarjala, 2008). Thus municipalities obtained authority for the whole local provision of general education. With the growing State subsidies municipalities also obtained the resources to manage their provisions (Sarjala, 2008). In addition, the 1968 Act on the Administration in the Local Provision of Education mandated municipalities to establish a separate office for the director or secretary of the local provision of education, i.e., the office of the superintendent (Laki kunnan opetustoimen hallinnosta, 1968/467). With this act the office of the superintendent was established in Finland.

By the end of the 1970s the State had completely unified the system of general education. The unification was conducted with the State's norm-based, system-oriented and centralized steering apparatus. One can claim that with that apparatus the State was able to reach its goal of social equity in general education. As that took place, the world around began to alter in fundamental ways, and the apparatus could no longer meet the new demands.

A general change in thinking about the redistribution of power from the State to local authorities and schools came about already in the late 1970s (Niemelä, 2008; Pihlajanniemi, 2006). Many of the international trends, like neo-liberalism, democratic individualism and New Public Management, influenced the public debate on how to develop Finnish society (Laitila, 1999; Rinne, Kivirauma & Simola, 2002; Ryynänen, 2004; Varjo, 2007).

After the 1980s Finnish society began meeting notable economic and demographic challenges. Neither the demographic nor the economic situation has become significantly less demanding during the 2000s either. The challenges have accelerated the redefinition of the relationship between the State and municipalities, which the State has regarded as the primary solution to meeting the challenges (Risku, 2011).

The previous cost-based and earmarked statutory government transfer system has been completely reformed into an index-based and non-earmarked one (Souri, 2009). In addition, the State and local authority allocations have almost been reversed. As the comprehensive educational system was implemented, the government transfer for education was 70% (Aho et al., 2006). In 2012 the State covered 34% of the estimated costs for basic education and 42% of those for upper secondary education (National Board of Education, 2013).

The 1995 Municipal Act gave municipalities a constitutional autonomy and made them main providers of public services (Kuntalaki, 1995/365; Pihlajaniemi, 2006). The 1998 aggregation of legislation merged the 26 disjointed separate education acts into nine acts, one for each different education form, from primary to higher education (Aho et al., 2006; Souri, 2009).

The constitutional autonomy and the reforms have provided municipalities with ample opportunities to reorganize their administration, and local authorities have used their freedom, too. Concerning superintendents, the consequences have been significant. The 1992 Act on the Administration in the Local Provision of Education (Laki kunnan opetustoimen hallinnosta, 1992/706) abolished the office of the superintendent in legislation. As the result, the 1990s saw a consistent decrease of full-time superintendents in municipalities (Rajanen, 2000).

## FINNISH EDUCATIONAL SYSTEM

The national educational system is the basic framework for Finnish superintendents, and will be presented next. The presentation is mainly based on the information given by the Ministry of Education (2013) and the National Board of Education (2013).

The Finnish educational system is divided into three main tiers, as illustrated in Figure 1 (Risku, 2011): basic education, upper secondary general or vocational education, and higher education.

| | Universities | | | Polytechnics |
|---|---|---|---|---|
| Age 25 | Doctor's Degree Master's Degree (2 years) | **Higher** | **Education** | Master's Degree (2 years) (3 year work experience) |
| | Bachelor's Degree (3 years) | | | Bachelor's Degree (3 years) |
| 19 | Matriculation Examination **Upper Secondary General Education** (2-4 years) | | | Vocational Qualifications **Upper Secondary Vocational Education** Apprenticeship |
| 16 | **Basic Education** (forms 1-9) | | | |
| 7 | | | | |
| 6 | **Pre-School Education** (1 year) | | | |

Source: Risku, 2011.

Figure 1. Finnish Educational System.

Municipalities have the obligation to provide basic education and assign each pupil a place in the local school. Pupils, on the other hand, are free to enroll in the school of their choice. Basic education comprises a nine-year comprehensive school, which is based on a single structure. In 2012, there were 2,789 comprehensive schools (Statistics Finland, 2103b). The number of schools has been declining steadily over the last decades. In 2009, about 45% of the schools had fewer than 100 pupils. The largest schools had over 900.

During the year before compulsory education begins, the child may participate in pre-school education, which is voluntary although municipalities are obligated to provide it. In 2009, 99.4% of 6-7-year-old children attended pre-school education, about 70% of whom also attended day care. Compulsory education begins when a child turns seven and ends when ten years have passed since the child started compulsory education.

Licenses to provide upper secondary education are supplied by the Ministry of Education and Culture. In 2012, there were 428 general upper secondary schools with a total of 107,412 students. As with basic education, the numbers of both general upper secondary students and schools have been consistently decreasing during the 2000s (Statistics Finland, 2013c).

The Government determines the overall national goals and the allocation of time for the various subjects. The goals and core contents of the subjects, as well as those of subject groups, thematic subject modules and student counseling are determined by the National Board of Education. Finally, it is up to the educational providers to compile and approve a local curriculum and a yearly work plan according to national guidelines.

The Ministry of Education and Culture determines the general framework for evaluation of education together with the Finnish Education Evaluation Council, Finnish Higher Education Evaluation Council and the National Board of Education. There is no inspection system or pre-inspection of text books (Opetus- ja kulttuuriministeriö, 2012a & b; Ministry of Education and Culture, 2013). The evaluation system includes an international, national, provincial and local level, and makes use of comprehensive information, not solely focusing on learning outcomes. The salient findings of evaluation are considered public information and have to be published (Opetus- ja kulttuuriministeriö, 2012b).

The learning outcomes of the Finnish educational system have been outstanding in all international evaluations in the 2000s. Finland had the best overall results in the 2000, 2003 and 2006 PISA surveys (OECD, 2001, 2003, 2004, 2006). In the 2009 PISA survey Finland obtained third place (OECD 2010a & b). When Finland participated in the 2011 PIRLS (Mullis, Martin, Foy & Drucker, 2012) and TIMMS (Martin, Mullis, Foy & Stanco, 2012; Mullis, Martin, Foy & Arora, 2012) surveys, the results were at the top as well. In all the above PISA, PIRLS and TIMMS surveys, Finland has had the smallest variation in the results of the schools. In addition, the Finnish educational system seems to be highly economical regarding both money and time spent on instruction (Sahlberg, 2011).

The national evaluation of learning outcomes is the responsibility of the National Board of Education (Opetus- ja kulttuuriministeriö, 2012a). In addition, a separate Matriculation Examination Board assesses the learning outcomes of all general upper secondary schools biannually (Finnish Matriculation Examination, 2012). The National Board of Education does not provide ranking lists, because they are regarded as unreliable, and they do not seem to consider the operational environments of the schools (Kuusela, 2008).

National level evaluation is often criticized for not being able to pay sufficient attention to societal changes and to the everyday challenges of schools. Educational policies and their objectives are deemed to have starting-points that are too theoretical and idealistic and that do not take into consideration the real situations of schools (Hannus et al., 2010).

Local education providers are obligated by law to evaluate their education and to participate in external evaluations as stated in legislation (Opetus- ja kulttuuriministeriö, 2012b). The purpose of local evaluation is to develop education at the local level and to connect local evaluation results with national ones (Kupiainen et al., 2009; Lapiolahti, 2007).

Local authorities often seem to have difficulty making concrete decisions to develop their provisions of education on the basis of evaluations (Lapiolahti, 2007; Löfström, Metsämuuronen, Niemi, Salmio & Stenvall, 2005; Rajanen, 2000; Svedlin, 2003). One of the reasons may be that educational administration outside schools was cut by 40% between 1990 and 1995 as the centralized governance system was dismantled (Hirvi, 1996).

In general, education in Finland is free of charge and funded by the statutory government transfer system, determined as a unit price for each student by the Ministry of Education and Culture. As earlier described, it is estimated to cover 34% of the operating costs of basic education and 42% of those of upper secondary education. The subsidy is paid directly to the education provider and is not earmarked for any particular purposes. Local authorities have to cover the remaining costs.

Concerning both basic and general upper secondary education, the main education providers are municipalities. In 2012, 96% of comprehensive schools were maintained by local authorities (Statistics Finland, 2013b). Local authorities also maintain most general upper secondary schools. Only a few are managed by private organizations (8% in 2009).

# MUNICIPALITIES AND LOCAL PROVISIONS AS FINNISH SUPERINTENDENTS' OPERATIONAL ENVIRONMENTS

Municipalities and local provisions of education form the most fundamental operating environments for Finnish superintendents. Finnish superintendents serve the local authorities in their efforts to provide education as State legislation requires them to do. They do not serve the State as such. In addition, legislation, as a norm, mostly obligates the education providers, not superintendents, principals or teachers (Souri, 2009). Furthermore, the present legislation does not even recognize the office of superintendent.

As previously stated, the size of municipalities varies a lot. In 2012, the variation was between 603,928 and 101 inhabitants. About 68% of the 320 municipalities had fewer than 10,000. There were only nine cities with more than 100,000 inhabitants. About half (46%) of the population lived in municipalities of between 10,000–100,000 (Local Finland, 2013a).

As the sizes of municipalities vary, the sizes of the local provisions of general education do, too. Concerning basic education, the average number of pupils was 1,605 in 2012. The numbers varied between 8 and 46,185. About 70% (226) of municipalities had less than 1,000 basic education pupils in their local provisions (Statistics Finland, 2013b).

The Municipal Act (Kuntalaki, 1995/365) mandates municipalities to have a municipal council, an executive board, an inspection board and a municipal manager. Furthermore, both the Basic Education Act (628/1998) and the General Upper Secondary Education Act (Lukiolaki 629/1998) require every school to have a principal and a sufficient number of teachers and other personnel. Otherwise municipalities may decide freely on their organization.

Because municipalities and their local provisions of education are of such varying sizes and municipalities can organize themselves with a lot of autonomy, their organizations differ a lot from each other. Small municipalities often have a very basic and limited administration, merely to meet legal requirements and to be able to manage necessities. Larger municipalities may comprise very complicated and multi-faceted administrations.

According to Kanervio and Risku (2009), almost every municipality has a separate board of education in Finland. In 2008, only 0.5% of the municipalities did not have a separate school board. In those municipalities, education was managed by the executive board. A few (2.4%) municipalities provided education jointly, and thus also shared the same school board.

Usually boards cannot concentrate solely on general education (26.6% in 2008). Most typically (56.8%) their areas of responsibility also include culture, library, sports and youth services. Some (4.8%) have even broader responsibilities with services like daycare, public transport or information technology (Kanervio & Risku, 2009). The area of responsibility of the school board seems to affect the responsibilities of the superintendent. The broader the area of the local board of education is, the broader also the scope of the superintendent appears to be.

In the same way as the sizes of municipalities and local provisions of education vary significantly, so do also the sizes of staffs in the local provisions. In 2008, the variation between the overall sizes of staffs working in local provisions of education was 1–4,031, the average being 186. The variation becomes even more considerable when examining the sizes of staff in local school offices. In 2008, the sizes of staff in local school offices varied between 0–100. Almost 5% of the municipalities had nobody, not even a superintendent, at the town hall to manage the local provision of education. In addition, in 21.9% of the municipalities there was only one person, often the one acting in the role of the superintendent, in the local school office. In 26.7% of the municipalities the superintendent had another member of staff to support his/her work in the local school office. Only 5.7% of superintendents had a local school office staff including more than 10 people. In addition, only 6.2% of the municipalities had district principals and 1.4% school principals to support the work of the superintendents (Kanervio & Risku, 2009).

## THE FINNISH SUPERINTENDENT

Next we shall concentrate on the Finnish superintendent. The examination is based on the report by Kanervio and Risku (2009), if not otherwise stated. The report is based on the first national study of superintendence in Finland. The study was funded by the Ministry of Education and Culture, and conducted by the Institute of Educational Leadership at the University of Jyväskylä in 2008.

## Demographics of Finnish Superintendents

Most Finnish municipalities (about 89% in 2008) have a superintendent for their local provisions of education. The gender distribution of superintendents is very even, with 50.5% men and 49.5% women in 2008. In general, larger and urban municipalities have a greater number of male superintendents, and smaller and rural municipalities more female superintendents. Comparing the results of Kanervio and Risku's report (2009) with those of Pirhonen and Janhunen (1995), one notices a significant increase in the number of female superintendents in the 2000s. In 1995, only 32% of the superintendents were female.

The average age of superintendents was 50.2 years in 2008, with no major difference between the genders. Over half (51.9%) of the superintendents were older than 50, and only a few (1.0%) younger than 30. The overall age distribution was 27–67. Again, there were no significant differences between the genders.

Most superintendents have experience working as a teacher (83.8% in 2008), a vice or assistant principal (18.1%) and/or principal (57.6%). Men have most typically worked both as teachers and principals before becoming superintendents. Women, on the other hand, have had a more direct career path to superintendence with less experience of working as a teacher and/or principal.

As the present legislation does not recognize the office of the superintendent, there are no stated requirements for the qualification of the superintendent, nor is there a qualifying educational level. Finnish superintendents, however, seem to be quite well educated, particularly in educational sciences. In 2008, altogether 98.1% had a teacher's qualification. Most (81.4%) had higher university degrees, and some a licentiate (7.1%) or doctoral (4.3%) degree. The most common major in the degrees appears to be educational sciences (37.5% in 2008), which is the typical major for class teachers. Concerning superintendents with a subject teacher's background, the major seems to vary a lot, with history (11.2%) and Finnish language (6.5%) the most favored.

As there is neither qualification nor qualifying education for superintendents, one may expect their administrative education to be very heterogeneous. That also is the case. Superintendents appear to have very diverse combinations of often fairly brief administrative training, in very different fields. As a result, less than half (45.0% in 2008) of superintendents are satisfied with their administrative education, and many consider that they learned the profession on the job. Thus, it is no surprise that most Finnish superintendents (69.2% in 2008) would like to have a national qualification for superintendents determined in legislation that would guarantee them sufficient pre-service education.

In the same way as the sizes of municipalities vary, so do superintendents' salaries. There is a significant correlation between the size of the municipality and the superintendent's salary. As female superintendents more typically work in smaller rural municipalities, their average monthly gross salary is significantly lower (4,094.40€ in 2008) than that of male superintendents (4,608.50€). Not surprisingly, the overall variation in superintendents' salaries (1,100€ – 10,000€) also well reflects the very different kind of positions people working in the office of the superintendent have in Finland.

## Role of Finnish Superintendents

Thanks to their constitutional autonomy, local authorities may decide with broad autonomy whether to have a superintendent and how to determine his/her job description. Furthermore as earlier described, municipalities are very different from each other, and they use their constitutional autonomy to arrange their local provisions of education very independently. As a result, the role of superintendent varies a lot from one municipality to the other. As one indication of the variation, one may note that in total 35 different titles were found for the superintendent in 2008.

As previously mentioned, most (about 89% in 2008) municipalities in Finland have a superintendent. Most often the superintendent is called the Director of Education and Culture (64.5%) or the Director of Education (24.2%), and he/she has a written job description (89.5%) decided by the municipal council. Almost always the job description determines that the superintendent is in charge of the whole local provision of general education.

Furthermore, superintendents are typically members of the municipal management team, manage the local school office, and act as principals' superior. Concerning the last task, it is noteworthy that superintendents very rarely (6.7% in 2008) select the principals. Most often the selection is made by the school board (77.1%). Then again, one of the superintendents' essential tasks is to prepare issues for the local education board to decide.

The superintendent selection processes reflect the superintendent's key role in the central administration of the municipality. The selection is most commonly made by the municipal council (57.1% in 2008) or the executive board (32.9%). Very rarely it is the municipal director (4.8%) or the school board (3.3%) that makes the decision. Most municipalities select their superintendents using open public application processes (60.0% in 2008), but also internal transfers (26.7%) and applications (3.8%) inside municipalities take place. The position of the superintendent is usually tenured (83.8% in 2008). Fixed-term arrangements (16.2%) appear to be used mainly only in exceptional situations, as when hiring a substitute.

When selecting the superintendent, the selectors seem to be looking especially at the applicant's qualification ($\overline{X}$=4.44 – on a 5-point scale), experience ($\overline{X}$=4.25) and personality ($\overline{X}$=4.09). It also appears to be important that the applicant's views correspond to the strategies of the municipality ($\overline{X}$=4.09). On the other hand, the applicant's gender, political stands and age do not seem to have much influence on the selection process.

The superintendent's area of responsibility seems to correspond to the one of the school board. Thus, in the same way as most school boards have very broad responsibilities, so also do the superintendents. In 2008, 70.5% of superintendents were responsible, besides education, also for culture, youth and sports services. Only 27.1% could concentrate solely on general education. Besides, 21.4% of those working in the office of the superintendent worked also as principals, 6% as administrative directors and 2% as office secretaries. Similarly to school boards, superintendents' responsibilities in small rural municipalities were very significantly broader than in larger urban municipalities, and significantly broader than in semi-urban municipalities.

Local school boards expect superintendents primarily to manage financial and general administration. The second most significant expectation concerns the development of the local provision of education, followed by pedagogical leadership and collaboration with the school board. Only 21.4% of superintendents believe that the expectations of the board change after municipal elections.

What superintendents themselves consider as their most essential tasks and what they describe doing in reality corresponds only partly with what school board members expect them to do. As their five most central tasks, superintendents name management of finances (15.7% of mentions), management of educational services (13.6%), general administration (12.5%), supervision and evaluation (12.3%) and staff management (9.9%).

When the superintendents were asked how they really spend their time, a somewhat different kind of list was created. It seems that staff management (21.5% of mentions) is the most time-consuming task. It is followed by management of finances (14.0%), general administration (11.7%), networking (8.1%), management of support services (8.0%) and working with the school board (8.0%).

Particularly considering the radical changes taking place in Finnish society, it is surprising that strategic planning and leadership do not seem to be among superintendents' most central tasks (6.4% of mentions) or to take much of their time (7.8%). Also, although almost all superintendents have a teacher's qualification, most of them do not seem to consider pedagogical leadership as one of their most central tasks (2.2%) or spend much time on it (4.3%).

The prevalence of managerial tasks may reflect at least three issues. Firstly, it seems that the role of leading public office holders today includes many characteristics of the New Public Management ideology (Aho et al., 2006; Alava, Halttunen & Risku, 2012). Superintendents are no longer public servants implementing guidelines and reporting their implementation according to the centralized system-oriented State administration. They serve local authorities which have both constitutional autonomy and responsibility for providing public services. In that administration they are the general managers of the local provisions of education with an inclusive responsibility of their organizations.

Secondly, the tight financial situation that has prevailed in Finland since the 1990s together with the reform of the statutory government transfer system has made financial management a key area in municipalities. Local authorities now cover 66% of costs for basic education and 58% of those for secondary education. In addition, the State subsidies are based on the number of pupils/students and are not earmarked (Ministry of Education and Culture, 2013; National Board of Education, 2013). The system requires exact forecasts and follow-ups of the numbers of pupils/students, and constant conflict with the other branches of administration in the municipalities to ensure local provisions of education the optimal resources.

Thirdly, superintendents often seem to have very little staff to support their work. It is no wonder that the everyday management and administration appears to fill their working days. By examining superintendents' answers about their use of time more closely in Kanervio and Risku's (2009) research it is apparent that 25.7% of the answers concern very basic everyday chores, like ensuring that the required services are provided, handling acute changes and problems, answering surveys and producing statistics, having meetings, and merely dealing with all kinds of routine issues. Also, 82.2% of superintendents are responsible for school transport, 71.9% for school premises, 66.6% for student care, 37.1% for school lunches and 22.4% for janitorial services. Some superintendents' comments on how routine or acute issues and emails fill their working days can be described as heart-breaking, to say the least.

Most (84.3% in 2008) superintendents report that their work is evaluated by somebody. The most common primary evaluator appears to be the municipal director (64.7%). Some superintendents (15.6%) also name the internal inspection board as their most central evaluator. Otherwise, politically appointed organs very rarely evaluate superintendents' work: school board (5.6%), municipal council (3.9%) and executive board (3.4%).

More than half (64.2% in 2008) of superintendents consider their work to include a lot or very much stress. In addition, only very few (2.4%) think their work does not include stress at all, or only a little (5.2%). Stress seems to affect superintendents mainly psychologically (82.3%), but also physically (14.0%). The most common psychological symptoms appear to be sleeplessness (16.5%), fatigue (16.5%), reduced attention span (8.7%), frustration (5.4%) and anxiety (4.1%). Concerning physical symptoms, headaches and problems with blood pressure are the most frequently mentioned (both 4.2%)

As the most significant reasons for stress, superintendents name the disjointedness of work (32.6%), problematic tasks (28.3%) and being hurried (27.0%). Considering how most superintendents have to work alone it is surprising how few (4.6%) mention lack of staff as the reason for their stress. When probing superintendents' views on factors impeding their occupational welfare, the high number of non-essential tasks, the range of responsibilities and inadequate budgets come up. In addition, superintendents appear to regard mastering their own working time as one of the key factors affecting their work.

Although superintendents appear to consider their work both very challenging and stress-creating, most (82.8% in 2008) of them seem to think that they succeed well or very well in their job. A majority (68.1%) would also select the same profession again, if they were given the opportunity to reconsider. In 2008, about one fourth (24.3%) appeared to have plans to move to other tasks over the next five years.

## Finnish Superintendents in Local Decision Making: Position and Views

As already described, Finnish superintendents do not serve the state, rather local authorities, which have constitutional autonomy to arrange their organization and to decide how to provide the public services legislation mandates them to provide. Also, superintendents are almost always in charge of the whole local provision of general education, and typically are associated with the municipal management team. Thus, superintendents also participate in forming and enacting both the strategies of the municipality and the local provisions of education.

Concerning municipal strategies, superintendents consider local authorities primarily to aim at adapting to the changes in the operational environment (95.7%) and at anticipating future changes (84.3%). Most (74.8%) also seem to be of the opinion that strategic decisions are made through genuinely democratic decision making processes, and regard it as important as well. Quite a few (39.5%), too, consider strategies to meet the unavoidable necessities, and a few (14.8%) think strategies are created randomly. When deciding on strategies, fulfilling operational needs (86.2%) is the most often selected option, but also meeting economic needs is regarded as essential (77.6%).

Concerning the relationship between the State and local authorities, superintendents hold the opinion that strategic decisions by the State establish the framework in which local authorities operate, although municipal councils make the ultimate strategic decisions. According to superintendents, the State attempts to support local strategic thinking with both support and obligation. As support they name guidance (29.3% of mentions), education (11.7%) and projects (10.3%). Obligations comprise mainly funding (20.0%) and legislation

(8.8%). At least the national core curricula (10.7%) can be considered to include characteristics of both support and obligation. National curricula obligate local authorities, but also give them a lot of freedom to meet the statutes. One can conclude that according to the superintendents, the national governance system seems to correspond fairly well to the labor division between the State and local authorities, as it is determined in the Constitution and Municipal Act.

At the municipal level, strategic decisions concerning local provisions of education seem to be based on the decisions made by the municipal council and the executive board with an almost equal impact by the superintendent and school board. In the same way as with the general strategic decisions in municipalities, the strategic decisions of the school boards are, according to the superintendents, affected more by those of the municipal council and executive board than those by the State. School boards seem to confer quite a lot of value on the views of the municipal officials in their strategic decision making.

Superintendents consider economic factors to influence school board members' decisions most. Pedagogical factors are ranked second. As with other local decision making, party politics do not seem to have major significance. The most difficult issues with which school board members deal appear to be economic ones, pressures created by local inhabitants and meeting local strategic decisions.

Superintendents regard their own views as the most important for school board members' decision making. Board members also seem to value principals' views a great deal, particularly in rural municipalities. Significant, too, are the views of parents, the municipal central administration, teachers and local inhabitants. Again, the views of the State seem to have less importance than those of local actors.

Superintendents themselves seem to listen especially to the views of other municipal officials in their decision making. Principals seem to have the largest impact, followed by the municipal central administration, teachers and superintendents in other municipalities. Concerning other actors, school board members' and parents' views appear to be the most influential. Superintendents also seem to listen to students and local inhabitants. The views of the State, once more, seem to have less value.

What mostly seem to occupy superintendents' decision making are demographic changes and schools' increasing economic needs. Local expectations on effectiveness, caring for those at risk of marginalization, change in societal values and school safety seem to also create major challenges. The list can be supplemented with parents' problems with bringing up their children, the relationship with the school board and meeting local and national statues, staff management, evaluation of learning outcomes, teacher selections, changes in curricula and inadequate resources for technology.

## ON THE FUTURE OF FINNISH SUPERINTENDENCY

One can claim that Finnish society is in the process of radically and rapidly evolving change, which started in the 1990s and is still continuing. In the 1990s the relationship between the State and municipalities was completely reversed. Municipalities were made the main providers of public services, and they obtained constitutional autonomy. It is in many ways absurd that the office of the director of the local provision of education, which was created in 1968 to ensure the implementation of the comprehensive education system, was abolished from legislation in 1992 in the midst of the reformation of the relationship between the State and local authorities. It was exactly then that there began to be a real need for the superintendent to lead and manage the local provision of education.

Fortunately, most local authorities have maintained the office of the superintendent, and there seem to be superintendents who are well-educated, possess appropriate work experience, and are committed to their profession. The present Government is developing Finland as a competitive Nordic welfare state, based on strong municipalities (Valtioneuvosto, 2011). The year 2008 saw the merger of 99 municipalities, decreasing the number of municipalities from 415 to 348 (Local Finland, 2013b). In 2012, the Government approved a white paper to decrease the number of municipalities to 66-70 (Valtiovarainministeriö, 2012). At present, the number seems to be open, but will no doubt be notably smaller than the one today.

No doubt, the way local authorities arrange their provisions of education and provide education will change radically in the near future. In the study by Kanervio and Risku (2009), only 5.7% of superintendents did not expect their local provisions of education to change radically by 2015. Or in other words, 94.3% were anticipating radical changes to take place. What will happen to the superintendents amid the changes?

According to Kanervio and Risku (2009), superintendents themselves most commonly (41.0% in 2008) expect their position to remain more or less the same, or to strengthen (24.3%) in the near future. Only 11.9% believe their position will weaken. When superintendents were asked about what would happen to their job descriptions, 33.2% replied that they expected their areas of responsibilities to expand, 28.1% anticipated the priorities of their work to change, and 18.9% were looking forward to obtaining more explicit job descriptions.

The authors of the present chapter will present their own scenario in the following way. As the number of municipalities decreases, there will certainly be fewer superintendents. On the other hand, local provisions of education will be larger and more complex organizations, and will require superintendent-like office holders to lead and manage them. Most likely municipalities will continue to act as the main providers of general education. Nothing seems to challenge their constitutional autonomy either. Also, there are no indications of abolishing the index-based and non-earmarked statutory government transfer system, so there has to be somebody at the municipality to secure and manage resources for education. In addition, the anticipated changes taking place in local provisions of education require people who will lead and manage the change processes at the municipal level. Furthermore, local level social equity in education calls for somebody who will look at the municipality as a whole, ensuring that people in various parts of the municipality have equal access to education. One can conclude that there will be even more need for full-time, well-educated and experienced superintendents to lead and manage the local provisions of education than ever before.

Due to the economic and demographic challenges local authorities are facing today it will not be easy to have the office of superintendent legislated. Municipalities seem to be cautious about everything new that would increase their workloads or restrict their operations. Without having the office of superintendent legislated there can be neither national qualifications nor national qualifying training for superintendents. Those issues have to be resolved through novel ways to both guarantee that local authorities obtain the superintendents they require and that superintendents have the knowledge and skills they need when they start in the profession.

As the sizes of municipalities and local provisions of education grow, superintendents will hopefully have larger staffs to support their work. At the moment, most superintendents seem to be working without sufficient support staff, and with quite extensive workloads. This issue is not unproblematic to solve either, because the trend is to reduce the number of people working in administration. So, a novel way of thinking will be needed here as well. It seems to be as superintendents predict: things will change radically in local provisions of education. One could also add that they have to.

# REFERENCES

Aho, E., Pitkänen, K., & Sahlberg, P. (2006). *Policy development and reform principles of basic and secondary education in Finland since 1968.* Washington, DC: World Bank.

Alava, J., Halttunen, L., & Risku, M. (2012). *Changing School management. Status review - May 2012.* Helsinki: Finnish National Board of Education Vol.3.

Basic Education Act (628/1998).

Constitution of Finland (1999). Retrieved on 15.4.2012 from: http://www.finlex.fi/fi/ laki/ kaannokset/1999/en19990731.pdf.

Earth Institute (2012). Retrieved on 24.3.2013 from: http://issuu.com/earthinstitute/ docs/world-happiness-report.

European Union (2013). Retrieved on 24.3.2013 from: http://europa.eu/about-eu/countries /member-countries/finland/index_en.htm.

Finnish Government (2013). Retrieved on 28.3.2013 from: http://valtioneuvosto.fi/ hallitus/en.jsp.

Finnish Matriculation Examination (2012). Retrieved on 25.9.2012 from: http://www. ylioppilastutkinto.fi/en/index.html.

Halila, A. (1949a). *Suomen kansakoululaitoksen historia. Kolmas osa. Piirijakoasetuksesta oppivelvollisuuteen.* [History of Finnish Folkschool. Third Part. From District Act to Compulsory Education]. Suomalainen tiedeakatemia. Suomen tiedettä Nro 3,3. Helsinki: WSOY.

Halila, A. (1949b). *Suomen kansakoululaitoksen historia. Toinen osa. Kansakouluasetuksesta piirijakoon.* [History of Finnish Folkschool. Second Part. From Folkschool Act to District Act ]. Suomalainen tiedeakatemia. Suomen tiedettä Nro 3,2. Helsinki: WSOY.

Halila, A. (1950). *Suomen kansakoululaitoksen historia. Neljäs osa. Oppivelvollisuuskoulun alkuvaiheet (1921–1939).* [History of Finnish Folkschool. Fourth Part. First Phases of Compulsory Education School (1921-1939)]. Suomalainen tiedeakatemia. Suomen tiedettä Nro 3,4. Helsinki: WSOY.

Hannus, S., Kauko, J., Kynkäänniemi, H., Pitkänen, H., Simola, M. Varjo, J., & Väätäinen, E. (2010). A dream well planned: Discursive space and social positions in Finnish comprehensive education quality assurance. In: Kauko, J., Rinne, R., & Kynkäänniemi, H. (Eds.). *Restructuring the truth of schooling – Essays on discursive practices in the sociology and politics of education.* Finnish Education Research Association, Research in Educational Sciences 48, pp. 246-273.

Hirvi, V. (1996). *Koulutuksen rytminvaihdos. 1990-luvun koulutuspolitiikka Suomessa.* [The Change of Rhythm in Education]. Keuruu: Otava Publishing Company.

International Transparency (2012). Retrieved on 4.5.2013 from http://www. transparency.org/cpi2012/results.

Isosomppi, L. (1996). *Johtaja vai juoksupoika. Suomalaisen yleissivistävän koulun johtamiskulttuurin ja sen determinanttien tarkastelua.* [Leader or Errand Boy. Examination on Leadership Culture and its Determinants in Finnish General Education School]. Tampere: Acta Universitatis Tamperensis ser A vol. 514.

Jussila, O. (2007). *Suomen historian suuret myytit.* [The great myths of Finnish history]. Helsinki: WSOY.

Kanervio, P., & Risku, M. (2009). *Tutkimus kuntien yleissivistävän koulutuksen opetustoimen johtamisen tilasta ja muutoksista Suomessa.* Opetusministeriön julkaisuja 2009:16. [A study on educational leadership in general education in Finnish municipalities. Publications of the Ministry of Education Vol. 16].

Kivinen, O. (1988). *Koulutuksen järjestelmäkehitys. Peruskoulutus ja valtiollinen koulutusdoktriini Suomessa 1800- ja 1900- luvuilla.* [System Development of Education. Basic Education and State Education Doctrine in Finland in the 1800s and 1900s]. Turun yliopiston julkaisusarja C 67 [Turku University Publications Vol. C 67].

Kuikka, M. (1992). *Suomalaisen koulutuksen vaiheet.* [Phases of Finnish Education]. Helsinki: Otava Publishing Company.

Kupiainen, S., Hautamäki, J., & Karjalainen, T. (2009). *The Finnish education system and PISA.* Ministry of Education Publications, Finland Vol. 46.

Kuntalaki (1995/365). [Municipal Act].

Kuusela, J. (2008). *Koulukohtaisten keskiarvojen tulkinnoista.* [On the Evaluation of School-specific Means]. Helsinki: Opetushallituksen muistio. [Helsinki: National Board of Education Memorandum].

Laitila, T. (1999). *Siirtoja Koulutuksen Ohjauskentällä Suomen yleissivistävän koulutuksen ohjaus 1980- ja 1990-luvuilla.* [Shifts in the Control Domain. Control of Finnish education system in the 1980s and 1990s]. Turun yliopiston julkaisuja C146. Turku: Turun yliopisto.

Laki kunnan opetustoimen hallinnosta (1968/467). [Act on the Administration in the Local Provision of Education].

Laki kunnan opetustoimen hallinnosta (1992/706). [Act on the Administration in the Local Provision of Education].

Lapiolahti, R. (2007). *Koulutuksen arviointi kunnallisen koulutuksen järjestäjän tehtävänä – Paikallisen arvioinnin toteutumisedellytysten arviointia erään kuntaorganisaation näkökulmasta.* [The evaluation of schooling as a task of the communal maintainer of schooling – what are the presuppositions of the execution of evaluation in one specific communal organization]. Jyväskylä: Jyväskylä Studies in Education, Psychology and Social Research Vol. 308.

Lappalainen, A. (1991). *Suomi kouluttajana.* [Finland as Educator]. Helsinki: WSOY.

Legatum Institution (2012). Retrieved on 8.4.2013 from http://www.prosperity.com/ Ranking.aspx.

Lehtonen, T. (2004). Epilogi: Suomi ja suomalainen sivistys. [Epilogue: Finland and Finnish Civilization]. In: Schwanitz, D. (2004). *Sivistyksen käsikirja.* [Handbook of Civilization]. Helsinki: Gummerus Publishing Company, pp. 571-602.

Local Finland (2013a). Retrieved on 16.5.2013 from http://www.kunnat.net/fi/tietopankit/tilastot/vaestotietoja/Sivut/default.aspx.

Local Finland (2013b). Retrieved on 20.5.2013 from http://www.kunnat.net/fi/tietopankit/tilastot/aluejaot/kuntien-lukumaara/Sivut/default.aspx

Lukiolaki (629/1998). [General Upper Secondary Education Act].

Löfström, E., Metsämuuronen, J., Niemi, E.K., Salmio, K., & Stenvall, K. (2005). *Koulutuksen paikallinen arviointi vuonna 2004.* [Local Evaluation of Education in Year 2004]. Opetushallitus. Arviointi 2/2005. Helsinki: Hakapaino.

Lyytinen, H., & Lukkarinen, E. (2010). Arvioinnin lakia niin kuin sitä luetaan historiasta nykypäivään [Legislation on Evaluation as It Is Read in History till Today]. In: Korkeakoski, E., & Tynjälä, P. (Eds.). *Hyötyä ja vaikuttavuutta arvioinnista* [Benefit and Effectiveness with Evaluation]. Koulutuksen arviointineuvoston julkaisuja 50. Jyväskylä: Koulutuksen arviointineuvosto, pp. 77-100. [Education Evaluation Council Publications Vol. 50. Jyväskylä: Education Evaluation Council, pp. 77-100].

Martin, M. O., Mullis, I.V.S., Foy, P., & Stanco, G.M. (2012). *Timss 2011 International Results in Science.* Chestnut Hill, Mass.: TIMSS & PIRLS International Study Center, Lynch School of Education, Boston College.

Ministry of Education and Culture (2013). Retrieved on 20.4.2013 from http://www.minedu.fi/OPM/Koulutus/koulutuspolitiikka/koulutuksen_arviointi/?lang=en.

Mullis, I. V. S., Martin, M. O., Foy, P., & Arora, A. (2012). *Timss 2011 International Results in Mathematics.* Chestnut Hill, Mass.: TIMSS & PIRLS International Study Center, Lynch School of Education, Boston College.

Mullis, I. V. S., Martin, M. O., Foy, P., & Drucker, K. T. (2012). *PIRLs 2011 International Results in Reading.* Chestnut Hill, Mass.: TIMSS & PIRLS International Study Center, Lynch School of Education, Boston College.

National Board of Education (2013). Education. Retrieved 25.4. 2013 from: http://www.oph.fi/english/education.

Newsweek (2010). Retrieved 15.10.2011 from: http://www.thedailybeast.com/newsweek/2010/08/15/interactive-infographic-of-the-worlds-best-countries.html.

Niemelä, M. (2008). *Julkisen sektorin reformin pitkä kaari Valtava-uudistuksesta Paras-hankkeeseen.* [The Long Reform of Public Sector from Valtava-reform to PARAS-project]. Helsinki: Kela, Sosiaali- ja terveysturvan tutkimuksia 102.

Nikki, M. L. (2001). Hallinto- ja toimintakulttuurin kehittyminen perusopetusta antavissa kouluissa 2000- luvun alkuun [Development of Administration and Organizational Culture in Basic Education Schools till the Beginning of 2000s]. In: Kari, J., Moilanen, P., & Räihä, P. (Eds.). *Opettajan taipaleelle.* [For Teacher's Career]. Jyväskylä: University of Jyväskylä, pp. 169-186.

OECD (2001). *Knowledge and Skills for Life - First Results from The OECD Programme for International Student Assessment (PISA), 2000.*

OECD (2003). *First Results from PISA, 2003, Executive Summary.*

OECD (2004). *Messages from PISA, 2000.*

OECD (2006). *PISA 2006: Science Competencies for Tomorrow's World Executive Summary.*

OECD (2010a). *PISA 2009 Results: What Students Know and Can Do, Student Performance in Reading, Mathematics and Science, Volume II.* Retrieved on 5.4.2011 from: http://www.oecd.org/pisa/pisaproducts/48852548.pdf.

OECD (2010b). *PISA 2009 Results: Overcoming Social Background, Equity in Learning Opportunities and Outcomes, Volume II.* Retrieved on 5.4.2011 from: http://www.oecd.org/pisa/pisaproducts/48852584.pdf

Opetus- ja kulttuuriministeriö (2012a). *Koulutuksen arviointisuunnitelma vuosille 2012–2015* [Evaluation Plan for Education for Years 2012-2015]. Opetus- ja kulttuuriministeriön julkaisuja 2012:14.

Opetus- ja kulttuuriministeriö (2012b). *Koulutuksen arviointi* [Evaluation of Education]. Retrieved on 20.9.2012 from : http://www.minedu.fi/OPM/Koulutus/ koulutuspolitiikka/ koulutuksen_arviointi/?lang=fi.

Peltonen, T. (2002). *Pienten koulujen esiopetuksen kehittäminen – entisajan alakoulusta esikouluun* [Development of Pre-school in Small Schools – from Old-time Schools to Pre-school]. Faculty of Education. Kajaani Department of Education. Oulu: University of Oulu Press.

Pihlajanniemi, T. (2006). *Kuntarakenne muutoksessa.* [Municipal Structure in Change]. Kunnallisalan kehittamissäätiön tutkimusjulkaisut, nro 53 [Research Publications of the Foundation of Municipal Development Nr. 53].

Pirhonen, E. V., & Janhunen, P. (1995). *Kuntien sivistystoimen hallinto 1995* [Administration in Local Provisions of Education and Culture]. Helsinki: Suomen kuntaliitto.

Rajanen, J. (2000). Selvitys koulutuksen paikallisen tason arvioinnin tilasta [Report on the Status of Local Evaluation on Education]. Helsinki: Opetushallitus. Arviointi 11/2000.

Rinne, R., Kivirauma, J., & Simola, H. (2002). Shoots of revisionist education policy or just slow readjustment? The Finnish case of educational reconstruction. *Journal of Education Policy*, 2002, Vol. 17, No. 6, pp. 643-658.

Risku, M. (2011). Superintendency in the historical development of education in Finland. In: Beckmann, J. (Ed.). *Effective schools in effective systems: Proceedings of the 6th Annual ISER Conference South Africa 2010.* Pretoria, South Africa: Department of Education Management, University of Pretoria with the International Symposium of Educational Reform (ISER), pp. 182-210.

Ryynänen, A. (2004). *Kuntien ja alueiden itsehallinto – kehittämisvaihtoehdot* [Autonomy of Municipalities and Areas – Options for Development]. Helsinki: Edita Publishing.

Sahlberg, P. (2011). *Finnish Lessons. What can the world learn from educational change in Finland?* New York: Teachers College, Columbia University.

Salmela, A. (1946). *Kansakoululautakunta. Lainsäädäntö selityksineen* [Folkschoolboard. Legislation with Explanations]. Helsinki: Otava Publishing Company.

Sarjala, J. (1982). *Suomalainen koulutuspolitiikka* [Finnish Education Policy]. Helsinki: WSOY.

Sarjala, J. (2008). *Järki hyvä herätetty Koulu politiikan pyörteissä* [Good Sense Aroused School in the Turmoil of Politics]. Helsinki: Kirjapaja.

Somerkivi, U., & Laine, O.I. (1959). *Kansakoulun johtokunta ja kansakoululautakunta* [Folkschool Directorate and Folkschool Board]. Helsinki: Tammi.

Souri, L. (2009). *Rehtorin oikeudellinen asema – selvitys 2009* [Principal's Juridicial Position – Report 2009]. Helsinki: Suomen Rehtorit ry – Finlands rektotorer rf.

Statistics Finland (2013a). Retrieved on 24.6.2013 from: http://tilastokeskus.fi/tup/ suoluk/suoluk_vaesto_en.html.

Statistics Finland (2013b). Retrieved on 12.7.2013 from: https://www.tilastokeskus.fi/ til/pop/2012/pop_2012_2012-11-15_tie_001_fi.html.

Statistics Finland (2013c). Retrieved on 12.7.2013 from: https://www.tilastokeskus.fi/til/lop/2012/lop_2012_2013-06-12_tau_003_fi.html.

Svedlin, R. (2003). *Pedagogik: Utvärdering i skolan - mellan skolutveckling och styrpolitik* [Pedagogy: Evaluation at School – between School development and Steering Policy]. Helsingfors Universitet Pedagogiska Institutionen Forskningsrapport 185.

Tähtinen, J., & Hovi, R. (2007). Kansanopetuksen ja koulujen kehityslinjoja Suomessa 1500-luvulta 1800-luvun alkuun [Trajectories of Folkschool and Schools in Finland from 16th Century to the Beginning of the 19th Century]. In: Tähtinen, J., & Skinnari, S. (Eds.). *Kasvatus- ja koulukysymys Suomessa vuosisatojen saatossa* [Upbringing and Education Issue in Finland during the Centuries]. Research in in Educational Sciences 29. Finnish Educational Research Association, pp. 13-54.

Unicef (2013). Retrieved on 14.5.2013 from http://www.unicef-irc.org/Report-Card-11/.

Valtioneuvosto (2011). Retrieved 15.4.2012 from: http://valtioneuvosto.fi/hallitus/hallitusohjelma/pdf/en334743.pdf.

Valtiovarainministeriö (2012). *Elinvoimainen kunta- ja palvelurakenne, osa 1 Selvitysosa* [Vital municipal and Service Structure, Part 1 Report]. Valtiovarainministeriön julkaisuja 5a/2012. Tampere: Juvenes Print, Tampereen Yliopistopaino Oy.

Varjo, J. (2007). *Kilpailukykyvaltion koululainsäädännön rakentuminen. Suomen eduskunta ja 1990-luvun koulutuspoliittinen käänne* [Drafting Education Legislation for the Competitive State. The Parliament of Finland and the 1990s Change in Education Policy]. Helsingin yliopisto. Kasvatustieteen laitoksen tutkimuksia 209 [Helsinki: University of Helsinki. Department of Education Research Vol. 209].

World Economic Forum (2012). Retrieved on 15.4.2013 from http://www3.weforum.org/docs/CSI/2012-13/GCR_Rankings_2012-13.pdf.

In: The Educational Superintendent
Editor: Adam E. Nir

ISBN: 978-1-62948-972-8
© 2014 Nova Science Publishers, Inc.

*Chapter 12*

# THE ROLE OF THE DIRECTOR OF EDUCATION IN SCOTTISH EDUCATION

## *Christine Forde*
University of Glasgow, UK

## INTRODUCTION

Although in Scotland the title "superintendent" is not used, local governments - the Local Authorities (LAs) - have responsibility for the provision of public education within their area and so there is an equivalent role, that of "Director of Education." In some LAs the Director of Education leads Pre-5 and school education while in other local authorities this function is combined with wider responsibilities and so there can be significant variations in the role. Nevertheless, both at local and national level the Directors of Education make a significant contribution to policy and practice in education. This chapter explores the role of the Director of Education in Scotland. The chapter begins with a brief overview of Scotland and its location in the United Kingdom (UK) and then moves onto a discussion of the key features of Scottish educational system which impact significantly on the role of the Director of Education. The final section of the chapter will discuss the role and significance of the Director of Education.

## CONTEXTUALIZATION: SCOTLAND IN THE UNITED KINGDOM

Scotland is one of the four "nations," that is the four jurisdictions in the United Kingdom, the others being England, Wales and Northern Ireland. Scotland's population has begun to rise again in recent years after a period of decline (National Records of Scotland, 2012) and has now a population of approximately 5,295,000 people. This rise is partly due to a slight increase in the birth rate and partly due to migration to Scotland from overseas (approximately 40,000). The first wave of immigration to Scotland in the modern era was from Ireland particularly in the wake of the Irish potato famine and with immigration from Ireland including Northern Ireland continues a substantial proportion of the Scottish population are of Irish heritage. The early 20th century saw the arrival of other European groups including Italians, Russian Jews and Ukrainians. Since the mid-1960s Scottish society has become increasingly diverse with significant immigration from elsewhere in the world, particularly Pakistan, West Africa, Hong Kong and more recently from Eastern Europe and the Middle East (McKinney, 2008). Scotland historically had significant periods of emigration particularly from the mid-19th to the mid-20th century which has resulted in the depopulation of rural areas. Scotland still experiences outward migration with approximately 16,000 going overseas and 40,000 moving to other parts of the UK.

Scotland is divided into 32 unitary authorities, local councils. Most of the population in Scotland lives in the local authorities in the urban "central belt" and here the capital city of Edinburgh is located on the east coast while on the west coast there is the largest city of Glasgow. The central belt made a significant contribution to the British industrial revolution but the large industries such as shipbuilding, steel and manufacturing went into decline in the 1970s and have been replaced largely with service industries. A substantial proportion of Scotland is rural with extensive mountainous areas in the Scottish highlands in addition to large rural authorities in the southeast and southwest which are also sparsely populated areas. Included in the 32 authorities are three island authorities: the Western Isles, Orkney Islands and the Shetlands. In their management of education at local authority level the Director of Education has to ensure that the educational provision addresses the learning needs of diverse groups of pupils who come from different ethnic, cultural and faith backgrounds and who live in very different locations.

## THE SCOTTISH EDUCATIONAL SYSTEM

Scotland has a separate legislative framework and policies relating to its own education system and these are distinctive from public education in other parts of the UK. Compulsory education was established in Scotland as a result of the *1872 Education (Scotland) Act* (Anderson, 2003). Historically Scottish education was administered through the Scottish Office of the Westminster Government in London. While legislation for the English education system is still administered through the Westminster Parliament, education is now a devolved function to the Scottish Parliament as it is in Wales and Northern Ireland, to their respective Assemblies. As part of the Scottish Government there is the Cabinet Secretary for Education and Lifelong Learning and two junior Ministers, the Minister for Children and Young People and the Minister for Learning, Science and Scotland's Languages. Education is administered at national level through the Learning Directorate which has oversight of all levels of education from early childhood education to tertiary education including further education (vocationally oriented third level education) and higher education (the universities).

School education is predominantly in the public sector with the LAs responsible for over 95% of educational provision for ages 5 to 18 in Scotland. LAs also provide Pre-5 (ages 3-5) education and have oversight of any private provision for this age group. School attendance is compulsory from ages 5 to 16 though increasing numbers of pupils are remaining in school beyond that age to complete the final stages of secondary education or are going into further education. Children begin primary school at aged 5 and then transfer to a secondary school at aged 12. Public education is non-selective and comprehensive, and so schools are provided on a neighborhood basis where a catchment area is specified for each school. However, parents can make placing requests to the LA to attend another school if they do not live in the catchment area. This system of placing requests can be a significant issue for the LAs, particularly when some schools are more popular and there is no capacity to take additional pupils, and it is part of the wider task of the Director of Education to manage local provision effectively.

Under the *Standards in Scotland's Schools Etc. Act* of 2000 (SE, 2000) for all children there is "a presumption of mainstream education," that is children will attend their local school unless their educational needs are such that they require specialist provision. In the past this specialist provision has been provided in special schools which operated as a separate sector. However, increasingly such provision is integrated into mainstream schools through specialist units for example, units for pupils with autism or for pupils experiencing social, emotional and behavioral difficulties in order to enable these pupils to integrate wherever possible in mainstream education.

| 0-3 | 0-3 child care nurseries: public | 0-3 child care nurseries: private | Voluntary groups such as play groups | | |
|-----|-----|-----|-----|-----|-----|
| 3-5 | LA Nursery classes in the local primary | LA Nursery schools | Private nurseries | Voluntary groups such as play groups LA Nursery classes attached to local primary | |
| 5-12 | Primary schools | Primary divisions in all through 5-18 schools (in remote areas) | Primary special provision units | Private primary schools | |
| 12-18 | Secondary schools | Secondary divisions in all through schools (in remote areas) | Secondary special provision units | Further education colleges | Private secondary schools |

Figure 1. The Structure of Scottish Education by Age.

**Table 1. Number of Schools in Scotland**

| Sector | Number of schools | Number of pupils |
|--------|-------------------|------------------|
| Primary | 2,153 | 370,839 |
| Secondary | 376 | 303,978 |
| Special | 193 | 6,756 |
| Total | 2,722 | 681,57 |

Scot Gov, 2013.

Within the public education system there are three parallel sets of provision, which are often referred to as "non-denominational," "denominational" and "Gaelic medium" education. The non-denominational/denominational distinction reflects the historic populations of Scotland. Under the *Education (Scotland) Act 1918* denominations could, where there were sufficient numbers in the population to warrant this, seek the establishment of a denominational school (Kenneth, 1968). At that point there was a wholesale transfer to the public sector of all existing Roman Catholic schools particularly in the west of Scotland and the majority of "denominational schools" today are Catholic. There are in the public sector 373 Catholic primary and secondary schools; three Scottish Episcopalian primary schools and one Jewish primary school (ScotGov, 2011). The Gaelic medium primary schools also reflect Scotland's history where Gaelic was until the late 19th century the spoken language of Scots living in the Highlands and Islands, but this culture and language was actively discriminated against. Since the mid-20th century there has been a resurgence of activity related to the Gaelic culture part of which has been to preserve and revive the Gaelic language particularly through Gaelic medium schools. There are over 60 Gaelic medium primary schools and units serving 2,418 pupils (Bord na Gaidhlig, 2011) located not only in rural areas where there remain native Gaelic speakers but in urban areas where parents opt for this form of education for their children. This range of schools - non-denominational, denominational and Gaelic-medium - is part of the task of the Director of Education who has responsibility not only for education aged 3-18 but, within this, these different types of provision, all of which are fully state funded and work within the broad national and local educational policies.

## EDUCATIONAL POLICY CONTEXT

National educational policy in Scotland begins at national government level but there is an increasing emphasis on partnership working for the development of educational policy to create genuine engagement in order to foster improvements in the outcomes achieved by learners. Educational policy is, therefore, set within the wider framework of the arrangements between national and local government. In addition, there is a range of stakeholders in education who also contribute to the policy making process. The Commission for School Reform (2013), in its report on reform in Scottish education, *By Diverse Means,* notes that there is a high degree of conformity across a range of powerful bodies exercising influence. This partnership working is evident in the most recent area of policy making in Scottish education. Following *Teaching Scotland's Future: Report of the review of teacher education in Scotland* (Donaldson, 2010), the recommendations have become part of a system-wide program of reform and development, to be achieved through partnerships of the main bodies in education. Thus the chief executive or chair of each stakeholder group is a member of the National Implementation Board (ScotGov, 2012), the body now overseeing the implementation of these reforms.

Scottish Government (ScotGov) through the Scottish Parliament can bring forward legislation. However, a substantial element of educational policy is below legislation with the ScotGov working in partnership with other stakeholders in education.

The Convention of Scottish Local Authorities (COSLA) is the representative group for the local councils that have responsibility for the provision of education within their area. COSLA is also the employer of the teaching workforce and other staff in schools.

Education Scotland was formed in 2010 through the merger of Her Majesty's Inspectorate for Education and the curriculum development agency, Learning Teaching Scotland. Education Scotland now has responsibility for leading the development of curriculum, teaching and learning and for quality assurance of educational provision in the Pre-5, school and further education sectors.

Scottish Teacher Education Group (STEG) is the representative group for the Universities that provide initial teacher education qualification programs and continuing professional development programs including the professional qualification for aspiring headteachers, the Scottish Qualification for Headship.

General Teaching Council of Scotland (GTCS) is the professional body for teaching in Scotland. It was established in 1965 and is the first independent teaching council in the world. All teachers in Scotland must be registered with the GTCS and to do so must complete successfully a recognized initial teacher education program and the induction year. The GTCS holds the professional standards for teaching and accredits initial teacher education programs and programs leading to the professional qualification of the Scottish Qualification for Headship (SQH).

Teacher Unions: there are a number of trade unions representing teachers in Scotland, the largest being the Educational Institute of Scotland (EIS), but UK wide trade unions such as the NASUWT have Scottish members. There are also representative groups for promoted staff, for example: School Leadership Scotland (SLS) and the Association of Headteachers and Deputies in Scotland (AHDS).

In addition, the Directors of Education are part of this partnership process through their association and so as a group have a significant role in the educational policy community.

Association of Directors of Education (ADES) is "an independent professional network for leaders and managers in education and children's services" (ADES, 2011) and is involved in policy making with local and national government. Through the Committees of ADES such as the ADES Personnel Committee there is considerable exploration of issues and sharing of practice.

## TEACHING AND LEARNING

Scottish education is currently undergoing a period of generational reform, firstly to the curriculum, and secondly in relation to the teaching profession. Both these reform programs illustrate the ways in which, through engagement with the range of stakeholders, policy is developed and then implemented. The development of the curriculum is based on the work of the Curriculum Reform Group established in 2003 which brought together stakeholders to consider how the early years and school curriculum needed to be developed in order to better match changing societal demands. The outcome of this review was a proposal for the *Curriculum for Excellence* (SE, 2004, 2006) for ages 3-18. The *Curriculum for Excellence* is a broad based and interdisciplinary framework at the heart of which are the four capacities.

This framework is intended to result in pupils becoming: "successful learners, confident individuals, responsible citizenships and contributing individuals" (SE, 2004, p. 4).

This curriculum program has had a significant impact on the national assessment program. There is one examination board in Scotland, the Scottish Qualifications Authority, which has articulated a qualifications framework from level 1 to level 11 (doctorate level). The SQA sets the national school examinations taken by pupils in the later stages of secondary school and in the light of the Curriculum for Excellence, the SQA has recently launched a new set of National Qualifications (SQA, 2013).

The same principle of "partnership" is reflected in leading this program of reform in the curriculum at both local and school level. Consequently for individual Directors of Education the implementation of the *Curriculum for Excellence* has been a major focus. In this engaging with schools and teachers has been one facet, another facet has been engaging with parents in order to address issues related to the implementation process, particularly questions of the pace of change and the securing the quality of education for each cohort of pupils while the change process is underway. Another facet is the task of reporting on progress in implementing the *Curriculum for Excellence* to both their respective local councils and to national government, a particularly important issue given the political drive behind these reforms.

Alongside overseeing the reforms on curriculum and assessment and on teacher policy another major area of responsibility for Directors of Education is quality assurance. There is a clear expectation on Directors of Education to have oversight of the quality of provision offered in the Pre-5 establishments and schools in their authority. Quality assurance in the school sector in Scotland is led by Education Scotland. Schools are all subject to external audit now through Education Scotland using a set of quality indicators, *The Journey to Excellence: How Good is Our School* (HMIe, 2006a) from which a public report is published. The outcomes of inspections of schools are reported to the Director and may contain action points related to the facilities and to the quality of teaching and learning which must be addressed at local authority level as well as school level.

## LOCAL GOVERNMENT IN SCOTLAND

Scottish education has been managed at three levels - central government, local government and school - since 1929 when a statutory responsibility was given to Local Authorities to manage schools. However, this tripartite arrangement is not without tensions particularly the balance between centralized direction and local policy making. One of the first pieces of legislation of the Scottish Parliament was concerned with school education: *Standards in Scotland's Schools etc. 2000* (SE, 2000). This Act gave the Minister of Education the power to set the national priorities in education. As Bloomer (2008, p. 933) observes: "That the policy making was delegated to the minister rather than being incorporated into primary legislation could be seen as an even more emphatic growth of centralized authority." While schools and headteachers in particular are accountable to the Director of Education, as Bloomer notes: "a more powerful line of accountability lies through inspection to the national level" (p. 936). There are, therefore, issues around the role of local government and education which have an impact on the role and work of a Director of

Education. In addition, the local context also has had a significant impact on the specific role and responsibilities of an individual Director of Education.

The 32 unitary authorities in Scotland which have local responsibility for education vary significantly in geographical size, composition of population and urban/rural make up. Each local authority has an elected body, the local council, which has responsibility for a range of local services, for example, cleaning, sports and leisure, museums and libraries. Education is by far the largest area of responsibility comprising on average 40% of the local budget (ScotGov, 2010).

### Table 2. Local Authorities and Size of Population

| Population (in thousands) | Number of local authorities | Local Authorities |
|---|---|---|
| 400k – 500k | 2 | Glasgow City<br>City of Edinburgh |
| 300k– 400k | 3 | Fife<br>North Lanarkshire<br>South Lanarkshire |
| 200k-300k | 3 | Aberdeen City<br>Aberdeenshire<br>Highland |
| 100k-200k | 11 | Angus<br>Dumfries & Galloway<br>Dundee City<br>East Ayrshire<br>East Dunbartonshire<br>Falkirk<br>North Ayrshire<br>Perth & Kinross<br>Renfrewshire<br>Scottish Borders<br>South Ayrshire<br>West Lothian |
| 50k- 100k | 9 | Argyll & Bute<br>Clackmannanshire<br>East Lothian<br>East Renfrewshire<br>Inverclyde<br>Midlothian<br>Moray<br>Stirling<br>West Dunbartonshire |
| less than 50k | 3 | Comhairle nan Eilean Siar (Western Isles)<br>Orkney Islands<br>Shetland Islands |

Based on information obtained from General Register Office for Scotland.

These local authorities administer Pre-5 education (including oversight of any private provision) and school education. The responsibilities of the local authorities with regard to the provision of education in their area include establishing and maintaining schools, employing staff, both teaching and ancillary staff, and the performance of schools in relation to the national quality assurance frameworks. Local authorities may also provide services such as educational psychological services and speech therapists. In addition, local authorities have responsibility for other activities broadly related to education, such as cultural activities including museums and libraries, leisure and sports facilities and care and welfare services and community development services. The Director of Education is the professional officer responsible for advising on policy and managing the range of local authorities services related to education and possibly other areas and reporting both to local and central governments. Third level education is not part of the local authority responsibilities: vocational training through the further education colleges is part of public provision but the colleges are independent and governed through Boards of Management. Similarly, the universities in Scotland are independent institutions and receive public funding from the Scottish Higher Education Funding Council.

Writing in 2003, Bloomer argued that at the beginning of the 21st century with the establishment of the Scottish Parliament, "the notion of a broad national sense of direction with increased encouragement for experiment and diversity at local level has become quite firmly established" (Bloomer, 2003, p. 162). However, more recently there have been debates about whether education should remain as part of the function of local authorities given the strengthening of centralized policy making, and increasing autonomy of schools, above all developing their own approaches to national policies shaping the *Curriculum for Excellence* (SE, 2004, 2006) for the particular groups of learners within their school. Pressure on the role of the local authorities and therefore on the role of Director of Education comes from two seemingly contradictory positions: on the one hand, there are arguments for greater powers to be delegated to schools and communities particularly with regard to strategies around community planning (ScotGov, 2006), while on the other hand there is a view that having 32 unitary authorities is inefficient (Gillies, 2008) given that many of these LAs serve populations of less than 200,000. Indeed there is growing pressure to make efficiency savings and the sharing of functions across smaller local authorities is now an option. Over the last two year some smaller local authorities have merged their education functions: Stirling and Clackmannanshire share a Director of Education and education service and East Lothian and Midlothian have set up a similar arrangement. There are counter arguments for maintaining local authorities: the local authorities provide some level of pluralism in educational provision, important given the extensive nature of public education in Scotland. Jeyes (2003) acknowledges the ongoing tensions between local authorities and central government in Scotland: "Some believe that local authorities should merely administer a national system while others support the view that there is a need for an alternative policy voice which supports and challenges schools and creates the capacity for creativity and diversity" (p. 180). Jeyes bases his argument for local leadership of education through the local government on four aspects:

> "linking community schools to community planning; social inclusion, not least
> through effective integration of services for children; local democracy through

participatory mechanisms and schools as democratic institutions; sustainability, both through active citizenship and environmental awareness"

(Jeyes, 2003, p. 180).

For Jeyes one of the crucial factors is greater working across local authority boundaries to facilitate sharing of practice and for the Convention of Scottish Local Authorities (COSLA) to actively take part in policy generation and the offering of alternative perspectives and strategies.

## THE ROLE OF THE DIRECTOR OF EDUCATION IN SCOTTISH EDUCATION

With four local authorities sharing functions there are now 30 Directors of Education. Most Directors of Education are "professional officers" and come from an education background, many of them having been teachers and headteachers. Where education is combined with other areas, particularly social work, the Director may have professional experience in that sector. A good proportion of Directors will have previously held other posts in the local authority such as Quality Improvement Officers or a management role in leading groups of officers. Directors of Education will be selected through competitive interview and appointments panels will be made up of elected members of the council and senior officials in the local authority. Prior to 1996 when, as part of local government reforms the 32 unitary authorities were established, there had been only one female Director of Education and so one of the noticeable changes over the last 20 years is an increase in the number of women in Director of Education roles.

There is significant variation in terms of the size, composition and geographical location of the 32 unitary authorities in Scotland and this has an impact on the role of the Director of Education. The role and the area of activity varies from authority to authority with some posts focusing solely on education whereas others posts will have a wider remit. There are also variations in the strategic role played by Directors; some hold an "Executive Director" post and so will be part of a senior management group in the Local Council. These Executive Directors have responsibility for several functions and will manage a number of distinct teams in each of these areas. In contrast there are Directors whose focus is specifically on early years and school education. A variety of titles is used for this role signaling the variations in the range of responsibilities particular posts in a particular local authorities will carry.

### Table 3. Directors of Education by Gender

| Gender | Number |
|--------|--------|
| Male | 21 |
| Female | 9 |

## Table 4. Areas of Activity of the Directors of Education

| Title | Number of posts |
|---|---|
| Executive Director of Education; and Community Services; and Social Services | 10 |
| Director of Education | 5 |
| Director of Children's Services; Children and Families | 4 |
| Director of Education and Social Care or Social Work or Communities | 3 |
| Director of Education and Lifelong Learning or Skills | 2 |
| Director of Education and Culture…Leisure…Sports | 6 |
| Head of Schools or Education | 1 |

Given the wide variation in title and areas of activity there is no typical role played by a Director of Education. Instead the functions are wide ranging and may include leading teams providing an integrated service particularly in relation to children and families or leading across a range of services including education, welfare, community development and criminal justice. Other Directors will have a responsibility for education and culture or sports and will manage services such as libraries, museums, sports facilities in the local area. Since the *Local Government Act* of 2003 there has also been increasing emphasis on community planning, particularly in areas of rural or urban deprivation and some directorships integrate functions related to educational provision with community development.

Some of responsibilities of the LAs are set out in *Standards in Schools Scotland Etc. Act 2000* (SE, 2000) and the *Local Government Act* (2003) which established a statutory framework for best value: "there are duties that are placed in local authorities to secure continuous improvement in the performance of their functions" (HMIe, 2006b, p. 4). The local authorities, like schools, are subject to inspections by Education Scotland (formerly, HMIe). This inspection process is framed by national legislation, particularly the LA's responsibility in addressing the agreed local education improvement objectives. The process of external review mirrors the inspection process of schools which is based on the principle of self-evaluation. The organization, whether this is an individual school or a local authority, is expected to engage routinely in the monitoring and evaluation of the core functions and the outcomes achieved using an agreed set of performance indicators. The framework for local authorities is *Quality Management in Education 2: Self-Evaluation for Quality Improvement* (HMIe, 2006b). This framework focuses on the management and delivery of educational provision within the local authority and includes a range of different aspects such as outcomes, impact on users, staff and the community, the delivery of education, policy development and planning, management and support of staff and partnership and resources. The final area is "leadership" which deals with strategic leadership within the LA. The illustrative example of effective strategic leadership in this framework gives a graphic indication of the expected joint workings of the elected members and the professional officers, particularly the Director of Education.

> Senior elected members provide officers with strong political leadership and direction and demonstrate a commitment to continuous improvement. Together, they communicate and demonstrate a very clear view of what the council is aiming to achieve. Senior officers develop effective and strategic business plans and identify key actions, intended outcomes and major targets. […] Senior elected members make transparent and

evidence-based decisions on the allocation of resources to education from local authority budget. Senior managers provide strong leadership targeting resources at key agreed objective and achieving Best Value (HMIe, 2006, p. 68).

While there is a debate around the role of local authorities in education, currently the LAs play a significant role in local provision. Education at this level is directed politically through either an executive cabinet or committee (for example, the Education and Culture Committee found in many local councils) which has delegated powers of decision making. This Committee then can instruct the Director of Education who, as the professional officer, is responsible and accountable for pursuing these policies. It is here that there can be tensions between national government policy and locally based decisions which directors have to balance to ensure the requirements of various legislative frameworks are met.

The expectation from Directors of Education is that they will lead change to bring about improvement particularly in terms of the learning outcomes of pupils. Relationships with schools are of critical importance in the local delivery of education. Working with schools and teachers is a focal point for Directors of Education in enhancing and ensuring high quality provision. Within the local authority the Director will have a team of professional officers to support and review schools - though the size and specific functions of this team vary enormously. Cameron (2008) argues that this element of the local education service is always vulnerable to financial cuts particularly in periods of economic constraint. Reductions in staffing is not the only issue. The role of Directors in leading the education service in a particular LA is summed up in the phrase "support and challenge" (HMIe, 2006b). There are considerable tensions about how far the role of the Director and of the LA officer staff is one of quality assurance or one of leading innovation and development particularly enabling schools the scope to experiment and innovate. The emphasis is more and more on quality improvement rather than the developmental role. Cameron (2008) charts the way in which the role of local authority education adviser has evolved from a responsibility to support development in schools into "Quality Improvement Officers" (QIOs) who "play a role in mediating the quality improvement processes devised at local and national level in the interests of public accountability and in helping schools and nurseries to provide a better educational experience for all children" (p. 163). There are two categories of professional posts that can be part of an LA's central team: Quality Improvement Officer (QIO), Education Support Officer (ESO) which can include areas such as staff development, curriculum development and staff tutor (SNCT/32, 2004), but within the current structures the QIO role attracts a higher salary and is often a permanent appointment at a senior level. In contrast, development officers will typically be on short-term transfer from school to another assignment. This raises questions about the increasing focus on accountability and the reduction in the capability of local authorities to support school-based innovation. Therefore, at a time when there is substantial reform both in terms of curriculum development and teacher development, the Directors of Education are having to take forward change with decreasing numbers of staff able to engage directly in supporting the development agendas of schools.

## THE CONTRIBUTION OF DIRECTORS OF EDUCATION

Directors of Education both collectively through the Association of Directors of Education in Scotland (ADES) and individually in their local authorities can bring about significant change. There are notable examples of Directors of Education shaping educational policy within their own authority and instituting innovation that also has a national significance. Jeyes (2003) argues that, "The chief officer [that is, the Director of Education] remains significant and can influence the content and style of education service management locally to a considerable extent" (p. 175). Jeyes himself was the first Director of Children's Services in the UK, pioneering the coordination of education and social, care, welfare and justice services. This has become the model for children's services in Scotland and across the UK. The Commission on School Reform (2013), led by a former Director of Education, notes examples of local authorities taking the lead in initiatives which have had an impact on education beyond the boundaries of the specific local authority, such as North Lanarkshire's authority wide approach to cooperative learning or Clackmannanshire's program of the use of synthetic phonics to raise literacy standards across all schools. In recent years a major responsibility of Directors of Education has been leading the rebuilding of schools and other facilities through the Public Private Partnerships (PPP) initiatives. An example is South Lanarkshire (South Lanarkshire Council, n.d.) where since 2004 successive Directors of Education have led the largest school modernization program undertaken in the UK, with 17 out of 19 secondary schools and 108 out of 124 primary schools being rebuilt and major refurbishments to the remaining schools.

Directors of Education have also been involved in more controversial issues, an example being around school closures. With a declining population in both some inner city areas and in rural areas different local authorities have undertaken programs of school closure. This has led in some cases to conflict with groups of local councilors and protests by parents and members of the local community where concerns ranged from the distance young children might have to travel, the quality of education provided in a larger school to a sense of loss in the community. School closures have been particularly controversial in rural areas where the closure of the school in a village might be the closure of the last remaining communal enterprise. Such is the significance of this issue in rural communities that any proposal put forward can be reviewed by the Cabinet Secretary. The process of school closure is set to become more complex with the proposal that any school closure be subject to an independent review which would allow parents and community members opportunities to participate (Sutherland, 2013). This proposal is itself controversial, seen by some in local government as a way of limiting the power of the local council and the Director of Education.

Relationships with the schools, the headteachers and teaching staff in particular are a crucial aspect of the role of the Director of Education. However, equally important is the engagement with the wider school community. A key element of the role of many Directors of Education is community development. One aspect of this is the engagement of the wider community in education but another aspect is looking to education to be part of a wider strategy of community development, particularly of communities that suffer from significant material deprivation. Again we can see examples of Directors of Education taking the lead in seeking to bring community development and education together. The work of the Director of Education in East Lothian is an example where he embarked on a program of consultation around community based management of education. This work illustrates the way in which Directors of Education can be instrumental in conceptualizing public education provision. In this proposal Ledingham (2010) argued that "We recognize that a one-size-fits-all approach to education does not work for communities that have widely different needs" (p. 1). Six clusters would be established each with a Board of Management and an allocated budget which would be responsible for overseeing educational provision and for setting targets and ensuring outcomes were achieved. The Board of Management would "include local representatives with a clear interest in education, for example teachers, parents, headteachers, community members, young people and elected members" (p. 1). This proposal would radically reshape the governance and management of education at local level, much reducing the role of the local authority and the Director of Education. However, this plan was not pursued largely because there was limited support across a wide range of stakeholders for taking on such responsibilities: there was a strong sense of confidence in those in professional roles taking these responsibilities forward. Though there has not been full implementation of this proposal, work continues on building genuine community involvement in education locally in this LA. This is an example of the continued work by Directors of Education to bring community development and education much closer together and illustrates the wide ranging roles that Directors play in Scottish education.

The role of the Director of Education is a complex one with often competing demands and expectations to be met. These tensions relate to the question whether the role of the LA and so of the leading professional officer, the Director of Education, is to manage national educational policy or to generate local strategies and policies to meet local circumstances. At the same time the relationship between LAs and the schools is evolving with schools gaining greater autonomy around matters such as the curriculum and teacher development. In many ways the Director of Education is the "connection" in Scottish education being the central point between national government and schools in the tripartite approach to managing Scottish education and between the profession and the elected members in the local council and between schools and the local communities. In this the Director of Education can help balance the demands of accountability and quality assurance by making space for the innovation vital for Scotland's education.

## REFERENCES

Anderson, R. D. (2003). The history of Scottish education pre-1980. In T. G. K. Bryce & W. M. Humes (Eds.). *Scottish education: Post-devolution.* Edinburgh: Edinburgh University Press. 2nd Edition, pp. 219-228.

Association of Directors of Education in Scotland (ADES) (2011). *Association of Directors of Education.* From:
http://www.adescotland.org.uk/index.php?option=http://www.gaidhlig.org.uk/bord/en/our-work/education_content&view=article&id=46&Itemid=58. retrieved 23.7.2013

Bloomer, K. (2003). The local governance of education: A political perspective. In T. G. K. Bryce & W. M. Humes (Eds.). *Scottish education.* Edinburgh: Edinburgh University Press. 2nd Edition, pp. 159-167.

Bloomer, K. (2008). Tensions between central and local government. In T.G.K. Bryce & W.M. Humes (Eds.). *Scottish education.* Edinburgh: Edinburgh University Press. 3rd Edition, pp. 931-938.

Bord na Gaidhlig (2011). *Gaelic education.* from http://www.gaidhlig.org.uk/bord/en/our-work/education

Cameron, A. (2008). Educational development services. In T.G.K. Bryce & W.M. Humes (Eds.). *Scottish education.* Edinburgh: Edinburgh University Press. 3rd Edition, pp. 162-172.

Commission for School Reform (2013). *By diverse means: Improving Scottish education.* Edinburgh: Centre for Scottish Public Policy & Reform, Scotland.

Donaldson, G. (2010). *Teaching Scotland's future: Review of teacher education.* Edinburgh: ScotGov.

General Register Office for Scotland (2013). *Council Area Profiles,* Edinburgh: GRO Scotland. From, http://www.gro-scotland.gov.uk/statistics/at-a-glance/council-areas-map.html

Gillies, D. (2008). The politics of Scottish education. In T.G.K. Bryce & W.M. Humes (Eds.) *Scottish education.* Edinburgh: Edinburgh University Press. 3rd Edition, 80-89.

Her Majesty's Inspectorate for Education (HMIe) (2006a). *Journey to excellence: How good is your school.* Livingston: HMIe.

Her Majesty's Inspectorate for Education (HMIe) (2006b). *Quality management in education 2: Self-evaluation for quality improvement.* Livingston: HMIe.

Jeyes, G. (2003). The local governance of education: An operational perspective. In T.G.K. Bryce & W.M. Humes (Eds.). *Scottish education.* Edinburgh: Edinburgh University Press. 2nd Edition, pp. 159-167.

Kenneth, Brother (1968). The Education (Scotland) Act, 1918, in the making. *Innes Review,* 19: 119-128.

Ledingham, D. (2010). Community-based management of schools – a migration, not a leap. East Lothian, East Lothian Council. From: www.eastlothian.gov.uk/downloads/file/3522/what_is_communitybased_management_of_schools_april_2010 retrieved 23.7.2013

McKinney, S.J. (2008). Immigrants and religious conflict. In M.A Peters, A. Britton & H. Blee (Eds.). *Global citizenship education: Philosophy, theory and pedagogy.* Rotterdam: Sense Publishers, pp. 333-350.

National Records of Scotland (2012). *Mid-2011 Population Estimates Scotland.* Edinburgh: National Statistics.

Scottish Executive (SE) (2000). *Standards in Scotland's Schools, etc. Act 2000.* Edinburgh: Scottish Executive.

Scottish Executive (SE) (2003). *Local Government Act 2003.* Edinburgh: Scottish Executive.

Scottish Executive (SE) (2004). *A Curriculum for Excellence: Report of the Curriculum Reform Group.* Edinburgh: Scottish Executive.

Scottish Executive (SE) (2006). *A Curriculum for Excellence: Agenda for Action.* Edinburgh: Scottish Executive.

Scottish Government (Scot Gov) (2010). *Expenditure on Scottish Education in Scotland 2008-2009.* Statistics Publication, Edinburgh: ScotGov.

Scottish Government (Scot Gov) (2011). *Schools in Scotland.* Edinburgh: Scottish Government. From, http://www.scotland.gov.uk/Topics/Education/Schools/FAQs

Scottish Government (ScotGov) (2012). *National Implementation Board Workplan.* from http://www.scotland.gov.uk/Topics/Education/Schools/Teaching/CPD/NationalImplemen tationBoard

Scottish Government (Scot Gov) (2013). *High Level Summary of Statistics Trend.* from, www.scotland.gov.uk/Topics/Statistics/Browse/School-Education/TrendSchoolEstate

Scottish Negotiation Committee on Teaching (2004). SNCT/32 March 2004, Edinburgh: SNCT. from http://www.snct.org.uk/library/268/SNCT%2032.pdf

Scottish Qualifications Authority (2013). *A Guide for Schools to the New National Qualifications.* Edinburgh: Scottish Qualifications Authority.

South Lanarkshire Council (n.d.). *Schools' Modernisation Programme.* From: http://www.southlanarkshire.gov.uk/info/878/schools/623/schools_modernisation_progra mme

Sutherland, D. O. (2013). *The commission on the delivery of rural education.* Edinburgh: Scottish Government and COSLA.

In: The Educational Superintendent
Editor: Adam E. Nir

ISBN: 978-1-62948-972-8
© 2014 Nova Science Publishers, Inc.

*Chapter 13*

# THE SWEDISH SUPERINTENDENT IN THE GOVERNING STRUCTURE OF THE SCHOOL SYSTEM

*Olof Johansson and Elisabet Nihlfors*
University of Umeå, Umeå, Sweden
University of Uppsala, Uppsala, Sweden

## INTRODUCTION

The regulation of the Swedish school system has during the last two decades changed in many ways. There has been a movement from central governance towards more local governance and back. The goal and result oriented system has given focus to the professional ability and responsibility of various role holders in the system, with special attention to teachers and principals. The more decentralized system has changed the balance of responsibility and accountability. As a result, parents and pupils have a free choice both among different schools in the municipality and between private and independent schools.

The changes in Sweden are in many ways a mirror of changes in the global perspective, like for example changes in the world economy, the Bologna process and the increase of international comparisons in different subjects, etc.

This paper starts with a short description of the Swedish school system, the governance system at present and a short historical background of the superintendent. Thereafter we present some data on today's superintendent and discuss the new relations among the different levels in the governing system from the viewpoint of the superintendence.

# THE SWEDISH SCHOOL SYSTEM[1]

The Parliament has the legislative power and the Government implements the decisions of the Parliament. The Education Act, regulations, curricula and syllabi are examples of national steering documents. The responsibilities of municipalities and the independent school organizations in relation to objectives and assignments for education for all children, young people and adults are described in the Education Act.

There are also rights and responsibilities for students and parents, for example, compulsory school attendance and the right to education described in the Education Act, which also apply to independent schools.

All curricula are compulsory for all schools and contain the comprehensive objectives and guidelines for the various operations. The curricula also describe the fundamental values and the tasks of each operation. There are three curricula, all determined by the Government:

- Curriculum for preschool. Children between 1 and 6 years of age.
- Curriculum for the compulsory school system, preschool classes and leisure-time centers (compulsory school, Sami school, special school and schools for students with intellectual disabilities). Children between 7 and 16 years of age.
- Curriculum for non-compulsory school system (upper secondary school, upper secondary school for students with intellectual disabilities, municipal adult education, government schools for adults and adult education for people with intellectual disabilities). Youth from 16 years of age.

Syllabi complement the curricula and state the objectives of education and educational targets in various subjects.

All municipalities are obliged to plan, monitor and follow up to develop education in a systematic way. This systematic work is documented. The National Agency for School Inspection inspects and controls a large number of schools every year. The evaluation from the school inspection is directed to the school organizers/owners and they have a stipulated time during which they have to revise their quality to an acceptable level. The National Agency for Education also carries out national follow-ups and evaluations of different aspects and policies in relation to the school system in a more abridged form.

## School Organizers/Owners

An organizer is the entity that is responsible for a certain educational program or operation within, for example, preschool, leisure-time centers, compulsory school, upper secondary school and adult education. The majority of schools are municipal, where the municipality is the organizer. Schools that are operated by private persons, companies or associations are called independent schools. The national agency for school inspections decides whether an independent school may receive its authorization and then it also has the right to receive grants for its operations.

---

[1] More information, in English, can be found on the web for the National Agency for Education. www.skolverket.se.

## School Organizer's/Owner's Responsibilities

Organizers run their operations based on those objectives and frameworks established by Parliament and Government. They have great freedom in determining how the operation is to be organized in order to achieve the objectives. For example: what resources will be used, how it will be organized, how the premises will be designed and what staff will run it. Regardless of how an organizer decides to run and organize the operation, all organizers must guarantee all children and students an equivalent education.

Children, students and their parents are able to select a preschool, school or education provider regardless of the organizer, and the municipality is responsible for ensuring that such operations exist and that everyone who requests a place and is entitled to it is offered one. Education is financed by tax money regardless of who organizes the school. The people who work in the schools have great freedom to organize their work and to choose methods and forms of teaching. This is done in cooperation with the children and students and for young children also in cooperation with their parents.

# THE GOVERNANCE SYSTEM

The government *formulates* and makes decisions regarding educational goals and content at the national level or arena. Out of this regulation each municipality is expected to be the arena where this regulation is actualized. In this work the municipality and the schools in a way reformulate the decisions taken at other levels. None of this is achieved in a linear way; it is a complicated process between political and professional actors but also with other stakeholders connected to the field. These stakeholders and others in the *mediation* arena mediate, interpret and transform decisions. There is from time to time tension between the different arenas due to the distribution of power.

The political governing system has been built up over a long period of time, being gradually interwoven into a very interactive system from 1958 up to 1990. With the passing of time, this system came to be interwoven through such things as timetables, weekly periods, teaching loads and dimensions and government contributions per student group in different subjects and activities. By means of these different regulations, the government could influence such things as content, organization and the economic side of these activities. Control was built into the actual structure of the regulations, whereas evaluation was expected to be carried out at each level.

Decentralization efforts can be seen from at least the middle of 1970. There are several reasons behind this. Weiler (1988, 1990) gives three motives for decentralization, all intertwined with each other: The *democratization* motive argues for the renewal of democratic influence – through decentralization political decisions could be achieved close to where education is taking place. The *efficiency* motive argues that decentralization leads to better disposition of resources for reaching given goals. The *professional* motive argues that changes in knowledge volume and structure demand more professional control over educational content and methods for learning.

All these three motives have been argued for over time in the Swedish context. At the beginning of the 1990s the economic crises in society was the main driving force to more decentralization in the educational sector. The governance of an educational system can be described in two dimensions, illustrating where and who has the power in the system.

Quadrant A represents strong central control. Quadrant D has strong political control at the central level but with a more decentralized form. Strong professional control is shown in quadrant B. In this instance, educational administrators are in a strong position when it comes to formulating the national policy for education, as this is an administration built on experience, with well-trained officials (including teachers). Quadrant C typifies an educational system that is built upon a strong professional teaching establishment that bears the responsibility for formulating goals for curricula on the local level and realizing these goals (DuRietz, Lundgren & Wennås, 1987).

The Swedish governing system has from 1842 up until 1950 moved from model C via B to A and back to B. After 1970 we can see a movement towards C and D – more decentralization, fewer rules and increased local authority. During 1991-2000 the government expressed its ambition to increase local influence and responsibility within all areas. Timetable, curricula, syllabuses, criteria for marking results and demands regarding evaluation were still interwoven into the system, although in a somewhat different way than previously. Economic control was transformed into financial support, which was not meant to regulate activities. The government still mainly regulated other parts. Evaluation "changed" to questions about quality and appeared as national inspectors, quality reports and also as international comparisons (Lundgren, 2007).

The decades between 1990-2010 show a mix of both centralization with many new regulations, a strong national inspection, more focus on pupils' results in an international comparison and at the same time an increased autonomy for the principals by the school law. This move from centralization to decentralization and back to recentralization in different parts of the governing system changes the balance between professional and political power on all levels in the system.

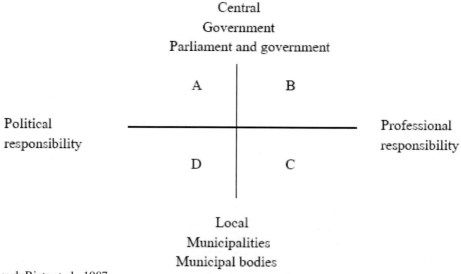

Source: duRietz et al., 1987.

Figure 1. Relationship of power dimensions and also two dimensions in the responsibility of the Swedish school sector.

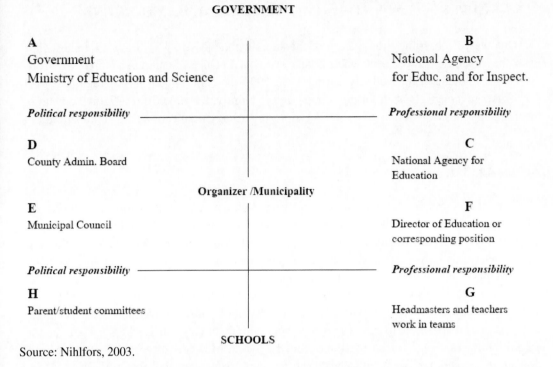

Source: Nihlfors, 2003.

Figure 2. Distribution of responsibility within the government's control system.

With the passing of time, the different parts of the control system have been managed on different levels in the school sector (Figure 1.2). The distribution of responsibility during the 1990s marks a period of professional control (G) with regard to curricula, as well as a move to the municipality's mandatory political responsibility (E). At the start of this, the National Agency for Education (B) supervised activities through its field organization via meetings with both political and professional representatives of the municipalities. From the middle of the 1990s, school inspectors (C) started to visit individual schools. Towards the end of the 1990s, development dialogues were formed as the National Agency for Education became active within all areas and responsible for distributing government contributions. At the same time, the Ministry of Education and Science (A) increased its resources for carrying out inquiries and conducted trial activities – for example, unscheduled activities at compulsory comprehensive schools. In this way, the Ministry of Education and Science dealt partly with the same areas as the National Agency for Education (E-H). All in all, during the 1990s principals and teachers (G), together with students and parents, were given clear responsibility for carrying out activities under the overall mandatory responsibility of the municipality (E).

Today the government addresses both the political and the professional arena. Principals and teachers are addressed directly via laws on education and curricula, as well as indirectly by means of regulations that are leveled at schools via municipal councils. According to the governmental bill on responsibility, the fact that curricula are primarily aimed at teachers does not mean that teachers are not under the direction of their respective municipalities. In describing the governing system we have not yet addressed the superintendent.

# SUPERINTENDENT – SOME HISTORICAL BACKGROUND[2]

One way of describing the history of the superintendent is to give a few examples, first from the situation before 1958 when a new law, the Local Education Authority Act from 1956, was implemented. Secondly during 1958-1990 the superintendent was regulated as a part of the governance system of the school sector. Thirdly, the time from 1991 and onwards, the municipalities have made their own decisions regarding organization and administration.

## Before 1958

This period can be seen to start as early as 1842, when the decision on compulsory schooling was taken and the government's interest in controlling the educational system increased, even if the influence of the church still was decisive. The influence of the government gradually increased, with legal and ideological control taking the form of standard plans that eventually became legislation for education, ordinances and curricula. Some schools that had started as private or municipal schools turned to the municipality and to the government for help in financing their activities. Special government contributions were made available to help pay wages to school administrators and teachers, as well as for school premises, school transport and for the acquisition of material. Follow-up and evaluation procedures were introduced at an early stage in the form of inspections. Government, county administrative boards and municipalities created positions for inspectors in order to increase their control of school activities. During the 1940s and 1950s, great changes took place in the way municipalities were organized, and there were many municipal mergers. The 2,300 rural districts were reduced to approximately 800 by the year 1955.

With different prerequisites and driving forces, schools developed with different forms of control and, at the outset, without any mutual coordination of school activities. In the middle of the 1950s there was a balance between strong central professional control and political responsibility and control. In 1958 all forms of schooling in the municipalities were gathered under common local education authorities and superintendents. One explanation to why the superintendent should be appointed by His Royal Highness the King for a shorter period was that the position of superintendent should be very important and therefore the person needed to be employed independently from local political contradictions and temporary group interests (SOU, 1980, p. 5). The position of superintendent was controlled by regulations stipulating that the position's scope was to be determined according to the size of the school system in the municipality, there were regulations as to the qualifications for this position, and the obligations of the position of superintendent were stated directly in the school law.

## The Period 1958 to 1990

In 1962 nine-year compulsory comprehensive schooling was introduced and several of the earlier forms of schooling were abolished. During the 1970s a number of changes were made in the way in which the school sector was governed. Experiments with local bodies and

---

[2] This part is built on the PhD thesis by Nihlfors (2003).

committees were ways of seeking new forms to engage more people in local efforts. For financial reasons, the government had to cut down on the transference of activities to the municipalities. This occurred when educational activities expanded and became more difficult to foresee and control. Recurring efforts to decentralize activities tend to create new issues. How much independence should be given to professionals on different levels? How should responsibility be distributed between the government and municipalities? Emphasis was laid upon the municipalities' responsibility to adapt activities to individual students. At the same time the government cut down on contributions and unemployment increased, causing an increase in the total cost incurred by the municipalities. Municipalities found themselves facing greater discontent among teachers, principals and municipal politicians.

The balance between the government and municipalities – concerning professional responsibility and political responsibility – underwent changes. The goal was to give more responsibility to politicians and professionals at the local level, but in many ways authority remained at the central level. Because of such things as new legislation regarding participation in the decision-making process on the labor market, more people were engaged in formulating matters. Government regulations on the position held by the superintendent were successively abolished. By the start of the 1990s there was no regulation to say that municipalities should have a local education authority or a superintendent. Each municipality could decide for itself what kind of organization it wanted.

## The Period 1991 until 2000

At the beginning of the 1990s, Parliament decreed a partly new distribution of responsibility between the government and municipalities. Among other things, the aim of this was to make the distribution of responsibility clearer. At the close of the 1990s, the distribution of responsibility can be regarded as somewhat obscure. There were fewer legal guidelines, but they were more explicit. Specially-destined resources or conditional contributions were made available parallel to standard government contributions. Ideological issues in the form of curricula were formulated to give greater room for local interpretation. The government drew up national objectives and expected an accounting in the way of results. During 1991-2009 several decisions were taken in Parliament regarding all parts of the school system, from preschool to adult education. These bills and regulations from the government are supposed to be implemented in municipalities and in that way were a question for the local board and the superintendent.

## The Period from 2000

The superintendent's formal position in the municipality has undergone a change process. In the late 1990s the superintendent usually worked directly under the supervision of a committee or board, and there was no other official level between them. At the same time, the superintendent was, as employed by the municipality, subordinate to the municipal director. A shift has taken place since 2000; today a majority of the superintendents work directly under the municipal director.

Another shift that has been implemented fully from 2000 is that the superintendent has a group of sub-superintendents responsible for different parts of the organization. In this way the superintendent does not meet regularly with the principals. From 2011 the principals obtained a stronger position under the new school law. Under the previous law the principal was mentioned 18 times and under the new law the state mentioned the principal 120 times. This is one example of how the national level has bypassed the municipal level, both the school board and the superintendent, giving the positions of the principal a much more important function in relation to the governance process of the local school.

## The Superintendent Today

When we started to investigate the role of superintendent our definition was: the position that is directly subordinate to a municipal political committee or board. The person holding this position is responsible for education within the entire municipality. Today we find different organizations in the municipalities and different titles for the person who holds the position responsible for the educational field in the municipality.

There are 290 municipalities in Sweden; in some of them all different school forms are included under the responsibility of one political board (from preschool to adult education), and in others there are different boards for preschool, compulsory school, upper secondary school and adult education. Preschool and compulsory school can be placed together under one board and upper secondary school and adult education under another. In some municipalities only upper secondary schools and adult education are placed together under a board at the municipality level, while the other school forms are divided into several different Municipal District Councils. There are also boards that combine education and culture in the municipality, or education and elderly care, for example.

There can be more than one superintendent in a municipality and they can be subordinate to one or two boards. Some municipalities are now revising these roles to have educational questions directed to the municipal council and removing the special boards. This alters the position of superintendent but as we mentioned above connects this role more closely to the municipality.

## THE SWEDISH SUPERINTENDENT -
## BACKGROUND DATA AND ON JOB OPINIONS[3]

In the position of Swedish superintendent the proportion of women has increased to around 35%. Most of the superintendents are between 46-66 years of age and have worked in the position between 1-26 years. Around 30% have been superintendent in 2-3 different municipalities but most of them have served in one municipality (64%).

Their backgrounds are traditional in that they have been teachers, principals and after that applied for the top position. A large proportion of the superintendents continued studies at the

---

[3] Data from the research program, National policy meets Local Implementation Structures, at the Center for Principal Development, Umeå University, financed by the Swedish Research Council.

university after their first degree and fewer than 10% of the superintendents have studied in fields other than education.

Most of the superintendents do not have any written mandate. Political decisions from the board, school or development plans, national steering documents, delegations, traditions, and their own experience guide their work. Most superintendents find themselves having high or very high autonomy. There are differences in autonomy as a consequence of the political boards, if there is an election and changes to the board and if the superintendents themselves are new in the positions, etc. Variations are apparent due to the increased responsibility of the local boards that affects the autonomy of the superintendent in some ways.

Superintendents are responsible for varying numbers of principals. Most of the superintendents (77%) oversee between 1 and 25 principals, but at the same time several superintendents oversee from 26 up to 150 principals. About than 40% of the superintendents have some leadership position between themselves and the principals, which means that the superintendents are most of the time talking through these leaders with the principals.

The superintendents are selected in an open search process and the positions are advertised nationally. Most positions have between 5 and 10 applicants. There is a tendency to have new superintendents come from a neighboring school district and move upwards to a district of a larger size. First time superintendents are more commonly placed in smaller school districts. There is no compulsory education for them but most of them come from a background of working as a principal and almost all have taken part in the National Principal Training Program (which today is obligatory for new principals). They are trained for the role and perhaps that is one reason why networking is important for them. What type of competence is needed for this position and function? If we ask the superintendents themselves the answer is *pedagogical knowledge, the person's potential to develop him or herself, good leadership that is documented, an entrepreneurial spirit and interpersonal skills.* After this comes administrative qualifications and earlier experience of leadership.

## Central School Office

Most superintendents have a central school office. In small municipalities (up to 15,000 inhabitants) the school districts' central office often consists only of the superintendent and an assistant and sometimes a person working specifically on school improvement. The economic and human resources support staff is part of the municipal office but works with the school district administration. When the municipality or school district has more than 20,000 inhabitants the number of staff increases and the larger cities have offices with 70 to 100 support staff members.

There is no clear evidence concerning the relationship between the size of the central office in the school district and the quality of schools in the school district. But we can almost see a reverse tendency, probably related to the fact that smaller school districts have fewer social challenges.

## THE SUPERINTENDENT AND THE SCHOOL BOARD

The superintendent is the top civil servant in the municipality for education and has the function to lead the administration and be responsible for implementing both the decisions of the school board and the municipal council. The latter has mostly to do with the overall economic frames while the school board decisions are more linked to educational matters.

The superintendent is not in a formal way responsible for educational outcomes but in practice the position is dependent on acceptable results. In Sweden there is no clear accountability link between children's school results and the function of the superintendents which clearly does concern the principals.

The ability to influence the board decisions is, according to 80% of the superintendents, held by the chairman of the school board. They also view themselves as holding a rather important position; 60% think they are important to decision-making of the board. Superintendents give principals a very low rating in relation to the possibility of influencing the board. When we compare the chairman's importance with the vice chairman, the superintendents give the latter about 30% chance to influence the board's decisions. Local lobbying organizations have approximately 10% chances to influence the board according to the superintendents. We also asked about some other relevant groups: parents, 12%, pupils, 3% and teachers, 2%. The data show us that the school board decision making is clearly only affected by the political and administrative discussion among the members and the central office.

Another way of measuring influence is by asking how many hours a week superintendents are in contact with the chairman of the board (outside the board meetings). Three hours a week (85%) is the most common answer. It is interesting to note that two to three hours per week dedicated to discussions between these two very central positions in the system can affect their professional behavior, making the differentiation between political policy making and administration less clear. They also report about the contact with the board vice chairman: 88% say they meet him/her for an hour every week outside meetings. We may suppose that many of these meetings have the purpose of explaining and arguing the proposals of the majority in order to find out how the minority will react to them. We can conclude that the superintendents have a clear mediator role in this policy process.

When we ask about how they would like to characterize the decision-making of the board, more than half of the group (56%) says that almost always decisions are unanimous and another 8% says that compromises are rather frequent. The fact that only 20% argue for partisan decisions with a slight majority might be explained through this mediator role of the superintendent. He or she creates a culture or a climate that builds on creating consensus and the superintendent's base argument is that his actions focus on finding the best solution for all pupils. Only 14% of the superintendents say that there is no clear trend.

What do superintendents think about the *district school board expectations* from them? The respondents took a position on different items or expectations: to lead school development, to lead the principals in their pedagogical leadership, to cooperate with the surrounding society, to create changes that lead to a better economic result, to create the conditions to reach better results on national tests, etc., to develop and implement national reforms, to develop and implement local initiatives and reforms, to evaluate the results of national decisions on the local level, to evaluate the results of local initiatives and reforms, to create prerequisites for cooperation with other municipality actors. We find that three of these alternatives were especially mentioned: to create changes in the organization that leads to better economical results, better results on national tests, etc. and cooperation with the board and the surrounding society.

Superintendents *respect politicians* and they do not think they are interfering in their work. Only about 10% think that a shift in political majority will affect their work. The position of superintendent seems to be stable as long as they are on speaking terms with the politicians; a shift in political majority on the district board will not affect their role and working conditions. But having said that, we must also recognize the fact that a number of Swedish superintendents have to leave their position every year because of relational problems and mistrust of the chairperson from the political majority.

The analysis of both the size of the municipality and the size of the central office does not show any relation to different types of decisions on the part of the board, except for the large cities that have many more majority decisions. The time the superintendent has had in office does only affect the response option *"no trend can be identified"* which is mentioned more frequently by newcomers in the office. We find no patterns in the responses provided to this question as far as gender is concerned.

## SUPERINTENDENTS AND NATIONAL EDUCATION REFORMS

The pace of reform in Sweden has been extremely rapid over the last two decades. Around 60 bills have been passed in Parliament concerning governing of schools and content issues (Education Act, Curricula, Grading system, etc.). The international influences on these decisions are stronger than they were in earlier times. One of the strong motives behind the reforms from the Parliament's point of view is to enhance learning or more frankly to get better results in international comparisons.

Only 41% of the superintendents are satisfied with the results students achieve in their school district. Among these superintendents only about 50% report that student achievements can be judged as good. We do not know if there is a relation between these answers and the fact that 83% of the superintendents think that national education reforms are of importance in relation to the ongoing development of our society.

It is interesting to find that only 42% agree that they use more and more time on implementing national reforms. This statement is supported by the fact that only 16% of them think the work with national reforms takes time that should have been dedicated to other important tasks. Those statements go hand in hand with the superintendents' opinions on how interested politicians are in these national reforms. We have asked the superintendents if they think that among the local politicians there is low interest in the evaluation of local reforms' effect: 37% said that this was the case. Therefore, it is not surprising that only 17% of the superintendents think that national reforms have had an intended effect on their school district. Rather, a majority of the respondents (54%) think that this is not the case. One explanation could also be that a majority of the superintendents think that principals are more in favor of the national reforms than teachers.

## Superintendent in the Policy Stream

Educational reform is a major tool for the political units to use when they want changes in the system. Decisions made by an elected political unit – national or local – are authoritative decrees on how the administration and, in the case of education, how the political unit wants the school districts and the schools to act. Reforms most of the time mean change in some important aspect.

To analyze what is happening in the policy stream is difficult and hazardous. It is difficult because the stream is global, national and local. And everything that passes, at least political decisions on different levels, are mediated in many different ways, in journals and magazines, in television programs and at the breakfast table. In these streams local officials such as superintendents together with principals and teachers are supposed to interpret or introduce the political decisions into reasonable everyday working life. When we try to isolate the superintendent, board members and principals in this policy stream by asking them about how they understand the "policy stream" and how they handle the situations, we encounter a difficulty as we are well aware that this fragments a very complex reality.

It is not only a question about what happens when the national level makes decisions and supposes that the different levels below will act as intended; it is a question about how the knowledge on the different levels is taken into account. It is also a question about how motivated different actors are to make changes.

As mentioned above, student outcomes have been one of the most obvious driving forces for educational reforms during the last decades. The OECD and the EU have had a "breakthrough" during the last two decades when it comes to international comparisons. Some call the last two decades changes for "the governance return" which is intimately connected with the growth of data and *the increase in possibilities for monitoring, targeting and shifting cultures and behavior that data apparently produce* (Ozga, Dahler-Larsen, Segerholm & Simola, 2011). Others think that when education has ceased to be invisible as a governed object in European policy, it will be transformed in its scope and governance. *The gradual shift from an indiscernible series of activities in the field of culture and education to a regulated space of learning via benchmarks and indicators is also a narrative about shift in governance in Europe* (Lawn & Grek, 2012).

One type of benchmarking is the international test created by the EU and the OECD. It is especially the PISA test that is coming back in the argumentation (PISA: the Program for International Student Assessment, OECD). Even if it is a more or less worldwide comparison, the results in the countries close to Sweden are of great importance. For example the comparisons with Finland have been frequent the last decade. At the beginning of the 1990s education in Finland was not considered as outstanding in international terms but when PISA results were published in 2001, Finland was one of the highest performing nations in the OECD (Sahlberg, 2011). During the same time Sweden was declining from its position in this test. These two countries chose partly different ways in the beginning of 1990s. Both gave municipalities great influence, but in Finland centrally organized inspection at the local level disappeared from the agenda, while it rather soon got a top priority on the Swedish agenda. These differences are used in the rhetoric for different arguments. Together with discussions about pupil outcomes, questions have been raised about the degree of trust and mistrust from and between different actors inside and outside the Swedish governing system. How the different ways of governing schools will turn out in the two countries needs longitudinal research.

Swedish superintendents work in different contexts to implement parts of the reforms in this policy stream. Some of the national policies are clearly educational policies while others are more general in character, but they still can have effects on the management of the field of education. Many different stakeholders in a highly political environment demand different actions from the superintendent and one of the main functions is to mediate between political and administrative managers on one side, and educational practitioners, especially the school leaders, on the other. The superintendent is in the crossfire between accountability, quality control and indirect steering from the state versus local government priorities (Johansson, et al., 2011).

# CLOSING REFLECTIONS

Based on the results presented above, we argue that it is obvious that the superintendent has a central position in the school district as policy-maker, implementer and gatekeeper. The gate-keeping function is what we mostly called a mediation function. Mediation occurs when the policy stress occurs while the gate-keeping function is related to the understanding of new reforms and the challenge they will bring into the system.

When the government in 1991 regulated the central municipality level as mandatory and left the municipality to decide regarding inner local organization, they did not mention the superintendent's position or function. The organizations, titles and areas of responsibility have changed in the municipalities, but all municipalities still have a position that can be compared with the earlier superintendents. One change that is obvious is that the superintendent today is clearly a civil servant in the municipality with the municipal director as head. A majority of the superintendents (77%) see themselves as members and active parts of the municipal administrative leadership. The superintendent is no longer the "voice of the state" employed independently from local political contradictions and temporary group interests, to quote the education minister back in the 1950s.

The structure of this public sector is complex. It is a hierarchical structure inasmuch as decisions made by Parliament and the government are more binding relative to those of the municipalities and the school sector. This does not automatically mean, however, that higher-level decisions are carried out in an uncomplicated way. Rather, the number of levels of responsibility as well as the different control processes point to the contrary. As the degree of expected participation in a democratic process rises, conflicts and negotiations become the rule rather than the exception.

When the regulation of the whole school system is changing it is important to study if and how the balance on different levels between the professional and the political arena is affected in relation to the outcomes of the curricula. We see today a tendency to more centralization on the local level at the same time as the national regulation in the Education Act of the principal's position and responsibility are becoming stronger. If and how this will affect the balance and trust between the local politicians and the superintendent when it comes to governing of schools is an empirical question requiring some further exploration.

# REFERENCES

DuRietz, L., Lundgren, U. P., & Wennås, O. (1987). *Ansvarsfördelning och styrning på skolområdet.* Ett beredningsunderlag utarbetat inom utbildningsdepartementet DsU 1987: 1. Stockholm: Allmänna Förlaget. (Division of responsibility and governing within the school sector. A paper created within the Ministry of Education.)

Johansson, O., Moos, L., Nihlfors, E., Paulsen, J. M., & Rsiku, M. (2011). The Nordic superintendents´ leadership roles: cross national comparisons. In J. McBeath & T. Townsend (eds.) *International handbook on leadership for learning.* Dordrecht: Springer.

Lawn, M., & Grek, S. (2012). *Europeanizing education governing a new policy space.* Oxford: Symposium Books Ltd.

Lundgren, U. P. (2007). To govern or not to govern: Some reflections on economics, ideology and governance of educational reform – Sweden's experience. In C. Odora Hoppers, et al. *Dilemmas of implementing education reforms. Explorations from South Africa and Sweden.* Uppsala: Uppsala Universitet, STEP, Research reports 11.

Nihlfors, E. (2003). The position of director of education in the control and administration of the school sector. *Acta Universitatis Upsaliensis. Uppsala Studies in Education,* 102.

Ozga, J., Dahler-Larsen, P., Segerholm, C., & Simola, H. (2011). *Fabricating quality in education. Data and governance in Europe.* London: Routledge.

Sahlberg, P. (2011). *Finnish lessons. What can the world learn from educational changes in Finland?* New York: Teachers College Press.

SOU 1980: 5: *Förenklad skoladministration.* Slutbetänkande av skoladministrativa kommittén. Stockholm: Utbildningsdepartementet. (Simplified school administration. Report from the school administrative committee.)

Weiler, H. (1988). *Education and power: The politics of educational decentralization in comparative perspective.* Palo Alto, Cal.: Stanford University Press.

Weiler, H. (1990). Decentralisation in educational governance: An exercise in contradiction? In M. Granheim, M. Kogan, U. P. Lundgren (eds.). *Evaluation as policymaking.* London: Jessica Kingsley.

In: The Educational Superintendent
Editor: Adam E. Nir

ISBN: 978-1-62948-972-8
© 2014 Nova Science Publishers, Inc.

*Chapter 14*

# THE ROLE OF THE DISTRICT DIRECTOR[*]
## IN EDUCATION DISTRICTS:
## A SOUTH AFRICAN PERSPECTIVE

### *Earle Chesterton Smith and Johan Beckmann*
University of Pretoria, Pretoria, South Africa

This chapter focuses on the District Directors in education district offices, providing both an "insider" and a "systems" perspective of the "superintendency" system in light of the South African national context and the structural, institutional and normative features of the South African educational system.

## SOUTH AFRICA'S NATIONAL CONTEXT

South Africa is the southernmost region of Africa, with a 2,500 km coastline along two oceans (the South Atlantic and the Indian). It is the 25th largest country in the world. South Africa is home to a population of more than 50 million people (48.7% male, 51.3% female) (Statistics South Africa, 2012), rich in cultural and ethnic diversity. From the streets of its metropolitan cities to the rural villages of its hinterlands, South Africa's predominantly young population is characterized by a wide range of languages, religious beliefs and customs.

Although Johannesburg is the largest city, South Africa has three capital cities: Pretoria is the administrative capital, the legislative capital is Cape Town in which the National Assembly (Parliament) is situated and the judicial capital is Bloemfontein. The country is divided into nine provinces and these are divided into 52 districts: eight metropolitan and 44 district municipalities. The district municipalities are further divided into 226 local municipalities.

South Africa has made significant strides since 1994 to reduce extreme poverty by providing basic services such as water, electricity, sanitation and housing to large segments of its population. But even with these efforts together with a social welfare system that has

---

[*] District Director is the closest South African fit to the commonly used title "Superintendent."

enabled many people access to education and food, many people living in South Africa still face various challenges such as access to health services and employment and confronting the high crime rate.

The country's economy displays both First and Third World dimensions. The developed part of the economy is similar to that of most developed nations. The rest of the economy is closer to that of poorer nations, such as the Democratic Republic of Congo. The main industries in South Africa are mining (mostly for gold, platinum, coal and diamonds), automotive industry, tourism and services such as insurance.

South Africa experienced an average growth rate of approximately 5% in real terms between 2004 and 2007. However, the period 2008 to 2012 recorded average growth just above 2%. Unemployment is very high (Statistics South Africa, 2012) and the income inequality is about the same as that of Brazil.

Most Black South Africans still suffer poor living conditions, and it is among this segment of the population that cultural traditions are the strongest. However, because many Black people have become urbanized and westernized, parts of their traditional culture have deteriorated. A growing middle class, mostly White with large numbers of Blacks, Coloureds and Indian people, is characterized by lifestyles similar in many ways to that of Western Europe, North America and Australasia. This is a result of the increased access to education and the greater exposure to world markets.

# THE EDUCATIONAL SYSTEM

Education in South Africa is governed by two national departments: the Department of Basic Education (DBE), responsible for primary (elementary) and secondary (high) schools, and the Department of Higher Education and Training (DHET), responsible for higher (tertiary) education and vocational training. Prior to 2009, these two departments were represented in a single Department of Education.

The DBE has responsibility for public schools, independent schools (private schools), early childhood development (ECD) centers, and schools for learners with special needs (LSEN). "Regular" public and independent schools comprise roughly 97% of schools in South Africa. The nine provinces in South Africa have their own education departments that are responsible for the actual provision of school education and implementing the policies of the national department, as well as policies developed to address contextual challenges.

In 2013, the South African government will spend 21% of the national budget on education.

During the period 2011 and 2012, the education sector provided public education to 11,923,674 learners in regular public and independent schools, who attended 24,255 schools and were served by 392,377 educators. According to the national census of 2011 (Statistics South Africa, 2012), among the South African population, 35.2% of Black/African, 32.6% of Coloureds, 61.6% of Indians/Asians and 76% of White citizens have completed a high school education or higher; 41.7% of the total population has completed a high school education or higher, whereas 8.6% of the population aged 20 years and older has not completed any schooling.

The DBE officially groups grades into two "bands" called General Education and Training (GET), which includes grade 0 plus grades 1 to 9, and Further Education and Training (FET), which includes grades 10-12 as well as non-higher education vocational training facilities. The GET band is subdivided further into "phases" called the Foundation Phase (grade 0 plus grade 1 to 3), the Intermediate Phase (grades 4 to 6), and the Senior Phase (grades 7 to 9). However, the administrative structure of most regular schools in South Africa does not reflect the division of bands and phases. For historical reasons, most schools are either "primary" schools (grade R plus grades 1 to 7) or "secondary" schools, also known as high schools (grades 8 to 12).

Since 1997 there has been legal provision in the South African Schools Act, No 84 of 1996 for some schools to levy school fees from parents to augment the money provided to schools by the state. There has always been provision for needy parents to be exempted from such fees partially or entirely. In 2006 the Department of Education declared some 40% of schools as "no-fee schools." They were no longer allowed to levy school fees from parents while the state subsidy to them was increased. At the moment the poorest 60% of public schools are "no fee schools." Table 1 shows the number of regular public and independent schools, learners and educators in 2012.

Teacher training and professional development training emphasize expectations regarding curriculum coverage, management and delivery as well as the use of existing texts available in schools. The new curriculum is central in the 2014 Action Plan for Schools: "Towards the Realisation of Schooling 2025" (Department of Basic Education, 2012a), which targets improving the quality and democratization of schooling. The Action Plan 2014 is an intervention initiative to improve the quality of basic education and is a part of the larger South African education vision of Schooling 2025.

**Table 1. Number of learners, educators and schools in the ordinary school sector, by province, in 2012**

| Province | Public | | | Independent | | |
|---|---|---|---|---|---|---|
| | Learners | Educators | Schools | Learners | Educators | Schools |
| Eastern Cape | 1,886,982 | 64,809 | 5,558 | 64,541 | 3,127 | 196 |
| Free State | 646,093 | 23,854 | 1,351 | 15,881 | 974 | 68 |
| Gauteng | 1,858,745 | 59,175 | 2,045 | 216,642 | 14,785 | 566 |
| KwaZulu-Natal | 2,812,844 | 90,251 | 5,955 | 65,125 | 4,681 | 221 |
| Limpopo | 1,665,013 | 55,277 | 3,935 | 50,765 | 2,393 | 143 |
| Mpumalanga | 1,027,851 | 33,059 | 1,807 | 26,932 | 1,605 | 113 |
| Northern Cape | 274,189 | 8,632 | 560 | 3,305 | 232 | 20 |
| North West | 760,272 | 24,881 | 1,591 | 14,870 | 1,043 | 54 |
| Western Cape | 991,685 | 32,439 | 1,453 | 46,334 | 3,950 | 190 |
| South Africa | 11,923,674 | 392,377 | 24,255 | 504,395 | 32,790 | 1,571 |

South Africa participates in four major categories of national and regional assessment, namely the Monitoring Learning Achievement (MLA) project, the Southern Africa Consortium for Monitoring Educational Quality (SACMEQ) project, the Annual National Assessment (ANA) and the Programme d'Analyse des Systèmes Educatifs des Pays de la

CONFEMEN (PASEC). The Education Department has also initiated diagnostic assessments of learner performance at the critical stages of the schooling cycle.

## THE DISTRICT DIRECTOR

The Minister of Basic Education in South Africa met with District Directors of 81 education districts across South Africa in Pretoria in April, 2012 (Department of Basic Education, 2012a) to highlight the pivotal role of District Directors in ensuring that all learners have access to high quality education. The Minister of Basic Education indicated that since district offices are the link between the National Department of Basic Education, Provincial Departments of Education, their education institutions and the public, it was important to strengthen educational programs and refine interventions from districts offices. Moreover, the educational mandate of District Directors is to be responsible for improving the performance levels of groups of school communities to comply with the demands of the Constitution of the country which manifests every person's right to education. To achieve this it is expected that District Directors focus on the performance levels during interaction with principals, educators, learners and parents in schools.

The objective of this chapter is to engage in the debate on how District Directors contribute to the South African public educational system. This discussion highlights the relation between the duties of District Directors and their ability to control education districts in accordance with articulated policies and plans while assisting in the district's professional development processes. The chapter does not attempt to determine what District Directors should do to strengthen education programs. Rather, the discussion focuses on issues such as control, supervision, professionalism and trust in public educational systems, in the past and present South African landscape, focusing on the supervision role of the District Director as superintendent.

## EDUCATION PROVISIONING IN SOUTH AFRICA

The District Director as pivotal employee in district offices has to lead the process of bringing about a schooling system that offers quality education to all learners in schools. This plainly requires careful planning by the District Director and a clear vision. Only through an understanding of the history of education in South Africa can one truly comprehend the challenges, the solutions needed and how to avoid past mistakes from the past (UNESCO, 2009). Figure 1 provides a graphical illustration of the segregated system of education at the different education levels.

South African educational leaders can be lauded for their ability to realize reconciliation and shared values (RSA, 2012a). In spite of the highly progressive Constitution, however, the legacy of division and segregation is still strong and is often reinforced by economic inequalities. The Action Plan 2014 to 2025 states that schools and the schooling system must continuously make a conscious effort to heal the divisions of the past, foster a sense of South African nationhood and, above all, provide educational opportunities that will break down the deep inequalities that still pervade South African society (Department of Basic Education, 2012b). This creates a huge professional challenge for the District Directors.

Figure 1 and 2 illustrate the changes made to address most of the structural inequalities. One such inequality is detected in research (Blum, Krishnan & Legovini, 2010; Kellaghan, Greaney & Murray, 2009) indicating that young children learn best if, during the first few years of their schooling, key concepts are taught in their mother tongue. But beyond these pedagogical considerations, promoting all languages in the educational system is a matter of national pride and of liberation from the legacy of colonialism.

For this reason, education provisioning takes place in two bands (General Education and Training and Further Education and Training) and in four stages. In the foundation phase (grade 0 and preschool to grade 3) education is provided in English and the mother tongue. During the second or Intermediate phase between grades 3 to 6, schools choose the Language of Teaching and Learning (LOLT). The senior phase consists of grade 7, 8, and 9 and is the end of compulsory education when a learner reaches the age of 16 (RSA, 1996b). Grade 12 is the conclusion of public school education.

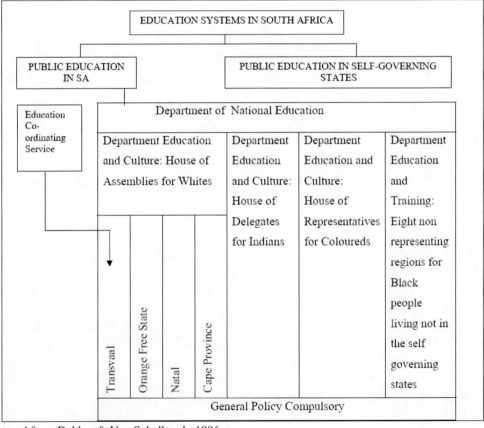

Adapted from Dekker & Van Schalkwyk, 1996.

Figure 1. Education system in South Africa prior to 1994.

| Department of Basic Education | | | | | | |
| :---: | :---: | :---: | :---: | :---: | :---: | :---: |
| Minister | | | | | | |
| Deputy Minister | | | | Needu: CEO | | |
| Director-General | | | | | | |
| Branch: Office of the DG | Branch: Strategy, Research and Communication | Branch: Curriculum Policy, Support and Monitoring | Branch: Teachers, Education Human Resources and Institutional Development | Branch: Planning, Information and Assessments | Branch: Social Mobilization and Support Services | Branch: Finance and Administration |
| 2 Chief Directorates | 3 Chief Directorates | 3 Chief Directorates | 3 Chief Directorates | 2 Chief Directorates | 2 Chief Directorates | 3 Chief Directorates |
| 7 Directorates | 9 Directorates | 8 Directorates | 10 Directorates | 6 Directorates | 7 Directorates | 9 Directorates |
| Nine Provincial Education Departments | | | | | | |

| Eastern Cape | Free State | Gauteng | KwaZulu Natal | Limpopo | Mpumalanga | North West | Northern Cape | Western Cape |
| :---: | :---: | :---: | :---: | :---: | :---: | :---: | :---: | :---: |
| Districts | Districts | Districts | Districts | Districts | Districts | Districts | Districts | Districts |
| District Director | District Director | District Director | District Director | District Director | District Director | District Director | District Director | District Director |

Figure 2. Current Structure of Education Department.

There are two Ministers of Education heading the Department of Higher Education and Training and the Department of Basic Education respectively. Each of these departments is headed by a Director General (DG). The Director General is responsible for the execution of all education policies for the relevant department. Funding for these departments is derived from central government taxes. Policies are set by the departments through their ministers and in terms of set procedures. The South African schooling system comprised 24,699 regular public schools, 418 special public schools and 1,207 independent schools in 2012 (RSA, 2012b). Regular public schools are responsible for 96% of learners in the system, or approximately 11.8 million learners.

In all of the nine provincial education departments there are a number of district offices. Schools in district offices are divided into primary schools (grades 1 to 7) and secondary schools (grades 8 to 12). Only 14,461 schools, accommodating two-thirds of all regular public school learners, are primary or secondary schools (RSA, 2012b). The remainder offer different combinations of grades and fall under the category of multi-grade schools (Mokhele, 2006). In 2011, schools fell under one of the 81 district offices distributed among the nine provinces.

Although the educational mandate of District Directors is to improve the quality of education provided by schools under their authority, boundaries of district education offices do not coincide with local boundaries of local government service sectors, such as health. To aid District Directors in prioritizing service delivery, schools are divided into one of five socio-economic quintiles, depending on the degree of poverty existing in the community surrounding the school (RSA, 2012b). Quintile 1 is the poorest while quintile 5 caters for the "least poor communities."

Provincial education departments are divided into districts with circuit offices and clusters of schools. The boundaries and even the number of districts are currently in a state of flux, due to the ongoing organizational restructuring process.

## DISTRICT OFFICES

District education offices in South Africa can be traced back to 1917 when the Jagger Commission and the Malherbe Commission of Education in the Union of South Africa advocated the idea of district education councils (Hofmeyr & Buckland, 1992).

Vos and Brits (1990) outline the history of districts in South Africa as a controlling mechanism of syllabuses, organized inspection, providing professional advice to teachers, issuing of certificates, and maintaining a proper standard of education. The number of inspection circuits that consisted of groups of schools within a certain radius or control proximity differed among the various racially based education departments before 1994.

Available literature on districts indicates that the concept of districts as a social construct developed during the previous decade as a result of decentralization (Narsee, 2006). The term "districts" began to be used around the 1980s and is rooted in the public administrative development paradigm of multinational agencies such as the World Bank (Rhoten, 2001). The decentralization literature of 1990 was marked by the redistribution of political and social power (Samoff, 1990). Decentralization is the process where system level decision making is shifted from national offices of government through bureaucratic channels to provincial offices to cluster groups of schools (Hannaway & Carnoy, 1993; Rhoten, 2001; Samoff, 1990).

The role of districts can also be articulated as management units of public leadership, management, administration and social support. District offices have a higher position in the hierarchy than schools and public leadership and management among various offices place different weights on the way they relate to schools (Buckland & De Wee, 1996). The delegated power from provincial government to district officials determines the management and administrative requirements (Narsee, 2006, p. 55) and prescribes the governmental mandate as an extension of the state (Buckland & De Wee, 1996). To fulfill the task of public education management it is expected of district management, and in particular of the District Director, to ensure that all learners have access to education of progressively high quality, since district offices are the link between the national Department of Basic Education, Provincial Departments of Education, their education institutions and the public.

The nature of district offices in the new wave of district reform after the initial years required delegation of authority (Malherbe & van Eck, 2009). In both eras, the common denominator remained the fact that directors of district education offices have both explicit and implicit power to decide on how they execute their mandates regarding administrative control and policy implementation. In this regard it would seem inappropriate to view them as mere replicas of the Provincial Education Department (PED) as they are mandated to develop context specific organizational structures and cultures (Kleine-Kracht & Wong, 1991). It is argued that authorities delegate powers and obligations to people and organizations which are expected in turn to develop their own unique climate and culture (Alvesson & Berg, 1992; Schein, 1993). It may therefore be stated that power is not delegated to district offices (organizations) per se, but to officers (people) in the district offices.

The renewed research interest in the different roles district management and district offices should and can play suggests that the place where educational change is most likely to be initiated is the district office. District offices have access to feedback reports from implementation processes, monitoring and evaluation of quality assurance during the process of implementation. All policy implementation requires leadership and management skills from officials in the district office as well as from the District Director who needs to carefully develop outcomes within a web of legislation. These skills include mandate analysis and the ability to create successful organizational processes and structures to execute their mandates.

## DISTRICT DIRECTORS

At the beginning of the 1980s inspectors were leading the education policy community in the racially divided education departments characterized by central decision making.

The different circuits formed part of the regional administrative councils. The responsibility of the regional administrative council was to advise the District Director, consult with the Provincial Advisory Board, audit or certify schools, allocate funds, recommend preferential admission, and exercise and perform other relevant powers, duties and functions with an education district (Vos & Brits, 1990, p. 80).

Over time the notion of districts has changed as a result of decentralization (Narsee, 2006, p. 16). Decentralization as the process where system-level decision making moves downward in the bureaucratic channels of central authorities of provincial offices to District Directors and schools (Hannaway & Carnoy, 1993; Rhoten, 2001; Samoff, 1990) is still prevalent in current public management systems. While the post-1994 restructuring focused primarily on examining the implications of decentralization for the educational system, there was a radical shift in the organization, management, governance and funding of schools (Narsee, 2006, p. 21). With the introduction of the South African Schools Act, 84 in 1996 (Republic of South Africa, 1996b) many of the roles that District Directors in district offices used to have were assigned to school level managers and school governing bodies in particular. Because of the complexity of restructuring in the young democracy, provincial departments had their own discretion to ensure the efficient flow of decision making from the provincial offices to schools.

Different formats were introduced by different provincial offices for education (Narsee, 2006). Some provinces like the Western Cape Education Department kept their circuit offices while the Gauteng Education Department introduced district offices by the start of 2000. With policy requirements similar for the entire public educational system, the amount of pressure on the District Director increased to comply with mandatory policy demands.

In the post-2000 wave, the district office had to evolve as an organization that develops a district culture around the policy implementation process. District Directors are at the front line of policy implementation. After policies have been formulated at national and provincial level management, these policies are distributed to key stakeholders for input. The key stakeholders in the various provincial education departments are the General Education and

Training Council (GETC), Civil Society Organizations (CSO), District Education and Training Councils (DETCs), Local Education and Training Units (LETUs), Specialist Advisory Council (SAC), Gauteng Provincial Action for Children (GPAC), the Education Labour Relations Council (ELRC) Provincial Chamber, and different associations of School Governing Bodies (SGBs) (Gauteng Department of Education, 2008) (see Figure 3). District Directors have to consult with all key stakeholders with regard to all matters concerning the realization of constitutional rights regarding education.

In the post-2000 era, the District Director at the district office is the superintendent of staff members employed at different levels within four sections of the District: Curriculum Development and Support, Institutional Development and Support, Human Resource Development, Educational Support Services, Policy and Planning, and Finance and Administration (Guateng Department of Education, 2008).

A total of 28 occupational categories are divided among the Curriculum Support, Institutional Development and Support, and Education Support Services (referred to as Civil Service staff or CS educators), and the Human Resource Development, Policy and Planning, and Finance Administration staff (employed as Public Service staff or PS staff). CS staff is employed by the Department of Education while PS staff is employed by the Department of Public Administration. The District Director has to sign contracts with all the staff members in the district office. The bureaucratic hierarchy in the district affords the District Director explicit and implicit power over all senior staff members in the district management team (see Figure 3).

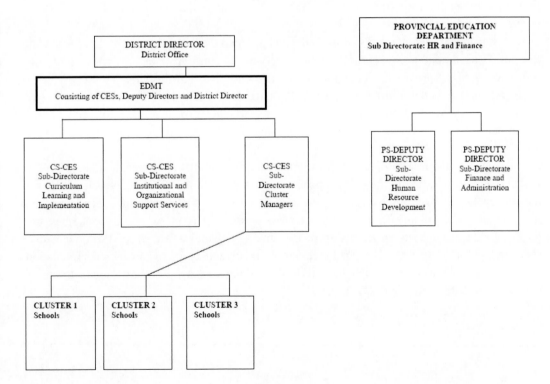

Figure 3. *District organogram 2012/13* (Gauteng Department of Education, 2012).

The focus of the district office is to execute and define the mandates of the Office of the District Director and implement it in schools. Decisions which inform most of the activities in the district are decided during the meeting of the Executive District Management Team (EDMT) for District Directors to operate a successful organization.

Although the district office largely became an extension of the provincial office during the post-2000 reform wave, the organization of management, governance and appropriation of funding was left to the discretion of the District Director who was now accountable to the MEC[1] (Hofmeyr & Buckland, 1992). Towards the end of 1998 this was changed and District Directors became accountable to the Head of Department for Education who reported to the MEC. District offices remained responsible for the organization, management, governance and funding of schools until the next wave of restructuring (Buckland & De Wee, 1996). Narsee (2006) states that by the beginning of the new century, plans were ready to take the financial responsibility from the district offices to a central shared service office. This was only implemented by the middle of the first decade of the 2000s.

The start of 2010 introduced a new wave of educational district restructuring as a result of continued research on the district function. This new approach to increase the quality of public education provisioning was first influenced by the alignment of political and municipality district boundaries and secondly by the need for a clearer policy framework for district functioning. It resulted in the draft document on the National Policy on the Organization, Roles and Responsibilities of Education Districts (Department of Basic Education, 2012a), which defined educational districts as administrative sub-units of the Provincial Education Departments. In provinces like Gauteng, the district educational director is expected to establish different circuits consisting of not more than 14 clusters of both public, subsidized and non-subsidized independent schools and schools for Learners with Special Educational Needs (LSEN). This structure is currently under review with the restructuring of the provincial education department initiative. This initiative could be viewed as an attempt to better utilize the District Management Team (DMT) and the Executive District Management Team (EDMT) structures to increase the pace of educational performance with the appointment of circuit managers and deputy directors who report to the District Director.

As much as the role of districts still remains public administrative management with the District Director occupying the highest position in the educational district hierarchy, it is still the delegated power from provincial government to district officials that determines the management and administrative requirements (Narsee, 2006, p. 55) and prescribes the governmental mandate as an extension of the state (Buckland & De Wee, 1996). It would seem inappropriate to view District Directors as mere replicas of the Provincial Education Department (PED) as they are mandated to develop context specific organizational structures and cultures (Kleine-Kracht & Wong, 1991).

---

[1] Member of the Executive Council (MEC) is the Education Political Head in the Provincial Government and Legislature and is responsible for school education in the specific province.

## LEGISLATIVE BACKGROUND

Policy culture refers to the intention which impacts decisively on the culture of organizations (Ball & Bowe, 1991). The culture of an organization consists of the assumptions (visible and invisible), values, norms and tangible signs (artefacts) operational in a district and explains the behaviors of employees in relation to the policies and laws as implemented by the District Director. The District Director therefore addresses the envisaged policy culture through different policy categories and acts that are clustered as follows:

1.  *Regulatory* (invisible) policies and acts – providing a legal framework for general operations.
2.  *Advisory* (behaviors) policies and acts - providing a framework for acceptable standards and quality for education provisioning.
3.  *Structural* (visible) policies and acts – determining the basis and outline for education provisioning and process for educational performance.
4.  *Developmental* (values, norms, tangible artefacts) policies and acts - collective bargaining structure for equal educational service delivery (Ball & Bowe, 1991; Marshall, 1991).

The categories of policies and acts envisage a particular kind of education system built on common regulations, advice, structures and development blocks within all educational institutions in South Africa (RSA, 1996b). If the policy requirements are common and the expectation of envisaged education culture is similar, then the education organizations like education districts and all employees including the District Directors should be operating in a similar manner (RSA, 1996a).

While recognizing the challenge of generalizability, the chapter focuses on the provincial legislative mandate for the Gauteng province. The policies and acts that govern public educational provisioning in this province include the Gauteng School Education, 6 of 1995 (Gauteng Provincial Government, 1995), the Gauteng Education Policy Act, 12 of 1998 (Gauteng Provincial Government, 1998) and the Examination and Assessment Act, 7 of 1997 (Gauteng Provincial Government, 1997). The provincial legislative mandates for District Directors in all district offices are similar. However, the context of the district will determine the need for the use of implicit or explicit power to ensure efficient service delivery.

The legislative conditions for the employment of District Directors are found in two main Acts: The Employment of Educators Act 76 of 1998 (RSA, 1998) and the Public Service Act 103 of 1994 (|RSA, 1994). District directors are appointed through the Employment of Educators Act 76 of 1998 (RSA, 1998), the Public Service Act 103 of 1994 (RSA, 1994), and the Public Service Regulations with Collective Agreement Resolution 3 of 1999 of the Education Labour Relations Council (ELRC) (RSA, 1999a). Executive power is assigned to the District Director as accounting officer by the Chief Director for Districts in the Provincial Education Department (PED) and the Head of Department in the PED. As a duly-appointed public service employee, the District Director has executive power with executive authority for the provisioning of education in schools in a province.

The District Directors are accountable for the successful implementation of education policy. This responsibility is linked to the Public Finance Management Act, 1 of 1999

(PFMA) (RSA, 1999b). The PFMA prescribes the responsibilities of leaders and managers as accounting officers. It is based on this act that the Minister of Education or the MEC can appoint or deploy accounting officers in the PEDs and to district offices.

District Directors can be expected to choose a particular leadership and management style that will influence the performance of the organization. The type of leadership and management style leads to a choice between mediation of policy implementation and compliance with policy requirements. It would be virtually impossible for district directors to operate outside a policy framework. Although researchers argue that the lack of a policy framework for districts causes district officials to perform at a lower level, policy fragments that collectively articulate some of the responsibilities of district officials do exist (Fleisch, 2002; Roberts, 2002). A comprehensive policy on the organization, roles and responsibilities of education districts has now been published (Department of Basic Education, 2013).

## THE ROLE OF THE DISTRICT DIRECTOR

The District Director has the power and authority to ensure the successful implementation of policy objectives. Examples of PED policy objectives include the vision of the PED, the strategic plans, and measures to ensure increased performance. The vision and mission statement for the GDE is delegated to the 16 different districts as their official mission and vision statements, thus providing these offices with common goals and values. The district education office as "sub-provincial" structures established by the provincial head office could therefore be classified as organizations populated by groups of individuals with common goals and values.

The Constitution of South Africa of 1996, as the supreme law, makes Parliament subject to this supreme law (Malherbe & Van Eck, 2009; Rautenbach & Malherbe, 2009). The Constitution of 1996 (RSA, 1996a) is the primary authority for all organs of the state.

A mandate is defined as written authorization to a person, group or organization to take a certain course of action (Ferejohn, Rakove & Riley, 2010). These researchers agree that a political mandate is the authority granted by a constituency to act as its representative. Any political mandate is subject to the Constitution of 1996.

According to Malherbe and van Eck (2009), the education provision in the Constitution of 1996 (RSA, 1996a) places a legal obligation on the mandator and the mandated to implement policies. Bray (1988) argues that the three forms of power delegation are mandates, deconcentration and decentralization. The primary education mandate according to the Constitution is the state's accountability for education provisioning (RSA, 1996a).

It can be argued that the mandate for district offices is formulated in the roles and responsibilities of government officials. The mandate of district officials includes accountability to perform in the areas of leadership, communication, financial planning and management, strategic planning and transformation, policy implementation, research and development, curriculum delivery, staff development and office administration. The difference between well-performing and underperforming districts could be a result of the manner in which officials and, particularly, senior officials in the district office use their explicit and implicit powers.

District Directors develop specific duties for subordinates and monitor and evaluate the execution of the duties based on the initial education mandate which District Directors receive from the PED. Explicit power in this instance would refer to the supervisor's ability to require subordinates to comply with rules, whether agreed upon or not (Caza, Tiedens & Lee, 2007). Implicit power, according to Brin~ol, Petty & Wheeler, (2006), would expect the supervisor to manage the accountability of these duties through subtle cues.

District management is accountable for the day-to-day operations of officials and subordinates. This accountability is based on the performance of officials. The expected performance of officials is managed through a Performance Management and Professional Development Agreement (PMDS) through a Collective Agreement on Performance. It can be argued that the district management should account for whether their implicit power leads people to assimilate behavior that is independent from others in the organization, and how explicit power cues lead people to act in ways that lead to a heightened sense of the self as being connected to others in the organization. Being accountable for the use of explicit and implicit power makes the district director responsible for the creation of a district Organizational Culture (OC).

## MANDATE OF PUBLIC EDUCATION

An extensive amount of research on the role of education districts has been done both locally and internationally (Anderson, 2003; Fullan, 2000; Narsee, 2006; Nenweli, 2011). The literature compellingly argues the pivotal role of education district offices as organizations in public educational systems. The role of the district in educational change in the 1970s and the 1980s was generally undertaken in relation to what Fullan characterized as the "innovation implementation" era of change (Fullan, 1985). Anderson (2003) argues that the primary difference between the early and current research relates to variation in the policy contexts and change environments in which the research was conducted. With the public educational system in South Africa the roles of district offices are argued by Narsee (2006) as either support bases for schools or aggressive monitoring agents. Nenweli (2011) writes that district offices are responsible for ensuring that public education needs are understood and addressed, and that national learning objectives are realized.

The Minister of Basic Education stated during a meeting with District Directors in April, 2012 (Department of Basic Education, 2012b) that "As District Directors, you play a crucial role as a direct link to schools." The purpose of the meeting with the Minister was to find out from District Directors how they can improve, what they are doing right and what issues at district level impact the delivery of the constitutional right of public education provisioning. The Constitution implies a social contract between the state and its citizens (RSA, 1996a). It functions like a performance manual that controls, instructs and directs the state in its actions. It limits the state's powers and prevents its abuse. It is therefore imperative that the state will comply with the provisions of the Constitution and comply with all the duties contained in it. The Constitution endeavors to structure South Africa's social and political system so as to achieve a society free of tyranny, inequality, poverty and violence, and empower the people to reach their full potential (RSA, 1996a). The Constitution was produced by the representatives of the people in a democratic process and was not imposed on the nation.

When District Directors as heads of education districts fail to comply with their constitutional duties, it impacts decisively on the quality of the democratic public education system (Malherbe & Van Eck, 2009).

## MANDATE OF CONTROL

The pattern of control in district offices was articulated by the Minister of Basic Education during the meeting with the District Directors. The Minister argued that new ways needed to be found in order to assist in finding ways to renew, resolve clearly, work differently, plan better, prepare fully, and better run districts and schools as centers of educational excellence. This brings about a new approach to traditional public administration which has been discredited theoretically and practically (Osborne & Gaebler, 1992).

This change supports arguments raised by several researchers regarding the emergence of a new paradigm in the public sector (Osborne & Gaebler, 1992; Taylor, 1911; Weber, 1970; Wilson, 1941). While the traditional model of district management is based on bureaucracy, the future of public management should be based on markets.

Hence, District Directors should apply control patterns likely to promote the quality of public education. Nenweli (2011) confirms that this should include services like curriculum support, institutional development and support, human resources development and education support services. Narsee (2006) argues that district management should allow district officials the choice to play a facilitating role in supporting schools or to be passive mediators between the provincial education offices and schools.

## MANDATE OF SUPERVISION

The current change in education that follows the presentation of the interim policy, the Policy on the Organization Roles and Responsibilities of Education Districts (Department of Basic Education, 2012a), introduced a new era for supervision by district offices. As noted by the Minister of Basic Education, the focal point of district planning should be on improving learner outcomes and performance, effective delivery of quality learning resources to schools, the filling of vacancies with qualified applicants and best utilization of available teachers. District Improvement Plans drawn up by District Directors should focus on these four cornerstones. The main objective of the District Improvement Plan should be to structure the way in which the district office function is performed.

The Director General of the Department of Basic Education (Department of Basic Education, 2012b) shared this view, highlighting that the District Improvement Plans are the key to effective leadership and management of schools in a district. The Director General said that district directors should ensure that their districts focus on District Improvement Plans to the point where every plan is clear and focused on what action is needed and what will cause this action to happen. The Director General said "Everything District Directors do must focus on our core business, which is improving learner performance!" This they should do while executing the prescribed functions using both explicit and implicit powers delegated by the Head of Department (HOD) in the Provincial Education Department (PED).

## MANDATE OF PROFESSIONALISM

District Directors should practice the principles of leadership that influence the culture of professionalism and the standard and quality of individual employees in the district office. As noted by the Director General for the Department of Basic Education (Department of Basic Education, 2012b), planning and intervention cannot stop at statements. Plans for professional development and for the increase of professionalism must be implemented and followed through at the district level, as they are key to the chain of implementation.

The Annual National Assessments (ANA) of 2012 (Department of Basic Education, 2012c) are a good example of the kind of professionalism development in education districts.

National and international assessments as tools for assessing the quality of district leadership and management are "at the core of our interventions, but District Directors should not be defensive about these results," said the Director General (Department of Basic Education, 2012b). "We cannot keep assessing and do nothing about the findings of assessments. What a District Director does and any planning that happens should be based on the analysis of results and feedback reports."

Some of the key responsibilities of District Directors are to understand district employees and the strategic importance of supporting schools with the use of learning and teaching support material in the classroom. Hence, District Directors need to strengthen and supply professional development and promote the quality of materials.

## TRUST IN THE PUBLIC EDUCATIONAL SYSTEMS

Public service professionals can no longer afford to be ethnocentric, inward looking, focused on the past, and defensive. They must be forward-looking, globally oriented, innovative, adaptable, and ready to take advantage of opportunities to serve the community more effectively (Alexandre, 2008). Public administration, if it is to be well done, must be aggressive, not a passive enterprise in the pursuit of public interest (Cooper, Ramachandran & Schoorman, 1998). The many decades of dormancy in the administrative and organizational structure of the public sector are reflected in and influenced by the unchanging nature of public service culture (Caiden, 1991).

In contrast, in South Africa there has been continuous reform during the past 12 years, reflected in new policies, structures, financial management frameworks and service outcomes aimed at enhancing public sector accountability, transparency and efficiency. This, however, has not been accompanied by a vision for a new public sector organizational culture, one of a more customer-driven and business-like mentality.

The kind of leadership and management styles in the South African education sector is a mandated style. The term mandate includes a judicial command or rule issued, directing the proper officer to enforce the contents of the ruling or law (O'Donell, 1994). Acemoglu and Robinson (2008) argue that the term mandate can also refer to an obligation handed down by an inter-governmental body; an official or authoritative command; an order or injunction; the power granted by an electorate; or an often controversial government requirement for the purchase of goods by individuals. The laws and policies are mandates enforced in a system that underwent transition government and that struggle to clearly distinguish between the use of explicit and implicit power and authority, as well as the difference between compliance and mediation during policy implementation. District Directors as deployed officials are expected to follow this kind of leadership and management style.

Research on the link between Organizational Culture (OC) and performance was conducted in order to investigate the underlying reasons for the differing performances in different districts within one PED (Smith, 2012). This study of the leadership and management function sought to understand OC in district offices in terms of the performance of employees in the district office. The study concluded, among other things, that District Directors have been functioning without a clear policy (Narsee, 2006; Smith, 2012). Neither District Directors nor national authorities are sure about the role that districts and in particular District Directors should play in enhancing the quality of public educational provisioning. Hence, these senior employees in the public education system do not manage education districts and district offices as they should.

## CONCLUSIONS AND RECOMMENDATIONS

The main aim of this chapter is to discuss the role of District Directors as Heads of Education Districts in South Africa. To achieve this goal the chapter focuses on the role of District Directors serving as superintendents in the South African educational system. It is argued that the District Director plays a decisive role in shaping the performance and achievement of education districts in South Africa. Nevertheless, two shortcomings typical of the District Director practices and roles are identified. There is a disparity in results of learners and schools in different districts within the South African system, indicating that the impact of District Directors on their district varies depending on the district's qualities as well as on their own leadership style. This poses a complicated professional challenge in considering that the key policy objectives of the new democratic South Africa are to provide free, basic, equal education to every child with particular emphasis on schools operating in disadvantaged areas. The implementation of such a policy seems crucial to overcome the past inequalities and segregation. Secondly, education district offices as service centers appear not to have consistent aims and prioritized goals resulting in a lack of support provided to schools, and disempowered officials. These challenges seem to accompany the transition from a segregating to a democratic society.

It is further argued that the District Director is accountable for the kind of Organizational Culture (OC) and performance in the entire district. He/she is also responsible to be the interface between the Provincial Education Department's (PED) mandates and the forms of power employed by district offices. Hence, the South African District Director pursues both policy mediation and policy compliance through the district management team. However, it appears that District Directors still need to find an appropriate balance between policy compliance and policy mediation while employing explicit and implicit forms of power.

The discussion also highlighted the relation between the duties of District Directors and their ability to control education districts in accordance with articulated policies and plans while contributing to the professional development of district employees. The District Directors' responsibility to account for performance in terms of centrally-enforced regulations may be reflected by the number of reports they are expected to submit to improve the implementation of the national government's strategic objectives. This conduct seems to undermine in many respects professional considerations and the initiation of changes required in a certain community or district. The District Director therefore never gets an opportunity to comply with the real professional challenges of his or her job which are relegated to the preparation of reports submitted to the central government.

However, it is important to note that movement from the bureaucratic to the professional continuum is not an easy task in considering that District Directors are not appointed as civil servants but are in fact public servants as defined above. Hence, further attention should be given to the formal status of District Directors' role if they are expected to foster and promote the professional dimensions of their districts. This should also have implications on the selection criteria for the position of District Director that may require some re-evaluation with more emphasis on professional qualifications and experience.

There is widespread belief that the quality of leadership makes a significant difference to school and student outcomes (Bush, 2007). In many parts of the world, including South Africa, there is recognition that district offices require effective leaders and managers if they are to provide the best possible education for their learners in an education district. The move towards shared leadership and management teams is a worldwide phenomenon may promote local needs and considerations and may, therefore, assist District Directors in their efforts to promote the performance of schools and districts operating in the South African educational system.

## REFERENCES

Acemoglu, D., & Robinson, J. (2008). Persistence of power, elites and institutions. *American Economic Review*, 98(1): 267-293.

Alexandre, C.S. (2008). *An idiographic analysis of new public management / leadership and traditional public management / leadership*. Unpublished DTech Thesis. Cape Town: Cape Peninsula University of Technology. http://digitalknowledge.cput.ac.za:8081/xmlui/handle/123456789/388. Accessed on 16 September 2013.

Alvesson, M., & Berg, O. P. (1992). *Corporate culture and organizational symbolism: An overview*. Berlin: Walter de Gruyter & Co.

Anderson, S. E. (2003). *The school district role in educational change: A review of the literature*. International Centre for Educational Change Ontario Institute for Studies in Education August 2003. *ICEC Working Paper #2 Anderson S.E.*

Ball, S. J., & Bowe, R. (1991). When the garment gapes: Policy and ethnography as process and practice. *Habitus*, 1 (1): 55-64.

Blum, J., Krishnan, N., & Legovini, A. (2010). *Expanding opportunities for South African youth through math and science: The impact of the Dinaledi programme*. Washington: World Bank.

Bray, W. (1988). *Juridiese aspekte van onderwys, skool en klasbestuur* (Juridical aspects of education, school and classroom management). Pretoria: Sigma Press.

Brin~ol, P., Petty, R. E., & Wheeler, S. C. (2006). Discrepancies between explicit and implicit self-concepts: Consequences for information processing. *Journal of Personality and Social Psychology* 91(1):154-170.

Buckland, P., & De Wee, K (1996). Education districts: The South African context. In: *Local/District governance in education: Lessons for South Africa*. Johannesburg: Center for Education Policy Department.

Bush, T. (2007). Educational leadership and management: Theory, policy, and practice. *South African Journal of Education* 27(3):391-406.

Caiden, G. E. (1991). *Administrative reform comes of age*. Berlin and New York: Walter de Gruyter.

Caza, B. B., Barker, B., Tiedens, C. L., & Lee, F. (2007). *Power becomes you: The effects of implicit and explicit power on the self*. School of Business, Wake Forest University, N.C., U.S.A. Organizational Behavior and Human Decision Processes, 114(1): 15-24. Available from http://www.sciencedirect.com/science/article/pii/S074959781000083X.

Cooper, A., Ramachandran, M., & Schoorman, D. (1998). *Time allocation patterns of craftsmen and administrative entrepreneurs: Implications for financial performance*. Entrepreneurship Theory & Practice, 22(2): 123-136.

Dekker, E., & Van Schalkwyk, O. J. (1996). *Modern education systems*. Cape Town: Butterworth.

Department of Basic Education (2012a). *Minister meets District Directors*. http://www. education.gov.za/Home/MinistermeetsDistrictDirectors/tabid/720/Default.aspx. Accessed on 13 September 2013.

Department of Basic Education (2012b). *The policy on the organisation roles and responsibilities of education districts. Call for comments*. General Notice 180 of 2012. Government Gazette No 3517, 5 March 2012. Pretoria: Department of Basic Education.

Department of Basic Education (2012c). Action plan to 2014 - Towards the realisation of schooling 2025. http://www.education.gov.za/LinkClick.aspx?fileticket=DmJw7rpw9wo%3d&tabid=418 &mid=1211. Accessed on 13 September 2013.

Department of Basic Education (2013). *Policy on the organisation, roles and responsibilities of education districts*. General Notice 300 of 3013, Government Gazette No 36324, 3 April 2013. Pretoria: Government Printers.

Ferejohn, F., Rakove, J. N., & Riley, J. (Eds.). (2010). *Constitutional culture and democratic rule (Murphy Institute Studies in Political Economy)*. Cambridge: Cambridge University Press.

Fleisch, B. D. (2002). *Managing educational change: The state and school reform in South Africa*. Sandown: Heinemann.

Fullan, M. (1985). Change processes and strategies at the local level. *Elementary School Journal*, 85, pp. 391- 421.

Fullan, M. G. (2000). *The new meaning of educational change*. London: Continuum.

Gauteng Department of Education (2012). *District organogram 2012/13*.

Gauteng Provincial Government (1995). *Gauteng School Education Act, 6 of 1995*. . Johannesburg: Gauteng Provincial Government.

Gauteng Provincial Government (1997). *Examination and Assessment Act, 7 of 1997*. Johannesburg: Gauteng Provincial Government.

Gauteng Provincial Government (1998). *Education Policy Act, 12 of 1998*. Johannesburg: Gauteng Provincial Government.

Gauteng Provincial Government (GDE) (2008). *Circular 68 of 2008: Under-performing schools*. Johannesburg: Gauteng Education Department.

Hannaway, J., & Carnoy, M. (1993). *Decentralization and school improvement: Can we fulfill the promise?* San Francisco: Jossey-Bass.

Hofmeyr, J. and Buckland, P. (1992). Education system change in South Africa. In: McGregor, R. (ed.). *Education Alternatives* (pp.15-59). Kenwyn: Juta.

Kellaghan, T., Greaney, V., & Murray, T.S. (2009). *Using the results of a national assessment of educational achievement.* National Assessments of Educational Achievement Volume 5. Washington: World Bank. http://www.uis. unesco.org/Education/Documents/ National_assessment_Vol5.pdf. Accessed on 16 September 2013.

Kleine-Kracht, P., & Wong, K.W. (1991). When district authority intrudes upon the local school. In Blasé, J. (ed.). *The politics of life in schools.* Thousand Oaks, Cal.: Corwin Press, pp. 96-119.

Malherbe, R., & Van Eck, M. (2009). The state's failure to comply with its constitutional duties and its impact on democracy. *Tydskrif vir Suid-Afrikaanese Reg* (Journal of South African Law) (TSAR) 2009; 2: 209-223.

Marshall, C. (1991). Teachers' learning styles: How they affect student learning. *The Clearing House*, 64(4): 225-227.

Mokhele, P. R. (2006). The teacher-learner relationship in the management of discipline in public high schools. *Africa Education Review* 3(1): 148-159.

Narsee, H. (2006). *The common and contested meaning of education districts in South Africa. E-thesis and dissertations*: Unpublished PhD thesis, Pretoria: University of Pretoria.

Nenweli, S. (2011). *The role of school districts in supporting underperforming schools in South Africa: A case of Gauteng province.* EDULEARN11 Proceedings (Proceedings of the Third International Conference on Education and New Learning Technologies held in Barcelona, Spain, 4-6 July 2011), pp. 7149-7156.

O'Donell, G. A. (1994). Delegative democracy. *Journal of Democracy* 5(1): 55-69.

Osborne, D., & Gaebler, T. (1992). *Reinventing government: How the entrepreneurial spirit is transforming the public sector.* Reading, Mass.: Addison-Wesley.

Rautenbach, I. M., & Malherbe, E. F. J. (2009). *Constitutional law.* Durban: LexisNexis Butherworths.

Republic of South Africa (RSA). (1994). *Public Service Act, 1994 Proclamation 103 published in Government Gazette 15791 of 3 June 1994.* Pretoria: Government Printers.

Republic of South Africa (RSA). (1996a). *Constitution of the Republic of South Africa, 108 of 1996.* Pretoria: Government Printers.

Republic of South Africa (RSA). (1996b). *South African Schools Act, 84 of 1996.* Pretoria: Government Printers.

Republic of South Africa (RSA). (1998). *Employment of Educators Act, 76 of 1998.* Pretoria: Government Printers.

Republic of South Africa (RSA). (1999a). *Public Service Regulations with Collective Agreement Resolution, 3 of 1999.* Pretoria: Government Printers.

Republic of South Africa (1999b). Public Finance Management Act, 1 of 1999. Pretoria: Government Printers.

Republic of South Africa. (RSA). (2012a). *Minister of Basic Education, Mrs Angie Motshekga, MP, Deputy Minister, Enver Surty, MP and Director-General Bobby Soobrayan and senior management at the Department of Basic Education met with*

*District Directors from each district across South Africa in Pretoria.* www.education.gov.za Accessed on 13 September 2013.

Republic of South Africa. (RSA, 2012b). *Action plan to 2014 - Towards the realisation of schooling 2025.* Department of Basic Education. Pretoria: Government Printers.

Roberts, J. (2002). *District development – The new hope for educational reform.* Paper presented at the conference of the Development Support Programme (DDSP). Johannesburg: Research Triangle Institute.

Rhoten, D. (2001). Education Decentralization in Argentina: A "Global–Local Conditions of Possibility" Approach to State, Market, and Society Change. *Journal of Education Policy* 15(6): 593-619.

Samoff, J. (1990). Decentralization: The politics of interventionism. *Development and Change,* 21(3): 513-530. http://onlinelibrary.wiley.com/doi/10.1111/j.1467-7660.1990. tb00387.x/pdf. Accessed on 13 September 2013.

Schein, E. (1993). *Organizational culture and leadership.* Thousand Oaks, Cal.: Sage Publications.

Smith, C. E. (2012). *Understanding organizational culture in district offices.* Unpublished PhD Thesis. Pretoria: University of Pretoria.

Statistics South Africa (2012). *Census 2011. Census in brief.* Report no. 03-01-41. http://www.statssa.gov.za/Census2011/Products/Census_2011_Census_in_brief.pdf. Accessed on 16 September 2013.

Taylor, F. W. (1911). *Principles and methods of scientific management.* New York: Harper.

UNESCO (2009). Education for All Global Monitoring Report 2009: Overcoming inequality: Why governance matters. http://unesdoc.unesco.org/images/0017/001776/177683e.pdf. Accessed on 16 September 2013.

Vos, A. J., & Brits, V. M. (1990). *Comparative education and national education systems.* Durban: Butterworths Professional Publishers.

Weber, M. (1970). *From Max Weber: Essays in sociology.* Translated and edited by Gerth, H. H. & Mills, C. W. London: Routledge & Kegan Paul.

Wilson, W. (1941). The study of administration. *American Political Science Quarterly* 56 (4): 481-506.

# ABOUT THE AUTHORS

**Adam Nir** is Associate Professor of Educational Administration, Policy and Leadership and the Abraham Shiffman Chair in Secondary Education at the Hebrew University of Jerusalem, Israel. He currently serves as the Chair of the Department of Education at the Hebrew University and is the elected President of the International Society for Educational Planning (ISEP). He is also Research Associate at the Van Leer Jerusalem Institute.

His research interests include school autonomy, decentralization and School-Based Management, educational planning, leadership and human resource management in public education. He is the editor of *Centralization and School Empowerment: From Rhetoric to Practice* (New York: Nova Science Publishers, 2009), and the author and editor of *Educational Accountability: Between Consolidation and Dissolution* (Jerusalem/Tel Aviv: Van Leer and Ha'kibbutz Ha'meuchad Publishers, forthcoming). Adam.nir@mail.huji.ac.il

**Lars Björk** is Professor in the Department of Educational Leadership Studies at the University of Kentucky. He was a Fulbright Scholar (2009) in Finland and was appointed Professor at the University of Jyväskylä, Finland, and East China Normal University, Ministry of Education, China. Dr. Björk has co-edited *Higher Education Research and Public Policy* (1988), *Minorities in Higher Education* (1994), *The New Superintendency: Advances in Research and Theories of School Management and Educational Policy* (2001), and *The Contemporary Superintendent: Preparation, Practice and Development* (2005). In addition, he has co-authored *The Superintendent as CEO: Standards-based Performance* (2005). lbjor1@uky.edu

**Theodore J. Kowalski** is Professor and the Kuntz Family Endowed Chair at the University of Dayton in Ohio. A former school superintendent and college of education dean, he taught previously at Purdue University, Saint Louis University, and Ball State University. He is editor of the *Journal of School Public Relations* and a member of several editorial boards including *Educational Administration Quarterly*. The author of numerous books and research articles, he received the 1993 Outstanding Faculty Research Award from Ball State University, the 2005 University of Dayton Alumni Award for Scholarship, and the 2011 Distinguished Service Award from the American Association of School Administrators.

**Tricia Browne-Ferrigno** is Professor of Educational Leadership Studies at the University of Kentucky who investigates leadership preparation, doctoral education, and school improvement. She has produced almost one hundred publications (e.g., journal articles, book chapters, evaluation reports, webinars) and been awarded three grants related to leadership development. Her research appears in the *Handbook of Research on the Education of School Leaders* (2009), *Learning-Centered Leadership: Policy, Research, and Practice* (2006), and *The Contemporary Superintendent: Preparation, Practice, and Development* (2005). She served as associate editor for *Educational Administration Quarterly* and currently serves as editor of the *UCEA Research Utilization Briefs.* tricia.ferrigno@uky.edu

**Jan Merok Paulsen** is Associate Professor in the Department of Business Administration at Hedmark University College, Norway. His professional interests are in the areas of educational governance and various forms of leadership and management practices related to renewal and organizational learning in schools. He is involved in a range of research projects on school board governance, superintendent leadership and school district policy analysis. jan.paulsen@hihm.no

**Guri Skedsmo** is Associate Professor at the University of Oslo, the Department of Teacher Education and School Research in Norway. She also holds a position as Senior Researcher at the Institute of the Management and Economic of Education, University of Teacher Education Zug in Switzerland. Her professional interests are in the areas of governance, assessment and school accountability. She is involved in a range of research projects on external evaluation and school inspection, data practices and school development. guri.skedsmo@ils.uio.no

**Joanna Madalińska-Michalak** is Professor of Education at the Faculty of Educational Sciences, University of Lodz, Poland, and Head of the Chair of Didactics and Teacher Education. She is vice-president of Polish Pedagogical Association and member of Council Board of European Educational Research Association. She is an advisor and a reviewer in scientific national and international journals. She has contributed in many EU projects and working groups as an expert. She has long-standing research interests in comparative education, teacher education, exemplary teachers and leaders, teacher's success and its conditions, teacher's and leader's professional development and learning, educational leadership. joanna.michalak@onet.pl

**Ronit Bogler** is Associate Professor and Head of Program in Educational Administration, Policy & Leadership at the Open University of Israel. She graduated from Haifa University, studied at the Technion - Israel Institute of Technology, and received her doctorate from Stanford University in California. Her research interests include educational leadership, teacher empowerment, job satisfaction, organizational citizenship behavior, and superintendents' work. Her publications appear in *Educational Administration Quarterly, Journal of Educational Administration, Educational Management Administration & Leadership* and *Teaching and Teacher Education.* ronitbo@openu.ac.il

**Philip Woods** is Professor of Educational Policy, Democracy and Leadership at the University of Hertfordshire, U.K. He is an internationally recognized scholar in the field of educational leadership and policy, with an extensive publication record and a particular focus on questions of democracy, educational policy and governance, leadership, alternative education and entrepreneurialism. He is Chair of the *British Educational Leadership*

*Management and Administration Society* (BELMAS). His books include *Democratic Leadership in Education* (London: Sage, 2005) and *Transforming Education Policy: Shaping a Democratic Future* (Bristol: Policy Press, 2011). Dr. Woods is co-editing a special issue of *Educational Management Administration and Leadership* on the theme of *Structural Reform in England: The New "Local" - Emerging Configurations of Governance, Leadership and Management*, to be published in 2014. p.a.woods@herts.ac.uk

**Amanda Roberts** worked in schools for 20 years, culminating in a headship in Hertfordshire, U.K. She moved on to run a consultancy company, providing support for learning in a variety of contexts including in schools in challenging circumstances and within the prison service. Roberts is currently Programme Director for the MSc in Practice-Based Research in the School of Education at the University of Hertfordshire. Her research interests encompass distributed leadership, teacher identity and the use of craft to support the development of individual and societal well-being. a.roberts2@herts.ac.uk

**Lejf Moos** is Professor of Educational Leadership at the Department of Education, Aarhus University, Denmark. He has for many years taught and researched in educational leadership and school development in Denmark and as partner in international research projects like the *International Successful School Principal Project* (ISSPP) and the *Superintendent Project*. He has published a number of research articles and books and has been a member of more than ten editorial boards and is the Co-Editor in Chief of the journal *Educational Assessment, Evaluation and Accountability* (Springer) with John MacBeath. He is the Series Editor of the Springer Book Series on *Educational Governance*. moos@dpu.dk

**David Gurr** is Senior Lecturer in Educational Leadership at the Melbourne Graduate School of Education, the University of Melbourne, Australia, and has a thirty-three-year background in secondary teaching, educational psychology, school supervision, and research in educational leadership. He is a founding member of the International Successful School Principalship Project. Gurr is a Fellow and has been the Vice-president of the Australian Council for Educational Leaders, past Editor of *Hot Topics*, *Monograph* and *Leading and Managing*, and was the Hedley Beare Educator of the Year in 2012. d.gurr@unimelb.edu.au

**Simon Clarke** is Professor of Education and Deputy Dean in the Graduate School of Education, The University of Western Australia. His teaching, supervision and research are located in the substantive area of educational leadership. simon.clarke@uwa.edu.au

**Lawrie Drysdale** is Senior Lecturer in Educational Leadership at the Graduate School of Education, the University of Melbourne, Australia, and has a forty-year background in primary teaching, professional development and academia. He coordinates postgraduate courses in educational management, and has research interests in marketing in education, and successful school leadership. He is a member of the International Successful School Principalship Project. Drysdale has written extensively in both academic and professional journals and he is a member and Fellow of the Australian Council for Educational Leaders. drysdale@unimelb.edu.au

**Helen Wildy** is Winthrop Professor and Dean of the Faculty of Education at the University of Western Australia. Her background as a student of a very small rural primary school in Western Australia underpins her commitment to education, particularly the leadership of small schools. She conducts research and supervises doctoral and Master's students in a range of leadership and school improvement topics, including the use of assessment data by school leaders. helen.wildy@uwa.edu.au

**Kadir Beycioglu** is Associate Professor at Dokuz Eylul University, Buca Faculty of Education, Turkey. His research interests are school leadership, teacher leadership, school improvement, principal preparation, educational change, and theoretical aspects in the field of educational administration. beycioglu@gmail.com

**Mehmet Sincar** is Assistant Professor at the University of Gaziantep, Turkey. His research interests include technology leadership, digital citizenship and cyber ethics. He earned his Bachelor's Degree in Electronics Education from University of Gazi, a Master's degree in Educational Administration from University of Gaziantep, and a PhD in Educational Administration from the University of İnönü. mehmetsincar@yahoo.com

**Niyazi Ozer** is Assistant Professor at Inonu University, Faculty of Education, Malatya, Turkey. His research interests are school leadership, organizational behavior in education [especially organizational justice & trust], school improvement, and dynamic schools, technology use in education and school safety and security. niyaziozer@gmail.com

**Celal Teyyar Uğurluis** is Assistant Professor at Cumhuriyet University, Turkey. His research interests include ethical leadership, instructional leadership, organizational leadership and internet ethics. He earned his Bachelor's degree, Master's degree and PhD in Educational Administration from the University of İnönü. cugurlu@cumhuriyet.edu.tr

**M. Cevat Yıldırım** is Assistant Professor at Department of Educational Administration, Supervision, Planning and Economics of Mardin Artuklu University, Turkey. He worked as a teacher, vice-principal and education supervisor. His research interests include organizational behavior, school-family cooperation, constructivist learning and leadership, environment management, and educational supervision. He has published several articles in national and international journals. He is currently a member of the Advisory Board of the *Kuram ve Uygulamada Egitim Bilimleri* Journal [Educational Sciences: Theory & Practice]. mcevatyildirim@gmail.com

**Rc Saravanabhavan** is Professor in the Department of Educational Leadership and Policy Studies at Howard University, Washington, DC, where he has also served as the Editor in Chief of the *Journal of Negro Education* and the Dean of the School of Education. He was an instructor at the collegiate level in Ethiopia and India and a visiting scholar at the Teacher Training University of Central Switzerland. His research agenda includes educational governance, leadership preparation, and administration of special education programs. rc.saravanabhavan@gmail.com

**N. Muthaiah** is Professor and Principal of the Sri Ramakrishna Vidyalaya College of Education, Coimbatore, India. He serves on the national board of accreditation of colleges of education in India. He is a leading voice for invigorating the role of District Education Officer (DEOs) in India.

**Sheila Saravanabhavan** is Professor in the Department of Special Education at Virginia State University. In 2008, she was a Fulbright senior fellow in India. Her research interests include attitudes toward disability and training parents and teachers to work with children who have a learning disability. She has also published works that emphasize the need for training school/district leaders in special education administration. SSaravanabhavan@vsu.edu

**Mika Risku** is Director of the Institute of Educational Leadership at the University of Jyväskylä, Finland. As a researcher he conducts a national research program funded by the Finnish Ministry of Education and Culture which looks at the educational leadership in the municipal, school and class level and is part of over ten international research networks. This program also conducted the first national superintendent and school board surveys in Finland. Mika Risku has written several publications, presents actively in conferences, teaches in many training programs and participates in many work groups which are interested in developing educational leadership. mika.risku@jyu.fi

**Pekka Kanervio** is a post doctorate researcher at the Institute of Educational Leadership in the University of Jyväskylä, Finland. Currently he is conducting a research project on educational leadership in the general education in Finnish municipalities for the Ministry of Education and Culture. He has worked as a principal in the general education for seven years and as a class teacher for fifteen years. He has been involved with the Institute of Educational Leadership since 1998. His PhD dissertation is titled *Crisis and Renewal in one Finnish Private School.* pekka.kanervio@jyu.fi

**Christine Forde** is Professor of Leadership and Professional Learning at the University of Glasgow, Scotland, and leads the Professional Learning Research Teaching Group. She works mainly in leadership and professional development including preparation for headship, middle and teacher leadership. She has published several books on professional development most recently *Mentoring and Coaching* (Dunedin Academic Press, 2011) and a range of chapters and articles on teacher and leadership development. In addition, Forde has published on issues related to gender and education. Among her recent research projects were the *Recruitment and Retention of Headteachers in Scotland* and *Developing Accomplished Teaching in Scotland.* Christine.Forde@glasgow.ac.uk

**Olof Johansson** is Professor of Political Science and Chair of the Centre for Principal Development at Umeå University, Sweden. His research interests are school leadership, principal training, school governance, school effectiveness, school improvement and values and ethics in relation to school leadership. He is working on five large research projects which all have international counterparts: *The International Successful School Principalship Project*; *Structure, Culture, Leadership*: *Prerequisites for Successful Schools?*; *National Policy Meets Local Implementation Structures*; and, *European Policy Network on School*

*Leadership and International School Leadership Development Network.* olof.johansson@pol.umu.se

**Elisabet Nihlfors** is Associate Professor of Education and Dean of Faculty of Education at Uppsala University, Sweden. She is Visiting Professor at Umeå University, Department of Political Science; Former Secretary General at the Swedish Research Council; a member of the research unit, Studies in Educational Policy and Educational Philosophy at Uppsala University. Her research interests include governance of schools, leadership, policymaking and democracy. elisabet.nihlfors@vr.se

**Johan Beckmann** studied at four different institutions of higher education, completing a doctorate at the University of Pretoria in 1985. He started his professional career as a high school teacher and joined the University of Pretoria as full professor in 1992. He served as Chair of the Department of Education Management and Policy Studies and as Director of the Interuniversity Centre for Education Law and Education Policy (CELP).

He is Adjunct Professor at East China Normal University in Shanghai, PRC, and a member of the International Advisory Board of the Institute of Educational Leadership at the University of Jyväskylä in Finland. johan.beckmann21@gmail.com

**Chesterton Smith** is a teacher by profession. He is working for the Gauteng Provincial Education Department as a Senior Education Specialist in one of the sixteen district offices. He completed his first degree at the University of the Western Cape, Cape Town, South Africa in 1995. He completed his Master's degree in music and later on his PhD in Education Policy Studies in 2012 at the University of Pretoria. He is a member of South African Music Rights Organization and the founder of the Theatre Awareness program and the Southern Ethos Community movement. earlechesterton@yahoo.com

# INDEX

## D

## E

## F

**J**

**K**

**L**